P9-BJG-351

GameChangers
The World's Leading Entrepreneurs

HOW THEY'RE CHANGING THE GAME & YOU CAN TOO!

Published by CelebrityPress™, Orlando, FL
A division of The Celebrity Branding Agency®

Celebrity Branding® is a registered trademark
Printed in the United States of America.

ISBN: 9780982908327
LCCN: 2010936905

For more information, please write:

CelebrityPress™,
520 N. Orlando Ave, #44,
Winter Park, FL 32789

or call 1.877.261.4930

Visit us online at www.**CelebrityPressPublishing**.com

GameChangers
The World's Leading Entrepreneurs

HOW THEY'RE CHANGING THE GAME & YOU CAN TOO!

TABLE OF CONTENTS:

CHAPTER 1

PERSONAL INTEGRITY – THE KEY

BY FLETCHER M. JOHNSON, JR., ESQ.

HERE'S THE TEST. THREE QUESTIONS – ANSWER YES OR NO.

1. You go to a fast food restaurant. Your order is taken and you pay the cashier - she gives you back incorrect change. She mistook a $1 bill for a $10 bill and gives nine dollars more than you deserve. Do you call her attention to this and return the money?

2. Early in the week, you've made Friday night plans with a friend. You'll grab a bite to eat and catch a movie. On Thursday another friend calls and informs you that he has tickets to an NCAA basketball playoff game and tip-off is 7 p.m. Friday night. Do you enjoy dinner and the movie?

3. Sherman works two doors down from your office and is a 'freaking' genius. But like many geniuses, he is shy and unassuming. There is a staff meeting and you mention one of Sherman's projects as the solution to a major problem. As everyone gets more excited you neglect to mention that it is

SHERMAN'S idea, not yours. Do you immediately correct this misconception and insure that Sherman gets the credit for the idea?

If you answered "yes" to each question then you possess that elusive quality known as personal integrity. If you didn't answer "Yes" to all three questions, you need to ask yourself why not.

According to common wisdom (and Chinese fortune cookies) integrity is doing the right thing even when nobody is looking.

* * * * * * *

The call came late one afternoon. I was tired at the end of a busy day in a week full of busy days. The voice on the phone belonged to a worried mother. Her twenty-something son had been arrested in Texas and was being extradited back to South Carolina. He was going to have to face the consequences of choices he had made and actions he had taken years earlier.

The mom told a tale of woe not very different from many I had heard before but something she said made me listen more closely instead of merely being polite.

"You know, Randall (not his real name) made some mistakes. He did wrong, but for the last few years he has done his best to do the right thing. If he hadn't gone to the Department of Motor Vehicles to renew his driver's license that was about to expire, he wouldn't have gotten arrested and we wouldn't even be having this conversation."

I figured if Randall was willing to go to prison for doing the right thing the least I could do was to agree to talk to his mother and to visit him when he arrived back in South Carolina.

As is my custom I asked Randall's mother how she came to contact our law firm. She mentioned a gentleman's name and said, "he said to call you, you would know what to do, and you would do the right thing."

Several months later Randall, his mother and I were standing in front of a judge in a South Carolina courtroom. Randall had originally been charged with burglary, possession and sale of illegal drugs. The judge had sentenced him to 15 years in prison, suspended upon completion of a drug rehabilitation program and five years probation. Randall had completed the drug rehabilitation program; however, he had neglected to check in with his probation officer and instead had moved to Texas with a friend. Once in Texas he had remained straight and sober, had gotten a job, and was well on the way to obtaining a master's license in one of the building trades. He had not even gotten a speeding ticket until that fateful day when he went to renew his driver's license.

On this day the judge was being asked to revoke Randall's probation and send him to prison to serve the balance of his 15 year sentence, which would be 14 years. It was clear that the judge had a serious decision to make. She was faced with difficult choices.

During the months since Randall's mother first called me I had thoroughly investigated the matter. I had learned that since he moved to Texas, Randall had made a daily habit of doing the right thing. He had impressed his boss and co-workers to the extent that they provided affidavits in his support, the boss swore that Randall's job was waiting for him, and he even went so far as to send a plane ticket so Randall would have a way to return to Texas and his job. Randall's files were filled with affidavits from his neighbors and others in his community who painted a picture of a young man who was 180 degrees removed from the drug-crazed thief he had been.

After the probation office director had testified and recommended that the judge revoke Randall's probation and sentence him to serve the balance of his 15 year sentence in the South Carolina Department of Directions, the judge turned to me and asked me what I would have her do.

I replied: "Your honor, I would like for you to do the right thing." I then explained how Randall had made daily, conscious decisions to do the right thing that had culminated in the affidavits and the plane ticket in his file. I reminded her that nothing could be better for the people of South Carolina than to send this young man back to Texas where he has a job and people who obviously love and care about him because if she incarcerated him, and did the perfectly permissible legal thing, it would cost the taxpayers $43,000.00 per year for the next 14 years.

I added that I would promise that Randall would never be a problem for the people of the State of South Carolina again.

The judge had every right to put Randall in prison for the next 14 years. It would have been the expedient thing. Instead, she chose to do the right thing. Randall walked out of that courtroom having had his probation terminated and ordered to immediately return to Texas and never to return to South Carolina except to visit his mother.

Randall had transformed himself from a drug addict who would do or say anything to feed his addiction to a young man who is building a life of success and the foundation of that life is personal integrity.

All too often this is a foreign concept in today's society. If our society is to survive it must not only become common, it must be the bedrock of our foundation.

On a regular basis people ask me how business is going. In our uncertain economy, I think they are hoping to get some sort of vicarious thrill when I spin a tail of woe. Instead, when I tell them that not only is my company surviving, it is thriving, they are amazed. Many of them ask "how? In this economy?"

When everything is distilled down, it is not rocket science or brain surgery. The basic fact is so simple, yet so complex. It is ancient, but refreshingly new to many. The key to our success, and the success of the vast majority of those enterprises that are thriving today is the concept of personal integrity.

"What is it?"

Simply put – <u>it's doing the right thing, every time, all the time</u>.

"That's impossible!"

Is it, really?

We represent clients that range from individuals in abject poverty to members of royalty and owners of multi-billion dollar businesses. They seek us out for one reason, and one reason alone. We do what we say we will do – no smoke, no mirrors, no drama, no B.S.

Often times I have had to look a client in the eye and tell him he was out of his mind, that he was reality-challenged. Those with intelligence will turn red in the face, swallow hard, and say "I hadn't thought of that." Others will get angry, ask me how I get the nerve to speak thusly to them, and complain about how they are paying me, etc., etc., …blah, blah, blah.

Those in the second group very quickly become "former clients" because if someone is paying us we expect them to take our advice.

Integrity shining through a business doesn't just happen. It begins literally on a cellular level in the business founder/owner, in the key members of the "team" and in all of the employees of the business.

In the beginning there must be a conscious choice – "I will do things the right way."

The immediate question always is, "won't that affect your bottom line? …won't it impact your profit?"

Regardless of how you define "profit" the answer is "yes."

If you realize that the accumulation of money is not the most important pursuit in life, then yes, doing the right thing may cost you money from time to time. By the same token, if you realize that the accumulation of money is not the most important pursuit in life, then yes, doing the right thing will bring you riches you cannot begin to imagine.

But how do I know what "the right thing" is?

We all have a moral compass. The question is "does yours point towards true North?"

My moral compass was calibrated by my parents and other adults who loved me and cared about me when I was a child. They drummed into me the teachings of Jesus Christ and the Boy Scouts of America.

When you check your moral compass you can't get much more basic than "Love God with all your heart, soul and mind and love your neighbor as yourself." Follow up with a good dose of "a Scout is trustworthy, loyal, helpful, friendly, courteous, kind, obedient, cheerful, thrifty, brave, clean and reverent" and you have the foundation for being able to discern what "the right thing" is in a given situation.

Many of the progressive minds in our society want to say this is old-fashioned, politically incorrect nonsense. I beg to disagree.

If you have a well-tuned moral compass and follow it, you will be viewed as being a person of integrity and moral character – one who can make a hard choice in a difficult situation and who can live with the consequences of that choice. You care about the people you work with – everyone from the janitor to your partners. You care immensely about your clients or customers. You want them to make wise choices and succeed beyond their dreams.

Or you can approach life like a sailboat without a rudder. This leads to decisions being made for reasons of political expediency and with situational ethics.

SEVEN STONES ON THE PATH OF INTEGRITY

1. Integrity is developed and learned over a lifetime.
2. Integrity is your moral compass, your reference point. It is the one true thing by which all else is measured.
3. At the end of one's life, integrity stands as a great cathedral. But it began as a hole in the ground and a single stone. Over time, raw building materials began to take shape until finally the cathedral stood against the sky.
4. Each day is a building process for integrity. It must be put on and worn like a coat anew each day.
5. Integrity is like a favorite firearm. It must be regularly maintained, regularly used and regularly tested. At the first sign of dirt, rust or corrosion, immediate action must be taken to clean it, oil it and polish it - to return it to pristine condition.
6. Integrity can be compromised or lost. If this happens it will be immediately obvious to you, and you would gladly pay any price to be able to turn back the hands of time.
7. If your integrity is compromised or lost, all is not lost. But you must prepare yourself for a conditioning process and a re-training process that will appear to be the most difficult thing you have ever undertaken. However, if you persevere, you will survive and you will once again be viewed as a man or woman of integrity.

For some time now, more and more people have become concerned over the lack of personal integrity and its impact on society. We regularly see the "perp walks" and the lying faces in front of Congressional committees until we deem them commonplace.

Therein lies the sadness. The great futurist Buckminster Fuller said it best. "*On personal integrity hangs humanity's fate.*"

ABOUT FLETCHER

Fletcher M. Johnson, Jr. is the managing partner and chief trial counsel of the Law Offices of Fletcher M. Johnson, LLC in Bluffton, South Carolina. A well-seasoned civil and criminal trial lawyer, Mr. Johnson's practice focuses on individuals and their small businesses with an emphasis on litigation avoidance. Mr. Johnson also serves as a municipal court judge for the Town of Bluffton.

Mr. Johnson and his wife, Elizabeth, also own a commercial real estate business and a music publishing business that manages the rights of their musical compositions.

When not involved in church or community activities or keeping up with his nine grand children and two cats, Mr. Johnson enjoys playing guitar and mandolin.

Fletcher Johnson can be reached at:
(843) 757.6444 or fletcher@fletcherjohnsonlaw.com

CHAPTER 2

SIGNING OFF – ONLINE

BY C. RICHARD TRIOLA

"No one would have crossed the ocean if he could have gotten off the ship in a storm"
~ Charles F. Kettering

A funny thing happened in my late forties. Out of nowhere I became a founder, president and CEO of a technology company. My friends thought this was hysterical (they have seen my VCR flashing 12 o'clock for months on end). Along the way I also added 'inventor/patent holder', which really sent my colleagues roaring. Doesn't that ring true of the 'career' path of a typical entrepreneur? How many of you are currently doing what you always thought you would be doing?

I haven't given much thought about my own personal journey until recently - I was asked to submit a resume for an investment group we were forming and quickly realized I was in trouble – how do you do that? I don't remember if I ever had to prepare one? My last regular paycheck was when I was a Wall Street investment banker – more than 30 years ago. I mentioned this at our last monthly CEO club meeting and we all realized that none of us are employable! Any serial entrepreneur would be hard pressed to put in writing all the things that they accomplished (better yet, attempted). Try this - pizza chain, multiplex cinemas, site locator, property syndicator, real estate professional, movie distributor, telecommunications marketer, sports writer, personal development trainer, etc.

Many years ago, I heard a successful businessman say that you must 'fail your way to the top' – I remember thinking: "Cool, I'm almost there!" Looking back, I feel blessed that I 'created' these opportunities to test and learn (fail) along the way. My life's goal became quite apparent 'to never make the same mistake twice'. On my never-ending quest to find the 'holy grail', I will certainly continue to make mistakes. As entrepreneurs, we are always testing limits and 'going out on a limb'. Every step we take is generally 'virgin' territory and one that requires you to blindly move forward –'flying without a net', or without the help of some off-the-shelf 'how to' book… where success can sometimes be expressed as follows: "As long as I keep falling forward, I'm 6 feet closer to my goal".

OK! Let's rewind back to 1999. I relocated from NY to So. Cal and met with a former real estate colleague. He asked for my help to expand his real estate escrow business from LA to Orange County. Although my only past experience with the escrow business was to pick up a commission check after my real estate deal closed, he hoped that with my sales, marketing and management background, I would figure out how to open this market. Instinctively, like most entrepreneurs, I accepted the challenge and knew I needed to quickly identify or create a 'differentiator' - to go up against the competing '800 lb. gorillas' and take/gain market share. The internet was coming into its own around the same time, so I thought: "Wouldn't it be great if we could take the entire real estate transaction, a cumbersome and paper intensive process - to say the least - and move it up over the web?" This way, all stakeholders, namely: buyers/sellers, borrowers, title, RE agents, escrow/settlement/closing agents, attorneys, county recorders, notaries and secondary investors (like Fannie Mae), could all streamline their entire processes by going completely electronic and digital - and thereby eliminate all paper, faxing and scanning (as well as toner, ink, etc.). This would collapse time frames and reduce costs dramatically - what a beautiful thing!

Although I jumped in before legislation was even in place, the 'trigger' that allowed this to develop was the passage of the Federal 'e-Sign Act '- signed into law in June 2000 and which became effective October 1, 2000. The essence of this legislation(as well as the States' passage of the Uniform Electronic Transactions Act - UETA) is that an electronic signature affixed to a contract/agreement would hold the same legal weight as a 'wet-signed ' original document in a court of law. Great – this would be a 'no –brainer'!! Why would anyone drive across town to get a document signed or use expensive couriers or overnight carriers, like USPS, FedEx or UPS (now identified as the new 'snail mail')? Why wouldn't everyone want to have their contracts, agreements, NDA's, etc. legally executed in minutes vs. days – anytime, anyplace? Well, after nearly 10 years - 'Hello, Houston, we have traction!"

As with most entrepreneurial ideas, there were plenty of naysayers (usually, the closest people you know). Early in the process I attended a venture capital forum, attended by approx. 900 entrepreneurs, and hosted by a panel of seasoned experts and investors. From the audience, a question was asked "I have this brilliant idea, but before I present it to you I would need you to sign a non-disclosure agreement (NDA) - will you do that?" An expert on the dais responded "if you have something so unique you should protect it and file a patent – I won't sign your NDA." Next step, I contacted one of my closest friends/classmates , an attorney, and he recommended another attorney friend, based in Seattle, who did quite a bit of patent work for Hewlett Packard. He flew down, the 3 of us had breakfast and before you knew it, I filed for my first patent. (By now it's hard to pick my friends off the floor - they can't believe it!) After I filed the patent, I pitched the same panelist. Amazingly, he said: "sounds great but you will never get your patent"- needless to say he was first person I went to when I did receive the patent (and he did offer congratulations). Over time, one of my best decisions was to not wait for the patent to be granted, but to also create the technology platform that would connect all parties and documents over the internet. Good thing… because it actually took almost 6 years for the U.S. patent to be issued. We could have waited until the patent was issued and then initiated a licensing campaign without writing a line of code, but our platform has served, and continues to serve, as a catalyst in moving this archaic industry forward.

Just think about how many thousands of decisions you have been confronted with in the past and will make during your lifetime, and how any 'different' decision would have possibly changed the course of your life. What school should I attend? Should I ask that girl for a dance? Do I accept this job offering? Do I move to the suburbs? etc. When you take a step back, you realize that if you perhaps made just one different choice you would not be where you are today. So let faith be your guide and understand that every decision you have ever made brought you to exactly where you are today - even down to reading this book - it is now from this place that you may move forward with a blank canvas!

So, moving on to electronic signatures. I was fortunate enough to have a friend, early in the process, who shared with me that I better hold on and 'bootstrap' the company. He was involved in the development/launch of the ATM machine and the 'war' stories were astonishing - rolling these machines into small towns, allowing folks to only take out $20.00 at a time and answering questions like "what happens if my money explodes when I put this card in the slot"? It took 17 years for mainstream adoption of these now ubiquitous machines. Isn't it amazing that we all still know at least one person who refuses to stick that plastic card 'in the wall' - in our vernacular we would not classify these folks as 'early adopters'! So here we are, 10 years after passage of the 'e-Sign Act', and 99% of companies have still yet to deploy e-signatures – which we profess will be as widespread and '*game changing*' as the cell phone and emailing.

I wouldn't exactly classify our persistence as 'genius', as it just made too much sense that if you could legally execute a contract/agreement electronically and not have to deal with all the paper, storage, human errors, etc., why would you ever be 'tethered' to pen and paper? '*Pen on paper is gone*' has been our mantra. As an 'out of the box' creative person, I challenge you to think about how many applications/processes you can think of that would be enhanced by eliminating the need to fax, print, scan or overnight documents by simply e-signing over the internet? (Just send your thoughts to me at: gamechangingideas@expressdox.com, and you just might be the lucky winner as we select the best overall entry – judged by the amount of time/ money saved as well as the overall impact on the environment).

Let's fast forward 2, 5 or 10 years when e-signing becomes the 'de facto standard'... what will this do for our environment? ... how many trees can we save, etc. According to the Mortgage Bankers Association (MBA) 'for every mortgage we process, we kill a tree'.

With the continuous rise of global e-commerce, I have no doubt adoption of e-signatures would be the one of the most significant 'game changers' in our lifetime. It is the 'glue' that will keep business growing without borders, and moving at the speed of light. If it is not the most important factor, it will certainly be right up there with oxygen! Look around - what would your life be like without cell phones, email, text messaging (ok - fax machines and scanners are 'so yesterday'). I often wondered about the first person who bought a fax machine and why? (Think about this for a few seconds.)

'Dare to be different' - go with your gut and instincts - do your research and then move forward. If I listened to the Harvard-educated patent holder/investor, I might not have ever received the most important asset and 'barrier to entry' we have today. (Now worth millions of dollars.)

Some additional thoughts on the top eight steps to improve your chances of success in any business:

1. Persistence – Get in the game and stay on the field – as a former president of a sports hall of fame, I had the privilege to personally know Joe DiMaggio, Dan Marino and Tommy Lasorda, to name drop a few. The common thread amongst these greats was that they were on the field, getting dirty and not in the stands. They immersed themselves in their profession and worked harder than anyone else - success only looks easy to the person in the bleachers.

2. Differentiate yourself – 'go out on a limb!' That's where all the fruit is, anyway.

3. 'Fail your way to the top' – don't worry about mistakes. The more mistakes you make, the closer you are to your goal. Let Thomas Edison and Colonel Sanders be your inspiration – they were the masters of mistakes.

4. Innovate, innovate, innovate – Go find your 'blue ocean' strategy!

5. Identify your 'why'? – If your reason is big enough you can

'run through walls' to get this done. Remember – When you hit the wall just 'hang a right'!!

6. Form a mastermind/advisory board - surround yourself with people who are smarter than you are (this was not hard for me to find) and those that "have been there and done that". They will shorten your road to success and help you avoid many costly mistakes you would make without them.

7. Prepare for a roller coaster ride – one day you receive a call that some 800 lb. gorilla is interested in your product/service – you are now on a roller coaster high… only to receive that call the next day and, for whatever reason, they are no longer interested – you plummet to a new roller coaster low – draining all your emotions. You need to become good at making certain that you stay middle of the road – highs should not be too high and lows should never be too low.

8. Never stop learning. Read books, attend classes/seminars – you may walk away with that one 'nugget' that will change your life… It did for me!

You were probably looking for my Top Ten - please refer back to #2 above and…

<u>**Go Make A Difference!**</u>

ABOUT RICHARD

C. Richard Triola has made a career of spotting emerging trends and capitalizing on them quickly. Whether it was trading stock options in the 70's, introducing 'take-and-bake' pizza's into the marketplace in the 80's, or pioneering e-Signatures in the late 90's, you can rest assured that 'Rick' is already working on the next 'Game Changer'.

Before he knew the definition of an entrepreneur, he began his career at the age of 12 with a paper route – moving on to establish a mobile hot dog business at the age of 16. The hardest thing about heading to college was the tremendous 'pay cut' he had to leave behind.

Having purchased his first stock at age 15, Rick pursued his dream career as a Wall St Investment Banker. After the market crashed in the mid 70's, Rick left Oppenheimer & Co and headed West to begin his Real Estate career – buying, selling, managing, and syndicating commercial properties – Rick mastered his profession over the next 25 years.

Rick started Settleware Secure Services, Inc. in 1999 and today provides the Real Estate/Mortgage Industry the first and only electronic/paperless and end-to-end transaction processed completely over the Internet. In 2006, Rick added 'Patent Holder' to his resume.

Today, Rick resides in Laguna Beach, Ca with his beautiful wife Gina and their Golden Retriever, Jackson.

CHAPTER 3

CHANGE YOUR HEALTH TO CHANGE YOUR GAME FOR GOOD...IT'S EASIER THAN YOU THINK TO LOSE WEIGHT!

BY THOMAS W. CLARK, MS, MD, FACS

Meet Renee – a successful entrepreneur who is intelligent, driven, ambitious, influential and successful. She seems to have it all except for one thing...optimal health. You see, Renee is overweight and has made multiple attempts to lose weight. On more than one occasion, she has lost a fair amount of weight, only to gain it all back and then some. It seems Renee has tried every weight loss program available. She is frustrated because she knows that her weight and overall health are barriers to attaining something she desires - her greatest personal and professional potential. Renee is my ideal patient.

I love my job because I get to help many people like Renee each and every day. She is motivated to lose weight and wants to understand how to finally overcome her barriers to successful weight loss so she can not only lose weight, but develop the habits to keep it off long-term. She realizes that a "quick fix" is not the long-term answer. She will soon realize that there is a new tool for her weight loss toolbox … *hormone manipulation.* Once she puts this simple tool to work, I will get to witness a transformation that brings great satisfaction. It is every physicians dream to help people attain their optimal health. I do this each and every day.

At any given time, an average of 50-65% of the American population state they are trying to lose weight. They desire the benefits of attaining optimal health but are frustrated by their inability to reach a healthy weight and keep it there long-term.

Something that works but not commonly discussed is how to change what often causes weight problems in the first place – our very own hormones – and specifically a master hormone called insulin. I will explain how to easily manipulate your hormones so that you can master your weight and change your game for good. In this chapter, I reveal 7 steps to long-term weight loss success. The information shared here is applicable to anyone who wants to lose weight. Better yet – it's easier than you think!

1. DECIDE, COMMIT AND MAKE IT HAPPEN.

The reasons you have for wanting to lose weight play a big part in your commitment to a weight loss regimen. For some, feeling good about their physical appearance is a priority. Poor self-esteem can prevent you from attaining what you want in life. Losing weight can have a significant impact on your health, increase your energy level and improve your overall sense of well-being. This is very empowering. Every step towards your goal increases your motivation and commitment to long term success. You are more than worth it!

We all have "wishes" such as being healthier, more beautiful, richer, happier, more successful, or retired by the age of 50. However, wishes do not result in change. The only people who will experience their wishes and dreams are those that clearly identify what they want and commit to it. However, commitment alone is not enough. Commitment with action produces results. I guarantee this is a journey worth making.

2. KEEP IT SIMPLE.

This applies to many areas of our life but particularly with weight loss. If you make your weight loss plan too elaborate or unrealistic, the likelihood of compliance is slim. This leads to feelings of frustration and failure. Your weight loss plan needs to be specific to your needs. At the end of the day, you need to be able to look in the mirror and be able to say with confidence that your plan is something you can realistically do…for life.

3. FOCUS YOUR ATTENTION ON WHAT MATTERS MOST.

Although exercise is very important, it is diet that is the key to weight loss success. I recommend that you focus on one thing at a time starting with what you eat, and then move on to your behavior and fitness. Here are general guidelines for eating:

- Concentrate on three meals a day and a snack in between meals.
- Do not skip breakfast.
- Each meal should have a good protein source such as lean meat, fish, seafood, eggs, and cheese
- Keep the carbohydrates to a minimum. Most people do not realize that you can survive without any carbohydrates but your body cannot survive without protein and fat. The carbohydrates you do eat should be fiber rich, complex carbohydrates (colorful vegetables and salad)
- Stick with healthy foods you like and will be able to eat long term.
- ***I typically see the best weight loss and improvement in other health parameters when a persons protein:carbohydrate ratio is at least 2:1 (i.e. 90 grams protein:45 grams carbohydrates/day) and they keep their overall carbohydrate intake <50 grams/day.***

Most weight loss plans are built around decreasing calories and fat. Well, as most of you know, it is not quite that simple. If it was, I would just tell you to eat less and you would lose weight very easily (and be hungry all the time). Unfortunately, it does not work that easily (and if it did I would not have a job). I like to think of it as being a "calorie ceiling" – if you eat more than a certain number of calories you will gain weight, but just because you eat less doesn't mean you will lose weight. Fat usually isn't a problem either…unless it drives your calories too high. You should concentrate on the good fats such as Omega 3's and avoid Trans fats.

4. MAXIMIZE YOUR METABOLISM.

One of the potential problems with restricting calorie intake (diets) is that your body will preferentially break down your lean body mass (LBM) instead of fatty tissue. This is an evolutionary survival mechanism since early man's food supplies were unpredictable at best. This allows you to slow your metabolism significantly when calories are restricted, making you resistant to weight loss and aiding survival during intermittent fasts. That works great for survival, but not well when you are trying to lose weight. For weight loss, you ideally want to keep your metabolism as high as possible when you cut down on calories.

It is your muscle mass which influences your overall metabolism the most. A simplified definition of metabolism is the total amount of energy needed to keep your body in a stable state. Muscle tissue burns more calories than fatty tissue. Therefore, the more LBM (muscle) you have, the higher your metabolism – "muscle burns calories". So, improving/keeping your LBM is critical to improving your metabolism. How is this done? Through exercise and taking in adequate amounts of quality protein.

The best exercise plans incorporate cardiovascular and resistance training. People often think that cardiovascular exercise helps the most with weight loss, but actually weight lifting does this more effectively. Building muscle increases your metabolism – muscle burns calories.

5. UNDERSTAND YOUR HORMONES BEFORE YOU TRY TO MANIPULATE THEM.

Now I don't want you to "glaze over" here but you need to understand your hormones - they hold the key to successful weight loss. Once you have a basic understanding, you can then focus on easily manipulating them so they work "for" your weight loss efforts instead of "against" them. It's about working smarter, not harder.

There are many hormones within your body that influence your weight, health and how you feel. Thyroid, estrogen, testosterone, cortisol and many others all play into this. But I am going to focus on just three – insulin, glucagon and growth hormone. I begin with insulin which is one of the most important hormones that affects your weight and overall health. Insulin is often thought of as the master hormone due to its far reaching influences.

Insulin is a hormone made by your pancreas. Its main function is to help keep blood sugar levels normal. When your blood sugar goes up, insulin is released into the blood stream. Insulin then helps facilitate the transfer of sugar molecules into your body's cells and consequently, your blood sugar will go down. Ideally this will keep blood sugar levels in a nice, narrow, healthy range (70-120 mg/dL).

From a weight loss perspective, insulin is a fat storage hormone. If insulin levels are elevated, you **will** store fat. Insulin works independently of caloric intake. Insulin does not care if you are eating low calorie. You will still gain weight if insulin levels remain high. When insulin levels are low, fat will be mobilized out of the fatty stores and burned for energy. This results in a higher energy level, less hunger/cravings and easier weight loss. Sounds great huh?

Other hormones that directly affect fat storage and subsequently weight (in a good way) are glucagon and growth hormone. ***Glucagon*** is another hormone made by your pancreas and can be thought of as the opposite of insulin. Glucagon helps mobilize fat molecules out of fatty tissue to be burned for energy (what I like to call "fat burning mode"). ***Growth hormone*** is naturally made by the pituitary gland in the base of our brains. Growth hormone helps build muscle thus increasing our overall metabolism. Growth hormone also shifts our metabolism into the preferential use of fat to be burned for energy (again "fat burning mode").

So the million dollar question is "How do I keep insulin levels low as possible and glucagon and growth hormone as high as possible?"

6. MANIPULATE YOUR HORMONES.

Ideally during a weight loss plan you want to manipulate your hormones in the right direction to facilitate weight loss. You can do this by changing what you eat. Food is more than just calories and nutrients. You can think of food as a medication. We need it to survive, but how your body reacts to food is different depending on which other hormones are released. What I like to say is "It's not what you eat; it's what your body does with what you eat." Now, let's learn how you can manipulate your insulin, glucagon and growth hormone levels. We will start with the master hormone – insulin.

One of the nice things about insulin is that you have some control over it. You can't control most other hormones. But insulin only increases in response to an increase in your blood sugar level. Blood sugar levels increase in response to what you eat-specifically the carbohydrate you eat. By decreasing your carbohydrate intake (decrease all carbohydrates, but especially simple carbohydrates) you can keep your blood sugars stable and subsequently manipulate your insulin levels down. I see the best weight loss when people keep their total carbohydrate intake <50 grams/day. This amount almost always keeps blood sugars stable and insulin levels low. If your insulin levels stay low, you will remain in what I described earlier as "fat burning mode" meaning you will mobilize fat molecules out of your fatty tissue and utilize it for energy (i.e. lose weight!).

Glucagon levels can also be improved by decreasing carbohydrate intake. The other way to improve glucagon levels is to increase your protein intake. Protein stimulates the release of glucagon from your pancreas resulting in improved fat mobilization – "fat burning mode."

Your body's natural growth hormone can be improved by increasing your protein intake as well. Growth hormone release is also stimulated by exercise and getting quality sleep.

The bottom line is that what you eat changes your hormonal response to food and can manipulate your hormones in the right direction to aid with weight loss. By decreasing your carbohydrate intake and increasing your protein intake, you can stimulate fat mobilization and weight loss since you will decrease your insulin production while increasing stimulation of glucagon and growth hormone production.

7. PUT IT ALL TOGETHER INTO A PLAN THAT WORKS FOR *YOU*.

- ***Decide you want to make a change*** (this will only work if you are doing this for yourself – not for anyone else or any other reason) and develop a plan (short and long term realistic goals) then make a commitment to making it happen. Remember that actions are what cause results.

- ***If you are only going to do one thing***, then count your carbohydrate intake and control it by eating less than 50 grams/day. The lower your carbohydrate intake, the lower your insulin levels will be and the easier it is to lose weight and control your hunger and cravings.

- ***If you are only going to do 2 things***, then count your carbohydrate intake and your protein intake. Get your protein into that 90-100+ grams/day range.

- ***Don't ignore the need for fitness***. Preserving/improving your lean body mass is critical for preserving/improving your metabolism. Mixing cardio and resistance training activities is best, but do NOT ignore resistance training.

- ***Don't skip meals (especially breakfast).*** Eat on a schedule. I like people to eat 3 meals, plus planned snacks. Be sure to remain hydrated with about 8 cups of water/day.

- ***Enlist support from others*** and surround yourself with positive people who desire or already possess the skills necessary for long-term weight control.

- ***Journal*** your way to success. Read labels and track your carbohydrate, protein and calorie intake. This is particularly important during your weight loss phase and anytime you need to "get back on track."

- ***Manipulate your hormones*** as described here – decrease insulin production and enhance glucagon and growth hormone production through controlled carbohydrate intake, adequate protein, getting enough sleep and resistance training.

- ***Believe in yourself – You can do it!*** Make gradual changes that fit into your life and before you know it, you are on your way to changing your barriers into opportunities for success.
- ***Seek professional help…everyone is unique.*** Make sure the professionals you choose are qualified and specialize in evaluating each individual and their personal medical problems/goals rather than just recommending the same plan for everyone. Be sure they are able to work with you to develop a realistic plan that addresses your particular barriers to weight loss, your medical problems, and changes that you can commit to for life.
- ***Remember, life is what we do minute to minute and day to day – don't forget to have fun and enjoy your transformation every step of the way.***

ABOUT THOMAS

Dr. Thomas W. Clark is one of the most experienced bariatric surgeons in the United States. He has dedicated his career to helping people successfully lose weight and keep it off for life. In addition to being board certified in surgery and performing more than 3,500 weight loss procedures, Dr. Clark is one of the elite few bariatric surgeons who have also achieved an additional board certification in the field of Bariatric Medicine. This makes him one of the first pioneers in the United States to provide the full continuum of weight loss services for anyone who wants to successfully lose weight.

Dr. Clark has a unique talent for taking the key medically-based principles of effective weight loss and making them easy to understand and implement so people not only lose weight, but have the education and skills/habits to keep it off for life. He emphasizes that there are many tools (such as surgery) that help with weight loss, but you must know how to utilize your tool(s) so that they are most effective and maximize your weight loss efforts. In order to help with this process, Dr. Clark founded Weight Management University™, a comprehensive educational program that focuses on the nutritional requirements, lifestyle behavior (habit) modification and fitness information necessary for long term weight loss success. The program is available to anyone online or on-site in Newport News, VA. This is a results-oriented prescription for weight loss success, especially when combined with individualized counseling by Dr. Clark and his professional staff.

Dr. Clark graduated from Davidson College and the Wake Forest University School of Medicine in North Carolina. Dr. Clark is a Fellow of the American College of Surgeons and a member of the American Society for Metabolic and Bariatric Surgery, American Society of Bariatric Physicians, the American Medical Association and the International Federation for the Surgery of Obesity. Dr. Clark resides in Virginia with his wife and four children. Providing a comprehensive weight loss and weight management continuum of care that finally allows people to live their dreams gives true meaning to what he does every day. Dr. Clark is the founder of the *Center for Weight Loss Success* where he and his professional staff provide individualized surgical and non-surgical weight loss services, fitness and nutritional products for anyone who wants to lose weight and keep it off for life.

To learn more about Dr. Thomas W. Clark and to receive his free special report "Dr. Clark's 9 Ways to Jump Start Your Weight Loss", visit www.cmhva.com and his blog at http://centerformetabolichealth.com/blg/ You can also follow him on Twitter at http://twitter.com/docweightloss and read his daily "Dr. Clark's Tip of the Day" on Facebook at http://www.facebook.com/pages/Center-for-Metabolic-Health-PLC/128058772979 He can also be found at www.centerforweightlosssuccess.com

CHAPTER 4

CLOSE THE RIGHT LOOPS, CHANGE THE GAME

BY STEPHEN LUNDIN PH.D, "THE BIG TUNA", CO-AUTHOR OF THE BEST SELLING BOOK – *FISH!*, AND MIKE CHAET PH.D, "THE LOOP GUY", CO-AUTHOR – *LOOPS: THE 7 KEYS TO SMALL BUSINESS SUCCESS*

Following the darkest days of the financial crisis, we heard from leaders that we have a "new normal" and that "the game has changed". Small business owners and managers don't need new jargon to tell them things change, they see it every day in their business because they are close to the customer, close to the ground, and in many ways, small business is the economy. Small business leaders are constantly changing their game to adopt and survive, as they are burdened less with bureaucracy and more with the amount of work to get done. The question for small business is "With limited time and a lot to do, are we closing the right loops first?"

In small businesses we know the importance of taking action. The best business leaders are action-oriented men and women. One phrase that has emerged from this action-orientation is "Close the Loop" which is short hand for getting things done, for finishing a task. "Have you closed the loop with Bob?" "Have we closed all the loops on the new advertising campaign?" In small business, action is critical, but one important question remains. Out of all the things we could be doing, are we focused on closing the loops that will lead to success?

In the recently released book, LOOPS: The Seven Keys to Small Business Success, Mike Chaet and Stephen Lundin introduce a framework that can be useful in identifying the loops that should get your first attention, the seven essential loops. After reading the story we used to convey our message in the book, many have told us they have not only applied the ideas to their business, but have also been inspired to take them home.

WHAT IS A LOOP?

A LOOP is simply a symbol that represents a task. Any task is either in progress or complete, it is either open or closed. Ultimately what we are talking about here is execution. For example: you may have asked an associate to make a telephone call, and set up a meeting for you at three o'clock tomorrow. Later you ask, "Did you ever get in touch with Mr. Jones about that three o'clock appointment for tomorrow?" We often hear a response like, "Well I couldn't get him, so I left him a phone message, sent several emails and spoke to his secretary, I think he probably will get back to me sometime soon." Sound familiar? Fair enough the person is doing their work, BUT… Make no mistake; this is still an OPEN LOOP! You can never let activity hide or mask execution. What is critical here is whether the loop is open or closed.

One way to make communication much clearer and effective is to school your associates on this simple fact. Loop Open. Loop Closed. I need help. You are typically not interested in the process, only the results. If you were interested in the process, you could ask, "What efforts have you made to get this done?" Care has to be taken with this approach for you may find 'the monkey has moved from the associate and is now', in the words of Bill Onken, 'firmly attached to your back'.

A different example of loop closing may come in the form of an apology. Apologies are one way of closing a LOOP that, if left open, may lead to negative, or even dire circumstances. An apology can bring closure to a whole host of situations, if in fact the person receiving the apology believes that it is genuine, and does in fact make the decision to accept it. If the person decides to accept it and confirms the acceptance, we have a closed LOOP. If the person chooses to accept it but never tells the first person that they accepted, we still have an open LOOP. Incomplete communications! LOOP still open. It is for this reason, that it is important in communications of all types, that the LOOP gets closed with full confirmation. Then and only then do you have a completely closed LOOP.

In small business some loops are more important than others. We have identified seven loops that have the highest leverage. In our research with small business and in the lifetime we have each spent running small businesses we have found these to be consistently the differentiator between success and failure. Baring some unforeseen act of nature or economic "Black Swan", these seven loops should be your first concern each and every day.

THE SEVEN STRATEGIC LOOPS THAT DESERVE YOUR ATTENTION

The following seven strategic LOOPS are described in detail in the book LOOPS. They provide a blueprint FOR ACTION. By constantly working on and improving these seven LOOPS you will be constantly improving ALL ASPECTS OF YOUR SMALL BUSINESS. They provide you with a way to separate the important from the less important, so you can focus your energy on the highest leverage items.

Loop One: Manage your Experience Zones

An experience zone is a place or space where you have a concentration of customer interactions and hence the most concentrated opportunity to deliver great customer experiences. Customer retention has more to do with making an emotional connection with customers than good customer service. Of course, having both would be ideal. To achieve either, you must know and understand the "experience zones" of your business. Understand your experience zones and constantly work to improve the customer interactions that take place in these zones. Be creative, and differentiate yourself from your competition.

Loop Two: Build a Winning Culture With Vision Moments

Create in your minds eye a picture of how you want your business to both look and feel. What would you like employees to say when they are with friends? How would you like customers to feel when they enter your shop? If you could identify connections between employees and customers that would best communicate your vision for the business, what would they look and feel like?

Employees create a winning culture moment to moment. These moments accumulate to build a culture, a brand, and a reputation. Vision moments are those conscious acts generated from a fundamental commitment to the vision of the enterprise. The fundamental commitment guides each employee to accept responsibility for recreating the vision every minute of every day by living the moments, and closing the LOOPS that must be closed to accomplish this. And your job is to keep the vision alive and keep the conversation going.

Loop Three: Monitor the Fundamentals and Use Loop Groups to Empower Your People to Support Yourself

There are certain basics in every business. All businesses make assumptions, establish direction, set goals, assign responsibilities, measure accomplishments, track progress, communicate results, and make necessary changes. And while these basics at times can seem routine and perhaps uninteresting, they must be mastered and monitored continuously. Fundamental loops must be constantly and continuously closed. Use Loop Groups to get the job done.

There are two basic types of loop groups. A team of employees who assemble on a regular basis to review results and discuss successes and failures is one kind of group. An outside loop group is formed by identifying other small business owners who are willing to meet once a month and discuss their business issues; seeking to learn from outside perspectives and grow from the interaction.

Loop Four: Standardize Every Major Process

One of the greatest inventions in business is the standardized process. Without a standardized process, each event would be treated as novel, and very little would get done—and what did get done would be inconsistent. Standardization and systems helps you close loops in a predictable manner.

Loop Five: Innovate with Passion

"Grow or die" is often misunderstood as a philosophy. It does not mean get *bigger* or die. Although scale can be a differentiator, size is the least important dimension. Grow or die means always get *better.* Standing still is a sure formula for moving backwards. Whether you call it *kaizen* or *continuous improvement* or some other name, innovation must be a key ingredient in any business. Steve has written a book titled *CATS: The Nine Lives of Innovation* that is full of things you can do to improve your personal innovation.

Loop Six: Live in the Real World

Living in the real world means planning for the unexpected by leaving margins. Plus having a plan B and maybe even a plan C. Flexibility must be part of every operating plan. By planning for the unexpected you are always ready for the inevitable surprises.

Loop Seven: Lead by Example

If you only have the time or interest to do one thing as a leader; lead by example. Leading by example sends such a powerful message of integrity and is such a profound source of inspiration for employees that if you can lead by example, the rest of leadership will be a cinch. As a leader in your small business you'll want to 'walk your talk' and be that which you ask your employees to be.

MORE ABOUT LOOPS

In this section we have looked at loops through the lens of common business issues.

LOOPS AND EMPOWERMENT

In small biz, we see the ongoing challenge to get all levels of workers to make good decisions. Workers can only make good decisions if they have the power to close LOOPS directly on the front line when they are 'belly to belly' with the customer. Consider also, that they don't need the power to close ALL LOOPS, ALL of the time, but, if they have the power to close a high percentage, if not most of the LOOPS, most of the time, it will make the customer feel good. If there are still LOOPS that need to be closed, then the worker can say to the customer, "We still have some open LOOPS to deal with, but *I* will take care of those tomorrow by talking to my supervisor." Or, "I'll get those closed right now if you give me five minutes. Let me call you right back." If you talk in terms of closed or open LOOPS with customers, they will understand that the process of helping them is underway. Good customer service.

You will always have a certain number of loops that have already been closed and a certain number that are yet to be closed. As you can see closing LOOPS and keeping them closed is a constant ongoing PROCESS. Accountability comes into play here, where workers must get their LOOPS closed on time. Remember it's the open LOOP that causes customer dissatisfaction creating delays, incorrect orders, poor service, untimely response, and so on. When you are talking LOOPS and empowerment, you have to allow employees, teach employees, and supervise employees, as well as train ourselves to have the discipline to CLOSE LOOPS EFFECTIVELY AND ON TIME. That in fact is true accountability.

The business that is successful today, empowers employees to close as many LOOPS in real time as possible. In other words, they give employees the tools to close LOOPS when they need to be closed. Each time a LOOP is handed off to somebody else there is a risk that, the LOOP may not get closed, which results once again in unhappy customers and dissatisfaction. This weakens the entire organization. The closer you are to the original source to closing the LOOP, the more likely it will get closed effectively and in a timely fashion. Let's review the three simple LOOP RULES.

1. LOOPS are either open or closed.
2. Close the LOOP as quickly as possible.
3. Get the LOOP closed right the first time.

LOOPS AND TIME MANAGEMENT

As a small businessperson you need to use your time wisely and well. People are not as patient today as they were 5, 10 or 15 years ago. They aren't even as patient as they were last year. Fax machines gave way to email which gave way to instant messaging, which gave way to social networks and so forth and so on. Fed Ex and UPS can deliver packages overnight. Time has become the most revered currency of the day. In the successful company today, LOOPS must be closed quickly. Your customers not only expect it, they demand it!

You must be the judge as to what is reasonable or not, in closing any given specific LOOP. Consider managing LOOPS by using a paradigm that we call MARGINS. A margin is allowing enough time and resources to complete projects and close LOOPS. Plan your day out properly. It is not good to have a collection of emergency type, high pressure LOOPS. It creates stress and inefficiency. Well managed LOOPS, with enough margins, and, given the proper time frame will result in superior productivity, customer service and overall efficiency. So, when you are talking about time management, leave sufficient margins and close your LOOPS as quickly as possible.

LOOPS AND COMMUNICATION

You may wish to use the rule of five. The rule of fives in communications states, "When you are empowered to communicate a message you need to remember that each person works on their own time frames and have their own communications style. Therefore you may wish to use up to five different forms of communications to get your message across."

For example, when communicating with someone 2000 miles away; you may make a phone call and not get them. It is not easy to get in touch with Mr. Jones, and the LOOP is still open, so you still have to find a way to get that LOOP closed in the most efficient manner. Here is where you may use the rule of fives, which once again states, you may need to use five different methods to communicate with Mr. Jones. Back to our example, we need to get in touch with Mr. Jones: make the phone call. If that doesn't close the LOOP, leave a message, however loop is still open so ask for a confirmation. Send an email if you don't get an immediate response, and once again, ask for a response on the email. Send a fax, even then you could call an associate or a friend of Mr. Jones to try to get the message through. You may even need to call Mr. Jones' mother and explain the situation. That's five ways to try to close the Mr. Jones LOOP. Of course if you need to use a few more, go for it!

Take the example of planning an event for your small biz, let's say a wine shop, and you want the customers of your small biz to know about the event, a wine tasting. We now know that one form of communications is not going to hit enough people to close all of the LOOPS. It's time to consider five additional ways to communicate the specifics of the event. In a sense this is a marketing challenge. Consider that almost everything depends on closing the LOOPS for ultimate success, otherwise you are going to have unsatisfied customers because they are going to say to you, "Well, nobody told me about the wine tasting – I wish I had known." You could respond with, "Well, we sent you a flyer." They might say, "I don't read my flyers because I get too much junk mail." You can say, "We also sent you an email." "Spam is a problem so I haven't read my email in two weeks." If that's all you can say, you have an unhappy customer, and a failed event, ouch!

So really the important part to remember is that the end user, or the recipient, has his or her own agenda, way or style of accepting information, plus, in our lives today, we are all in "information overload" so we may very well not get all our messages. We may travel, or be busy during the day, and not get to it until the end of the day, if at all. We live in a good world, but it's a busy and hectic world, even kind of crazy at times; there's always something going on. It's important, when we are trying to close a LOOP, for both parties to get that LOOP confirmed and closed. This becomes a reciprocal issue.

When accomplished, and LOOPS are successfully closed most people are appreciative and say, "Oh man, thanks for closing the LOOP. I'm glad I know about the meeting (or special event or whatever it may be)." With that in mind, and because people have their own individual ways of receiving information, and add to that, the fact we might be dealing with hundreds of people each day, we are the ones that have to be creative in how we're going to get that LOOP closed. Therefore, start with the rule of fives: keep trying until you get the LOOP closed. Usually within the fifth communication loop closed you are going to get it done as opposed to leaving one phone message and then thinking you are done. It's the RSVP, it's the resolved issue with your teenager, or employee. It's a closed loop, remember, "the closed loop has all of the answers".

LOOPS AND ACCOMPLISHMENT

When considering the LOOPS PARADIGM and the term accomplishment, we see that a closed LOOP is nothing more than an accomplishment, in other words a CLOSED LOOPS EQUALS ACCOMPLISHMENT. It is simply a matter of completing a task or series of tasks. Every open loop is nothing more, nothing less, than a task. The cumulative effect may be great, with great impact on your business or even your life. In our LOOPS LOG, (see loops4biz.com for Loops Logs) we have a section for each day that has room for five important LOOPS. Think about the cumulative effect of this total accomplishment.

Close five important LOOPS each day, that means, in a six day week you are closing: 30 per week, 120 per month, 14,400 per year.

Most people can close more than five a day. Now consider the cumulative effect throughout an entire organization, of 10 people, that's 140,000 important LOOPS closed per year, minimum. The cumulative effect is powerful when LOOPS get closed. Add another word to the term accomplishment, "closure" which means simply completing the project or task, no matter how large or small it is. Closing Loops brings closure. Good stuff!

LOOPS AND INFLUENCE

We have had the opportunity and privilege to talk and work with Steven Covey in the past, as part of his Executive Excellence Program. He states "that within what he calls your circle of influence are the things that you can control". Further he says, "Within your circle of concern are the things you cannot control". So work within your circle of influence. Take only YOUR OWN LOOPS into your circle of influence, and close them. Thus you are doing the things you can control and are starting to group, stack and link your LOOPS collection within the things you can do and accomplish. As you keep doing them, you don't have to worry too much about other people. We call this the LOOP OF INFLUENCE. Other people will automatically take notice.

YOU can only control the LOOPS that YOU can close. Once you start doing this successfully, people will look to you and say, "Man, that's a LOOP closer, maybe even a MASTER LOOP CLOSER". In other words, you become the go-to person. The person that can close LOOPS successfully influence other people because they are setting the example in terms of performance. This becomes a case of LEADING BY EXAMPLE and increases your "Loop of influence". This is important because, as we start increasing our Loop of influence, we start to see overlap to other people's loops. This gets everybody working together, helping each other out and builds a strong case for working as a team. Maybe even a LOOP GROUP.

LOOP STACKING AND PROJECTS

Stacking LOOPS is simply an accumulation of CLOSED LOOPS on a single job. Think of it as a pile of closed loops. The accumulation of these CLOSED LOOPS on a complex task allows us to break the job down into easier digestable parts (loops). Each LOOP builds on the one before it and stacks them up. This adds up to final, completed tasks. A great visual.

For example, putting out a finished graphic product, such as a poster, by a graphic artist: There are many different stages along the way. As the graphic artist moves forward, each stage becomes an open LOOP: they will have to have copy, select pictures, select layouts, size of the graphic, ultimate decisions, even colors and more. All of these things become their own LOOP to close. Think about accomplishing big jobs (Loops) by knowing that the little things (Loops) that we do add up to the big picture. You heard the old saying, "There is no such thing as a small task." This is explained by the assumption that all small things ultimately add up to the bigger one. Our big jobs will become reality as we close and stack our LOOPS. Thus we say that ALL LOOPS ARE CREATED EQUAL.

Another term that can be added to our LOOP PARADIGM GLOSSARY is "LOOP TIME." When people are procrastinating and not doing their work and not seeming to accomplish things that they should be able and willing to do, in other words, they're not being accountable. Use the term: It's LOOP TIME, or aptly put, it's time to get to work and close your loops! "Look guys, we have got to close these LOOPS, we're getting behind on our deadlines". This is what is called LOOP TIME, time to buckle down and get things done. Kick some Loops into gear!

USING LOOPS IN YOUR BUSINESS

The LOOPS process starts with everyone in the organization doing what is called: "THINKING AND SPEAKING LOOPS" meaning everyone is on the same page or "IN THE LOOP" and speaking the same language.

When we talk about LOOP process at our office, we sometimes use the term LOOPING. The LOOP Process starts with "THE COMMUNICATIONS LOOP." The LOOP process says that all people involved in the process must agree that LOOPS is the common language that everyone is going to use.

The common language of course starts with the symbol of the open LOOP and the closed LOOP. The understanding is that if we all use that, when we say to each other, "Did you close the LOOP?" everybody understands that the rule is: a task is either open or closed and that no one is interested in all the smoke and mirrors that used to accompany the answer. The LOOP PARADIGM usually starts with communications between people who are in your organization and gets them to agree to work more efficiently and use this language process. A good starting point in the process to integrating LOOPS is to first have everyone read the LOOPS book (loops4biz.com) and then, sit down and agree that this is going to be the way everyone will communicate so that nobody's feelings are hurt. This eliminates possible misunderstandings. People tend to always want to feel good about what people say to them, and this ultimately leads to excuses and explanations when a Loop is not closed. In the LOOP Paradigm, setting the base line communications is critically important to prevent this. It keeps the air clear all the time.

LOOPS AND TEAMWORK

The next part of the LOOPS paradigm is what we call "LOOP PROJECTS." The LOOP PROJECT is taking a snapshot of a bigger project and then breaking it down into its smaller LOOPS or jobs to be done. It is important to visibly link them together and stack them. The interesting thing about visibly linking and stacking them together (use visuals on the wall or white board) is that everybody involved sees how they are accountable to everybody else and they see the relative importance of the work they do. Even though their task maybe licking the postage stamps, which may seem mundane, they also get to see that if those stamps aren't licked, then the promotion doesn't go out. If the promotion doesn't go out, people don't attend the open house or workshop. So the licking of the postage stamps can be linked to the marketing effort which can be linked to the actual event and then everybody feels like they are an important part, and invested in, the whole project's success. Therein alleviating the problem that some jobs are considered insignificant and the person that licks the postage stamps is often considered the person on the low end of the totem pole, and not very important.

One of the important aspects of employee satisfaction is recognition for a job well done and having them feeling that their work has significant importance. If everybody in the organization is talking LOOPS, then everybody realizes that their LOOP is just as important as everybody else's LOOP. You can see how THE LOOP PARADIGM does have an awful lot to do with human behavior. It goes along with the old saying, "A chain is as strong as its weakest link." We now are going to adopt the new saying, "A CHAIN IS ONLY AS STRONG AS IT'S WEAKEST LOOP."

MORE ABOUT LOOP SYSTEMS

Consider your accounting and financial records? Much of what you do is governed by a strict set of rules. Therefore, you can establish a system to manage your finances. You may have a cash register or computer broken down into departmental buttons which you close out daily with receipts being turned over to a bookkeeper who follows the rules to make sure your books are in order before they are sent to your accountant, who follows more rules and systems before your returns are filed. That's closing a SYSTEM LOOP, even though it seems an automatic thing that you do every day, or every month or every year. It's simply a system, a stack of LOOPS. That's accountability, if in fact it is getting done.

When you are talking about general projects that have less stringent oversight, such as running an open house, it is most efficient to systematize the process by using tools such as check lists, meetings, brainstorming, reports, and so on. Be sure to use them as they are designed, which will help close a whole series of LOOPS, because once again the open house event is nothing more than just a bunch of open and closed LOOPS. It starts with a collection of open LOOPS, ends as a stack of closed LOOPS … best done through the use of systems. The more

LOOPS we close and stack, the closer we get to the end of the project. Everybody is involved, part of the whole project, adding to the stack of closed LOOPS and feeling like they are an integral part of the team.

PRIORITIZING LOOPS

Prioritizing Loops becomes a question of what is called leverage; is it a high or low leverage LOOP? When dealing with junk mail for example, the question becomes… 'are we going to close this LOOP now or leave it open?'

Maybe you even want to throw it away?

Keep it simple, when measuring the relative importance of LOOPS. Close the LOOPS first that impact your projects the most. They are the loops that are important and urgent. Next close the loops that are important but not urgent. The loops left are not important although some may be urgent and you may question whether to close them at all.

Prioritize your LOOPS:

1. Urgent and Important (Real emergencies)
2. Important and Not Urgent (Strategic Planning, Training workers)
3. Urgent and Nor Important (Telephone ringing)
4. Not Urgent and Not Important (Junk mail)

*This system was not developed by Stephen Covey but is associated with his work and *The 7 Habits of Highly Effective People*.

IMPLEMENTATION TIPS

It's a simple process to implement LOOPS in your business. Start with a training session where you introduce the LOOPS concepts. Have everyone read the LOOPS book before you do the training. Then lead a discussion by asking, "How can focusing more attention on closing loops help us accomplish our goals? After the discussion create a list of specific loops to close for your business. Once you have an overall list of LOOPS to close, have each person start their own personal LOOP list.

Once you have introduced LOOPS, your business needs to keep on LOOPING. Hold LOOP meetings on a regular basis, maybe even every day for the first few weeks. Check the progress and seek out ways to improve your LOOP PROCESS and drive the LOOP PARADIGM deeper and deeper into your business. Understand that LOOPS is a mind set as well as a process. Ultimately it becomes your culture, a culture of success.

Please email us and let us know how you are doing with LOOPS in your small business, we'll be glad to help in anyway we can: Reach Steve at Steve@loops4biz or Mike at loopmaster@loops4biz.com

ABOUT MIKE

Mike Chaet, Ph.D., founded the CMS International Consulting firm, M & M Properties, Loops4Biz.com, Hydromaniax inc., and many other successful small businesses. A lecturer, author, and small business consultant, he has been involved in the development and management of over 2,500 small businesses worldwide. He splits his residence between Bozeman, MT, and Phoenix Arizona, with his wife Mary and little black pug dog named Ozzy. He may be contacted at: mike@loops4biz.com.

ABOUT STEVE

Stephen Lundin, Ph.D., the bestselling author of the FISH! series of books, with over 7 million copies in print, has an inventory of work experience ranging from dishwasher to think tank executive; teacher to business school dean; golf caddy to camp director; and small business owner to national sales manager. Today, Steve Lundin spends his time writing, speaking and filmmaking. He has taken his powerful messages about *FISH!*, Top Performer, and Innovation to audiences all over the world. By sharing his powerful, personal and authentic message, Stephen Lundin awakens his audiences to the possibilities that already exist in every workplace, every home and every life. Stephen Lundin's best selling book, *FISH!*, has continuously been a weekly Wall Street Journal bestseller and monthly BusinessWeek bestseller for more than four years. The now business-staple has also appeared frequently on the New York Times Business, Publishers Weekly, USA Today and Barnes and Noble bestseller lists. Published in 34 languages with over 4 million copies in print worldwide, *FISH!* has taken the *FISH!* Philosophy to all corners of the world. His book *CATS: The Nine Lives of Innovation*, takes the position that organizations don't innovate, people do. So if you want to have a more innovative organization, develop more innovative employees. The curriculum for this employee development is The Nine Lives of Innovation. Stephen's most recent work, co-authored with Bob Nelson, is *UBUNTU*, a powerful story about the African philosophy of teamwork and collaboration that has the power to reshape our workplaces, our relationships with our coworkers, and our personal lives, written by the bestselling coauthor of *FISH!* and the bestselling author of *1001 Ways to Reward Employees*. Steve may be contacted at slrunner@aol.com.

CHAPTER 5

CREATIVITY AND THE REALITY OF EDUCATION

BY ROBERT REEDY, M.F.A., PROFESSOR OF ART,
DIRECTOR OF THE ADVANCED DESIGN LAB
UNIVERSITY OF CENTRAL FLORIDA

I recently received news that I was passed over for an award through my universities' Teacher Incentive Program (TIP), which awards professors that demonstrate excellence in their fields with a substantial, annual monetary raise. As a working artist and professor, I have learned over the years that with rejection comes opportunity. In fact, rejection is quite common if one is continually stretching the creative boundaries in our work and lives. The problem is that the institutions and communities in which we work have set standards for success and do not reward what they have come to define as failure; however, this is how mankind has greeted many awesome and creative innovations throughout history. Thus, we have the notion of something being "Ahead of its time".

Our institutions and communities have such unshakeable definitions of success and failure that I cannot recall anyone, other than my mother, ever telling me, "its okay Rob. Everyone makes mistakes. Give it another try." When is the last time you have ever heard a math or science teacher say, "Okay class, this is how we solve for X. Now you try to create another way." Instead, we expect students to memorize and execute without time to question or wonder, much less create.

So here lies the problem. Students spend more time memorizing answers than trying to find their own, unique solutions. Students are worried if not afraid of being incorrect. We have put them through an academic factory in which error is shameful. On the other hand, a temporary error in the pursuit of learning is not shameful; therefore I believe this vulnerability to be a strength and not a weakness. For us to maximize our creative output, we have to clearly understand our weaknesses and limitations in order to adapt, improvise, and ultimately overcome our challenges. These mass-produced students rely on their talent for quickly accessing prepackaged data and any misstep in logic or result can turn their world upside down. They are unprepared for a world that is not clear-cut and that requires a creative and spontaneous mind. As a professor, I have never given much credence to the traditional definitions of talent. In fact, I am certain it is highly overrated. In my mind, talent is a word referring to potential not necessarily performance. In my profession, as in any other, talent will merely open doors, whereas performance and results will get you in the room. However, I want to be clear on this point. I'm all about proven performance, but not at the expense of creativity and conceptual development. Therein lies the conflict.

On this matter people in higher education begin to divide into camps based on their methods for successful learning and development. And the argument becomes—is the performance derived from a students' creative prowess more or less valuable than results achieved by mechanical and methodical instruction? This is not unlike the left-brain/right-brain phenomena. However, people forget, or maybe underestimate, the beautiful, yet complicated, symbiotic relationship between both sides of the brain working in tandem as one coordinated unit.

This is where we begin to see the cracks in the educational structures of our nation. Indeed, what if the very institutions that accredit our educational programs are basing their standards on the same outdated criteria year after year? For all of our technological and philosophical advancements, we are still trapped in a system that is hundreds of years old. A system that uses an old model for educating that works, by their standards, and generates income. I argue that it doesn't work. Success as an educator is not merely the advancement of my students but the advancement of a creative, freethinking scholar that is prepared for lifelong learning. We constantly use the term "think outside the box", when in fact what we need to do is build an entirely new box. When products of this old system enroll in my design class, they produce work that is deserving of a D or an F. My critique of their work typically goes as, "Your design is clumsy, ineffective, poorly crafted, and clearly lacks imagination; start over!"

So now, in my twenty-eighth year as an administrator and instructor, I have decided to take my own advice and start over. I have come to realize that perhaps I, as a product of the same system as my students, was facilitating the problem or that I was not 'walking my talk'… so to speak. Why should I hold my students to a standard that I do not maintain for myself? What's more is whether or not we actually think our students cannot recognize this hypocrisy; they certainly do. Imagine how this affects a student's creativity and productivity. We have known for centuries that it is critical to human development to be skilled in math and science, fully aware of the arts and creativity, as well as being voracious readers and inquisitors. So why do we continue to develop and implement educational paradigms that work against these foundations of cognitive development? Why has the creative side of human development become the punching bag for irresponsible spending and management in education? Is this the example we wish to model for our students? A model of robotic methodology in which only results are praised and not the creative and unique means by which our pupils come to a working, successful end?

GETTING STARTED

The first thing I did was throw out everything I thought I knew about classroom formats and procedures. Unlike professor Kingsfield in the movie "The Paper Chase", I reversed my traditional role as professor/mentor. I became more of a coach and facilitator, doing everything I could to aid my students in finding answers to their questions as opposed to the role of the all-knowing demi-god. The best, exemplifying metaphor would be that of a parent closely observing their child who has just ventured off on their first ride without training wheels.

The second step to my classroom overhaul was to restructure my classes from the outdated academic setting in order to cultivate, as closely as possible, a classroom that resembled a professional working environment. The challenge was to do so without jeopardizing my emphasis on the creative process while still keeping students in tune with the integrity of their performance and ability to meet deadlines. I have found that the easiest and often most tempting option for a professor is to throw a textbook at a student as though it is some how-to book that has all the answers and that I, the professor, needn't be bothered. This reinforces a student's belief that all that is required for academic success and achievement is to be on time and to execute. The problem here is that our results-based educational system does not provide the student with a working model that clearly exemplifies what is necessary to work creatively and practically in the real world. This is because processes and deadlines are always predetermined in our outdated educational system, which is not always the case when students find themselves as young professionals in a business environment.

Our students are conditioned from first grade to college to exclusively put stock in to passing exams and achieving high academic standards based on scores and rankings. As a university professor, these rankings mean very little to me because exams do not measure a student's ability to perform consistently and creatively in a competitive, work environment. For instance, with very little effort I can teach anyone to create a painting; however, in no way does this prepare them for the rigors of life as a professional artist. So as parents, if we are paying for our sons and daughters to receive a college degree in order to prepare them for entry into the real world, then why are graduates being told that while they have impressive academic records, they are still lacking the training and experience required to hit the ground running in their professional lives? The reason is plain and simple—they aren't ready. Those responsible for approving university curriculum frown upon the type of integrated programming needed to prepare students for entry into the actual workplace. We see it as too "vo-techish", or so basic and practical that it is impractical. This attitude presupposes that by preparing students for entry into their professional lives, that integrated, programmed curriculum will infect their lofty, creative aspirations and thus diminish the academic reputation of the institution.

Third, I decided to rethink the demographics in my classes, allowing students from all studies, backgrounds, and grade levels to begin in an advanced design class. This created an environment that was satiated with different perspectives influenced by a multitude of different factors—age, creed, race, values, "left-brain" thinkers and "right-brain" thinkers all together, creating together. Up until this moment all of our classes had been segregated and very rarely worked together except for the occasional "interdisciplinary" creative assignments. The segregation of colleges and departments within universities, which has become the standard across the nation, does not make room for this kind of collaboration.

With this in mind I decided to open my enrollment. There are no prerequisites for non-art majors and any university student could take my class. This is in opposition to most curriculum development theories established by universities and accreditation agencies. A great example of this inside-the-box approach is the idea that first and second year students must wait until their third or fourth year to engage in advanced coursework. Where did this standard come from? Why wait? Raise the bar today! So this is exactly what my students and I did. One semester I challenged them to redesign and create a name for their course. I gave them complete creative freedom so long as they met with state and university curriculum requirements. This is how ADLab (Advanced Design Lab) and HIVE learning was born.

THE ADLAB/HIVE LEARNING METHOD

Visualize walking into your classroom to students who are not only eager to learn but have started working early and without being told to begin. Imagine a class where students establish the creative timeline for course objectives and are regarded as an equal visionary in the course; a course where students are talked to rather than talked at, and who aren't afraid to say "I don't know". They know there will be coaching and encouragement to find the answer. Students that are inspired and highly motivated to learn, challenged by the unknown and taking the necessary risks to solve problems in a creative, thoughtful, and professional manner. Sounds like the Twilight Zone doesn't it? Well, I've seen it, and it is indeed real. It's the ADLab and our HIVE Learning Method.

ADLab and Hive Learning is a matrix model we are using to prepare college art majors for the real world of art and design. The mission is to merge traditional teaching principles of design and the visual elements with practical, real-world business application and hands-on client interaction in a competitive classroom environment.

With this approach, old teaching paradigms are discarded and replaced with real contemporary issues and challenges. Students use both their creative and analytical skills, abolishing the notion that by preparing for the real world somehow we are diminishing their creative and conceptual development.

While the first several weeks are focused on teaching students the fundamental aspects of visual language and design, the latter portion of the semester is directed towards applying what we have covered in a competitive environment with a real client and design problem. The client agrees to purchase a design project selected from the student competition. ADLab acts as a liaison between the students and client. The students communicate directly with clients, coordinating resources and design tools, while actively balancing academic, administrative and legal impacts of the project. Some of AD Lab's past clients include—Hard Rock Park, Seminole Co. Harley Davidson, Harris Rosen Hotels and Resorts and Smooth Jazz WLOQ.

The Hive Learning Method was a class assignment given to my ADLab students. The assignment was clear: create a new learning model for studio art classes and in particular ART 2203 / Three Dimensional Design. The students researched pedagogy, the syllabi of other universities, even the learning patterns of bees. The latter triggered an interesting find in the study of the swarming of bees. The communication and productivity of bees that use a centralized hive and a smaller swarm pattern while working individually to serve a greater purpose would be converted to a classroom learning model. We have since implemented the results of our research in all my classes. Students are now working in groups to solve design problems while maintaining individual creative freedom and solutions. Additionally, we are covering twice the amount of material in half the time with increased quality and creative outcome.

In the fall of 2009, I introduced Hive Learning in my classroom. To date, there has been a substantial, positive increase in my teacher evaluations, a rise in the mean grade of the course, and absences decreased. I continue to use the Hive Learning methodology, syllabus, collateral, and workbooks created by my students. Some of the side effects have been remarkable. Because I was unable to find a text that would fit this learning method my students and I created a course pack, which acts as a visual journal for the course. This is not that unusual except for the fact the proceeds / royalties are placed in an auxiliary account in my department. This is important because now all my courses are financially stable and are unaffected by crushing budget cuts by the state and university. In other words, my students now understand that using broader interdisciplinary approaches to funding issues and curriculum development can solve any problem. So in effect, I am modeling sound business principles with creative problem solving.

What if there was actually very little difference across academic subject matter? Like tubes of paint in a box that share basic structure and purpose—pigment, binder, tube, cap all needed for painting. Aren't academic departments and programs generally the same shape, size and placed in the same container. We share similar structures and purpose – semester, quarters, years, dean's, chairs and so forth. Only our subject matter and content divides us. So why can't we change the box or the shapes and sizes of programs to fit the real needs of our students, replacing our outdated systems and models?

Here is the 'Catch 22'. In order to stay vital and on the creative edge of new learning paradigms, we must commit to a set of values that is generally not accepted by our society. We must understand that if we are truly breaking new ground we will only possess the answers for a brief moment before we encounter the next question. We must realize that if our current system is not meeting the needs of our students on a global level, then we must change the box - not rewrap the old one. Maybe the box is no longer a rigid square but more like a flexible amoeba.

My challenge to you is: start now, change the box and make a difference.

ABOUT ROBERT

Robert Reedy is Director of Advanced Design Lab and Professor of Art at The University of Central Florida in Orlando, Florida. Prior to this, Professor Reedy served as Chair of Fine Arts at Ringling School of Art and Design, Bradley University and The University of Central Florida. His leadership and academic prowess has made him a nationally recognized leader in entrepenural, cutting edge visual arts programming. As a former recipient of a National Endowment for the Arts Artist in Residence Fellowship, Reedy is recognized as an outstanding educator with over thirty years of experience teaching ceramics, design and creative business concepts in the world of art.

Reedy's work has been featured at numerous national and international galleries and museums, including The Museum of American Art at The Smithsonian Institute in Washington DC, The American Crafts Museum in New York, and The Museum of American Ceramics in Pomona, CA. Additionally, his work is in the private collections of former Vice President and Ambassador Walter Mondale and his wife Joan, and The Arrowmont School of Craft and Design.

CHAPTER 6

PASH-UH-WHAT? THE ULTIMATE GAME CHANGER

BY JENNIFER BRYDEN

PASSIOWATT

It's not a typo. It's a descriptive word I made up to explain a phenomenon for which I know no other word.

A *passiowatt*, (pash-uh-wot) is a unit of energy, like a megawatt that provides a limitless amount of positive energy. Powered by taking action, and doing those things in life you care about most, the *passiowatt* can get you out of bed at three o'clock in the morning and keep you working long into the night. Pulling from a personal reserve of *passiowatts* is the only way you can continue on, day after day, when the rest of the world appears to be pulling, slowing, and pressing you down.

The more you use this energy, the more of it you discover within yourself. The problem is, events happen that cause us to lose sight on the source of this energy in those moments we need them most.

When we lose that vision, our vocabulary changes and we start using words like "tired," "stressed" or in the worst cases, "depressed." All it takes is a slight shift in focus to bring back the limitless energy of the *passiowatt.*

Pacing the back of the hotel ballroom, I waited to take the stage and pour my heart out to an audience of one hundred strangers that were two, three, possibly FOUR times my age. I couldn't stand still. I tried to sit. The table shook because I couldn't keep my leg from jittering. The man to my right asked if I was nervous. I managed a reply "Nope, excited."

…I lied.

Yes, I was nervous! I was progressively losing control of my body, erupting with *passiowatts*, because *I COULD NOT WAIT to share my message and I didn't want to screw it up.*

This was it, my point of no return. The first moment in my adult life when I would publicly declare who I am and what I stand for. I took a deep breath and rose from my chair. As I did so, the conference moderator took the microphone and released the audience. Perfect, I was finally prepared to dive face first towards my destiny and the rest of the room was on potty break.

This is the story of how changing my focus, by shifting my energy to draw from my *passiowatt* reserve, revived my business, saved my family and resurrected a peace within myself.

When both of my parents became unemployed, I decided I would leave college to help support my family. We would start a business together. I transferred my skills in video production and storytelling to the world of marketing and sales. I left art school for the university of hard knocks; you know, that place of slick hair gel, cheesy grins, shiny watches and briefcases… a world I believed was defined by zeros and graphical reports, instead of standing ovations and genuine smiles.

My passion for storytelling became buried, along with my identity, under the burdens of financial stress. My videos lacked flavor and voice; business trickled in as the walls began to cave. My family was crumbling and I was lost somewhere in the long dark tunnel between who I was becoming, and who I wanted to be. I missed my art. I hated this business.

When Mike, one of my business coaches, first offered me a ten-minute time slot at his annual marketing event, I wasn't exactly sure what I would speak on. His offer was incredibly generous considering he had never heard me speak in front of an audience. While I was confident in my abilities, even I didn't know what would happen once I took the stage. Ten minutes on video marketing? I had one month to come up with something. I came up with:-

"THE BOTTOM LINE - THE TOP 5 REASONS VIDEO MARKETING IS THE ULTIMATE WAY TO GROW YOUR BUSINESS"

One week 'til show time. I had my presentation, but I was worn out. I was still editing lame videos that looked like everything else on the market because I was in a hurry to grow my business.

I had lost focus on crafting beautiful stories. I had gotten in a rush, trying to turn out as many sales as possible, listening to that constant voice of self-doubt and fear. If I didn't make enough, how would we survive?

The initial plan was to go into this conference, give a presentation on why use video marketing, generate a lot of leads and then make a lot of videos, really fast. With a large bulk order, we could put a small cap over our heads and buy food next month. It was all lined up.

The closer the date became, the more the knot in my stomach grew. Not because I was nervous, but because I hated myself for allowing the personality of my clients to get lost in transaction. I was making myself sick and tired. Then I chose to shift focus.

I decided to write a little guide that would teach people how to create better marketing content. How-to's on harnessing the power of your personal story and video to market your business. I would give this little workbook away as a gift to anyone who would take the time to fill out a short survey. It was a small thank you to any one who could provide a bit of insight into my next step.

By giving this workbook away, it released some kind of mental barrier I had placed on myself. I didn't have to worry about "professionalism." I could share my personal views and share what I felt was worth sharing. I called this guide "*Inside Matters*."

Ten minutes after the conference began, I sat at home guarding the printer as the first few pages fell into my hands. We shoved the assembled workbooks into a bag for the hour and a half drive into Dallas, where we were supposed to already be setting up our booth.

I was weeping from utter emotional and physical exhaustion. I made up horrid stories of why we couldn't make it to the event, because I would rather not show up at all, than be late. Still, I clambered into the truck with my box of Kleenex, my first run edition of *Inside Matters* and buckled up for the ride.

The little workbook was chock-full of typos and grammatical errors and the page numbers didn't line up. But, it was spunky. It was me. *Inside Matters* was a small piece of my vision; the content I WANTED to create. It was a manual on marketing; how I felt it should be.

I arrived at my booth with a handful of ink pens, a few strips of survey and a short stack of my precious little guides. And I waited for hours at my table in the corner for my ten-minute slot on stage.

Did they think I was a joke? My naked booth, my homemade books with sections like "Monkey See, Monkey Do," analogies about cookies, the whole thing decorated like a children's book. Two days, twenty-five books hand delivered. No response.

I sat in on parts of the conference when I could, listening to the other speakers and then reviewing my own little speech in turn. 5. Drive Traffic. 4. Get Attention… Tuning in and out. 3. Build Credibility. Scribbling disorderly notes 2. Harnessing Star Power… Fighting lethargy. 1. Make your life better. Make your life better.

Something clicked. In ten minutes, I could teach a trick about video marketing or maybe, just maybe, in ten minutes I could say one thing that would make someone's life better.

It took me all of thirty seconds to re-outline my entire speech.

At 3:00 a.m. the night before my highly anticipated presentation, I sat in front of my home computer rearranging slides, playing the movie in my head of how my presentation would go.

Paper coated the floor where carpet should have been. Disembodied workbook pages scratched in red ink pulled my attention away from the screen.

Self-doubt made its first assault. If someone didn't find value in my little workbook they would just stop reading and throw it away. I would never have to know.

If someone didn't like what I had to say on stage, if no one found value in what I bring to the table as a human being; then what happens?

I spoke with a friend late that night, looking for some kind of reassurance. Did I really need to take this leap of faith, pouring out my heart, which scared me just a little, or would it be a better to retreat and give the "boring business benefit presentation" I had already prepared.

This was his response:

If you are nervous, you are focusing too much on yourself. Focus on your message.

I played out every possible worst-case scenario. When I realized my biggest fear was not being able to deliver *my* true message, I was ready.

Sometimes we are forced to change focus. Other times we must find the strength to do so, of our own free will. If we try to resist this necessary shift, our business, our life and our story will become stale and die.

The bathroom break was over; everyone began filing into the room. As seats began to fill, I spotted one of the couples who had picked up my workbook the day before. I approached them and asked what they thought of my little guide? DUMB IDEA JENN. BAD TIMING. I was already on track for a heart attack. Why go looking for negative feedback right before I take the stage to give one of the most important presentations of my life?

I expected something along the lines of "oh…it was…uh cute?" Maybe a polite, "You know, I didn't get a chance to look at it yet." But I didn't get "sorry" or "cute", I got "Amazing." I got a smile! Someone LIKED what I had to say! Not only did they like it, they wanted to share it with more people! If *Inside Matters* could help even one person then it was worth it, and now it might help hundreds.

I had invested all of my energy, all of my "*passiowatts*" into that little guide. And somehow, just before I launched my business, the universe had returned them to me ten fold.

When Mike called me to the stage, I think I ran? I don't really remember how I got up there, but there was a flood of ENERGY and confidence within me.

So my presentation began. I shared how I had written this Presentation "Video Marketing is the most Epically Awesome Way to grow your business"... but how that wasn't enough!

The specific reason we go into business is different for each of us, but we all start for a reason OTHER than just to run a business. It's about pride, or family, or freedom. For some it's helping people, for others it's doing something new every day, It was never really about the bottom line at all. Even the title in my first little presentation was wrong. It's not about the bottom line; it's all about the big picture! Market With Passion was born.

My new presentation was titled: *"The big picture: Why Passion Marketing is the most Epically Awesome way to serve your clients."*

When my overtime, turbo-paced, yet highly passionate presentation was over, I was met in the hall by handshakes, hugs and high fives!

A handful of individuals came to me with tears in their eyes sharing what it was that they were most passionate about. One woman showed me pictures of beautiful custom aprons she designs. Another shared her plans to write a book with her mother about an African refugee in her hometown. Another man came to me with tears in his eyes, and told me about how much spending time with his family means to him. I watched another light up as he spoke of training injured marathon runners - how they could get a piece of their life back and run again pain-free.

This was my point of no return.

I discovered what it was that I am most passionate about. It's bringing out this side of people we so often keep locked away.

I am committed to using my talents, my skills and my *passiowatts* to assist you in bringing out your passion.

Are you ready to change your game? More importantly are you willing to shift your focus?

When you are ready, I invite you to join the community of small business owners like yourself, who are busy lighting up our world with ***PASSIOWATTS!!!***

ABOUT JENNIFER

Jennifer Bryden is the Chief Creative Officer and Owner of Market With Passion, a multi-media marketing firm serving business of all sizes across the country. Known as *The Story Chef*, Jenn specializes in cooking up content that sticks, spreads and sells.

Jenn has extensive experience in video production and social networking campaigns. In early 2010, she was hired by one of the largest risk management firms in the service contract industry to plan and implement a ten million-impression campaign targeting the real estate industry. She consulted in the creation of the message as well as corresponding web applications.

Jenn is an Apple Certified Pro in Final Cut Pro and Motion. She has produced commercials and video products for popular international clients such as the International Woman's Football league (IWFL). Her short films have been honored in several film festivals, including a spot as a top ten finalist in the prestigious South By South West in Austin and special recognition for her health education videos by the Juvenile Diabetes Research Foundation International. Jenn regularly speaks to groups in the Dallas/ Fort Worth area on small businesses marketing topics such as content and product creation, video production, social media implementation and of course, 'How to *market with passion!*'.

When she is not working to help small businesses save time and make more money, Jenn runs the Dirt Devil Fastpitch Training Organization, training young female athletes on the fundamentals for success on and off the field.

Discover the "Top 5" ways you can harness the most epically awesome marketing tools in the universe at www.MarketWithPassion.com/GameChanger and receive your free edition of *Inside Matters: The Ultimate Guide to Better Marketing Content.*

Got a mobile QR reader? Subscribe from your phone!

CHAPTER 7

FROM IDEA ...TO PRODUCT ...TO MARKET!

BY WILLIAM BENNER

Do you have an idea that you'd like to turn into a product, which can ultimately be marketed and sold to others? It could be that you do this only as a kind of hobby – as many people do by selling small things at the local flea market or on eBay. Or it could be that this becomes your primary source of income – perhaps even something that you build into a large company one day.

Within my own field of endeavor, I turn ideas into products which make a profit, and are the basis of multi-national company operations. If you've ever seen a professional laser show, you've probably seen one of my products – software called "Lasershow Designer 2000" – in action. For example, LD2000 is used to create shows at the world's top theme parks and events like the Super Bowl and Olympics. I know how to go from an idea to a award-winning product because I have done this over and over again.

It is my hope that this chapter will not only provide information necessary to turn your ideas into products, but also provides the inspiration and motivation to follow through on your own ideas, and not get lost in procrastination or the distractions of everyday life.

STEP 1
COME UP WITH AN IDEA – PREFERABLY ONE THAT IS CLOSE TO YOUR HEART

Usually, you can find an idea for a marketable product or service close to your own experience. Is there something you work with every day that is frustrating or poorly designed? As they say on infomercials, "there must be a better way!" In my own experience, I found that tiny, expensive laser diodes were too sensitive to everyday static shocks that could destroy them. So I came up with a special component that absorbs even immense lightning-like shocks.

Or perhaps you can take an idea or process from one field, and apply it to another. I met a couple who were on the Simon Cowell-produced reality TV show "American Inventor". Their idea was to replace the basket in coffee machines with a special insert designed to infuse tea instead. In my own experience, I took ideas used in computer graphics software for TV monitors, and used them instead for the very different task of making laser beams draw out shapes and graphics.

At this stage, don't worry about not being an expert in all areas of your invention. Having an idea that is close to your heart will help to provide drive and passion, and these will be necessary to carry the idea through the following steps to becoming a saleable product.

STEP 2
MAKE SURE YOUR IDEA IS NOT PROTECTED IN SOME WAY

Before investing time, energy, and money into turning your idea into a product, find out whether or not your idea has already been thought of. Do an Internet search for keywords related to your idea, such as "coffee basket tea infuser" or "laser computer graphics". Even if there are some matches, perhaps your idea is an improvement or has a particular approach in manufacturing or marketing that can give you an advantage.

You should find out if your idea has already been patented by someone else. U.S. patents are found online at: www.uspto.gov and through Google at: patents.google.com. International patents can be found at: www.wipo.org. Search using terms that would be applicable to your idea. You might be surprised what you turn up within the patent databases! If nothing else, searching the patent database can give you additional input to help refine your own idea.

Even if your idea has already been patented, the patent may be expired or abandoned. Also, you can "design around" an existing patent by significantly changing some aspect of the invention. If you do find that you need to design around a patent, work with a reputable patent attorney to help you avoid patent infringement.

STEP 3
CREATE DRAWINGS AND WRITTEN DOCUMENTATION

The next step is to refine your idea using drawings or sketches, that can communicate the concept to someone outside of your field. For a patentable product, your drawings will eventually be conveyed to a professional draftsman, so the clearer they are, the less time and money you will have to spend later.

Another useful part of this step is to create a written description of everything that is on your mind regarding the project. For example, you should not only write about how to make the product, or what it will look like, but also write about how it will be used by others, how it would be marketed, the potential sale price, and everything else. This helps make sure the idea is clear within your own mind, and will also be useful for later steps, including collaborating with others, creating a business plan, and possibly applying for a patent.

STEP 4
PROTECT THE IDEA (IF APPLICABLE)

If, while creating the drawings and written documentation, you find that the idea isn't clear enough, or if you discover holes in the idea that you can't figure out for yourself, you could talk with someone who has expertise in the field of interest, to try to get additional information and help fill in the missing details. But this must be done carefully.

If the idea is unique, then it is certainly worthwhile to think about how to protect it. In fact, you should start thinking about this relatively early in the process – and definitely before you start discussing the idea with others.

One easy way to protect the idea is to create a non-disclosure agreement or "NDA". This is an agreement between you and potential collaborators stating that you may freely exchange information with each other, but the information that you discuss won't be shared with outsiders. For example, you can employ a machinist or CAD operator to turn your sketches into prototype devices. Or, you may want to enter into discussions with an established company to have them make and market your idea. A well-written NDA protects your idea from being misappropriated.

NDAs are very common, and you can find examples of these for free on the Internet. If you are on a budget, modify one to suit your needs. For a few hundred bucks, hire an attorney and have them draft the NDA for you, or at least review what you've created and make sure it is as bullet-proof as it needs to be for your application.

Any professional is quite accustomed to signing NDAs before entering into further discussions and in fact, if someone balks about signing the NDA, it is an indication that they are not a professional, and I would advise you to steer clear of such people.

MOVING BEYOND NDAS – DESIGN PATENTS, UTILITY PATENTS AND PROVISIONAL PATENTS

NDA's protect you only with specific contractors and potential partners. For full protection, if you have a patentable idea you will need some form of patent protection. These include design patents, utility patents and provisional patents.

Further discussion about patents is beyond the scope of this chapter, but I will give a few recommendations. First, be sure to work with a reputable patent attorney. There are some "patent shops" out there that will guarantee you a patent, but in such a case, they most often simply deliver a design patent which generally offers little protection for products. And second, don't be afraid to discuss your idea with a reputable patent attorney. One individual who approached me with an idea told me that they were afraid to discuss their idea with an attorney, for fear that they would run off with the idea themselves. There is nothing to fear when working with professionals.

STEP 5
CREATE A PROTOTYPE

Few products work exactly the way their creators originally intend. Therefore, you should create a prototype to help identify potential problems. It doesn't necessarily need to be made out of the final materials that an end-product will use. Instead, I find it useful to make a prototype out of common, easy-to-find materials, such as wood, cardboard and paper.

Some products may require you to get the help of others in order to create the prototype. For example, it may be necessary to have a local machine shop create some or all of the parts necessary. This is no problem since small machine shops are accustomed to working with individuals, and these machine shops may also have the capability to turn your crude sketches into formal drawings to produce the parts.

STEP 6
PERFORM TESTING USING REAL-WORLD SUBJECTS IF POSSIBLE

Once you've created a prototype, the next step is to test it and make sure it works as intended. As with the steps above, this step provides valuable insight into the completeness of the idea and will help to identify where further refinements are needed.

In the case of the couple with the tea insert for coffee makers, they found that some coffee makers did not heat water to the higher temperature required for tea. So they came up with a few ideas for solving this, including a separately heated insert.

If the testing reveals that further changes are needed, simply continue to refine the idea, and repeat some of the steps above until your product suits the requirement well.

STEP 7
CREATE A FINAL, PRODUCTION VERSION

Once you have a prototype that has been tested and seems to work well, you'll want to create a final version using the real materials for production such as metal, fiberglass, plastic, and other legitimate structural materials that will be expected in a finished product. As was the case in steps above, often times creating the final version will reveal holes or missing elements in the idea that don't show up until close to the end.

For the final version, it is most likely that you will need to involve the help of others, such as material suppliers and machine shops.

A WORD TO THE WISE – DON'T GET BOGGED DOWN TRYING TO MAKE A PERFECT PRODUCT

Make your first product as simple and basic as possible. It does not need to be "gold-plated", and perfect in every way. By keeping your initial product as simple and basic as possible, it will allow you to move out fast and get initial exposure to the marketplace, where you'll be able to gauge interest as soon as possible. If the market and interest is strong, you can always come out with an improved version later on. If the market interest is not as strong as you hoped, then you will not have wasted time on "gold plated" features initially.

TO MAKE IT YOURSELF, OR PARTNER WITH SOMEONE ELSE?

If the product is simple enough, you could likely make it yourself and perhaps have your family members or friends help with the assembly. You could fund initial production runs out of your savings, or even using a credit card to buy parts.

If the product is complicated, or if ramping up for production will be difficult, you might want to consider partnering with others, such as an 'angel' investor that has money to fund production quantities, or a partner company who is already established in the market. Obviously partnering with others involves risks, so this should be done very cautiously.

STEP 8
FORMULATE A BUSINESS PLAN

Although a business plan could be done at almost any point in the process, I am choosing to put it here – at a point after you know you have a manufacturable product that works as intended.

Creating a business plan will help you to identify if there are holes in your idea for bringing the product to market. And, as was the case with the drawings and documentation above, if you discover holes in the business plan while you are writing it, you should keep on working on it until the plan is refined.

There are many great resources available, including the Small Business Administration guidelines available for free online at: www.sba.gov.

STEP 9
BRING YOUR PRODUCT TO MARKET (IF YOU BUILD IT THEY WILL COME?)

Once you have your product ready to go, how can you bring it to market. In many fields, tradeshows are a great way to demonstrate your product directly to potential buyers. Tradeshows are often relatively inexpensive – perhaps $1000 to $3500 for a booth space.

Online marketing can be relatively inexpensive. Your website should completely describe and demonstrate your product, and include ways to purchase the product (online sales, a dealer list, etc.). Work with a web expert to help your site and product be found in search engines. And there are the obvious things that can be done with social media, such as Facebook, Twitter and YouTube.

You may need to use other marketing approaches, such as advertising in relevant magazines and trade journals, and perhaps even direct mail.

For my laser shock absorbing component, it takes a combination of "all of the above". I demonstrate LASORB at tradeshows (the lightning-generating ESD gun we use helps draw people into the booth!), there is a website and YouTube videos online, and I hired a public relations agency to help place articles in appropriate electronics-industry magazines.

STEP 10
ENJOY THE FRUITS OF YOUR LABOR

The ideal product is one that you create once, and can replicate many times at low cost and effort. You don't have to put much effort into making the actual item, such as our software that we duplicate on computer discs, or LASORB which we order in runs of many thousands from an overseas supplier.

This lets you move to the next step: further improvements to your product to keep ahead of competition, or even additional new products. Once you have successfully created one product, the next one will be much easier!

ABOUT WILLIAM

As President and CTO of Pangolin Laser Systems, a multi-national organization with offices in the United States, Central Europe and China, William R. Benner Jr. sets the general strategic direction for the company and oversees all company operations. As CTO, he supervises all hardware and software development as well as research and development on new products, which tend to strongly influence the future direction of the laser- and SMS-display industries.

In addition to having received more than 20 international awards for technical achievement, Benner's products are used by some of the best-known companies in the world, including Walt Disney World, Universal Studios, DreamWorks, Boeing, Samsung, and Lawrence Livermore Labs.

Beyond his work at Pangolin, Benner has served as a director on several boards as well as Technical Committee Chairman for the International Laser Display Association. He has also consulted for companies outside of Pangolin including NEOS, Cambridge Technologies, RMB Miniature Bearings and many others.

Benner holds numerous Patents, and has received personal letters of commendation from President Ronald Reagan and Florida Governor Bob Graham. He has also been published in the SMPTE Journal, The Laserist, LaserFX, EDN magazine and Motorola's Embedded Connection magazine. He represented the state of Florida in the United States Skill Olympics and represented the U.S. in International Skill Olympics trials, receiving gold medals for each. Benner has also received the International Laser Display Association's highest accolade, the Career Achievement Award.

CHAPTER 8

THE NEW PR: A VIRTUAL NECESSITY!

BY LINDSAY DICKS

Up until a few years ago, public relations was all about sending out press releases (in an envelope with a stamp amazingly enough!) to magazines and newspapers and trying to get clients booked on radio and TV interview shows.

The ONLY way to get "the word" out was through newspapers, magazines, TV and radio shows.

Now, those newspapers and magazines are rapidly shrinking in size – the ones that are still in business, that is. And the average age of network news viewers is *over 60.*

And even though these offline media still have the clout of tradition as well as their long-established brand names, their actual power to persuade and dominate the overall public conversation diminishes year by year. Ratings and readership continue to show slow, steady year-to-year declines.

For entrepreneurs, professionals and marketers out to seize the latest internet opportunities, performing purely old-school public relations doesn't do the job anymore. You must utilize the newest revolutionary online public relations tools to build your brand and your business. Let's discuss how these strategies can be a "Game Changer" for you as well!

PR DOESN'T STAND STILL

In countless old movies, you often see fast-talking public relations guys wearing hats and ties, calling newspapers and gossip columnists in a desperate attempt to get their clients some much-needed "ink." They all knew that newspapers are where they could get noticed and get the needed boost to their careers

That changed with the rise of TV journalism. In the 60's, 70's and to this day, for those wanting to reach the public, getting on the nightly news was the Holy Grail. Activists and government officials alike made sure their announcements and press conferences were timed to make the 6 pm news.

Now? What's the point of waiting for the 6 pm news, if anyone's even watching it anymore? Any time is the right time to tweet!

The point is that public relations progresses with technology – and it's only natural that the rise of online PR has been swift and dramatic. PR is there to present its clients and companies as the newest "Big Thing." Why then, would outdated media be used to deliver an ultra-modern message?

And actually, that's just the start of the argument for changing things up and embracing online PR. Because it's about a lot more than appearances and trends.

It's about your bottom line.

There's a reason many businesspeople are abandoning the (offline) Yellow Pages for advertising. It's not worth the cost anymore – most people, now that they are using the internet on a regular basis, consistently use Google, Yahoo!, and Bing, among other search engines, to find just the right product or service that they're searching for.

And it's why SEO (Search Engine Optimization) is THE way to make your online business boom. When you find yourself or your business consistently coming up on the first page of Google search results for your keywords, you know you've pretty much got it made.

That's why the ultimate aim of today's online public relations is SEO-oriented. If your PR doesn't have an SEO pay-off, it can be a waste of time, effort and money – no matter how big a splash you make in of-fline media.

For example, let's say you did get a story about yourself on the local news. Let's go a little further – wouldn't you like a front-page story in "The Wall Street Journal?" Who wouldn't?

And yes, while they may even post this article online, believe it or not, that's not really enough.

Although it's indeed cool to be featured in one of the nation's leading newspapers - and momentarily might grant you SOME new traffic to your website - the idea that it will really boost your website numbers is really putting a lot of faith in the idea that your particularly unique prospects will happen to be on "The Wall Street Journal" website and see your article in the first place. Not likely.

But, c'mon. A "Wall Street Journal" piece? That has to be good for *something,* right?

You're absolutely right - it's a giant accomplishment. And it becomes an even greater accomplishment if you use it to not only bring qualified traffic back to your website, but also to boost your Google rankings!

PUTTING ONLINE PR TO WORK

As I noted earlier, there's no denying that many traditional media out-lets still have a very powerful brand. So, let's say you want to leverage that imaginary "Wall Street Journal" story - and use it to boost your site's SEO.

There are several ways to do just that…so let's take a look!

- **PUT IT ON YOUR WEBSITE**

Create a section on your website and feature the article. That way, when you begin to circulate a link to the article, it goes to *your* website, not the newspaper's. That's great for Google's purposes, as well as your own.

- **PUT OUT AN ONLINE PRESS RELEASE ABOUT IT**

By putting out a press release about your WSJ story, you can not only let as many other media outlets know about your newfound celebrity, but you can also insert keywords and website links that will boost your Google results. Many online services will submit the press release to a large number of outlets that will ensure your story gets out. And again, in the press release, link to the story where it's placed on YOUR website. And don't forget to put the press release on your site too!

- **BLOG ABOUT IT**

If you don't already have a blog going (and hopefully through WordPress.org – Google really, really likes Word Press!), you should; it's a very important element to your overall SEO strategy. Blogging about things like your WSJ story and, again, including keywords (and if the blog is external to your website make sure to include links back to your main site), will also improve your search engine scores.

- **BE INTERVIEWED ABOUT IT**

Offer yourself for interviews on online radio shows, podcasts, videos, etc. Use keywords often in your conversation and mention your website address several times – and try to arrange a transcript of the conversation to be posted, if it already isn't automatically done by the online media outlet. Do it yourself and put it on your own website or as a blog entry.

- **USE SOCIAL MEDIA TO ANNOUNCE IT**

Twitter, Facebook, LinkedIn and other social media sites are great to announce the WSJ story and, of course, insert the link to your website! If someone comments on the story, send that out in a new Tweet or Status Update. Keep the conversation going and keep traffic moving to you.

- **USE SOCIAL BOOKMARKING SITES TO KEEP IT ALIVE**

By using bookmarking sites such as Digg.com and Delicious.com to bookmark and give a big thumbs-up to your article (on your website of course!), and encouraging friends and colleagues to do the same, you end up creating more traffic to your site and more recognition of you and your business.

- **CREATE A VIDEO ABOUT IT**

Have someone interview you on camera about the article – or just talk about it by yourself to the camera. Place the video on YouTube, on your social media pages and, most importantly, on the homepage of your website. Placing videos on websites have been proven to keep visitors there longer – another factor that helps you rate higher in Google search results.

Now, just because we used the example of a "Wall Street Journal" story obviously doesn't mean you can't go through this whole process with some other interesting, noteworthy or newsworthy item about you or your business. Other online PR opportunities include:

- Moving your office or expanding to another location
- Offering a new product or service
- Being recognized by a trade or marketing association
- A unique client success story
- The release of a new informational product, such as a free report, webinar, article, book, etc.
- A new JV or partnership
- A big charitable project your business is backing

…and so on and so on. Just like traditional PR, there are about a million possibilities for interesting stories that give you an excuse to draw attention to you and your business. We do it for our own clients every month – and we make sure the word gets out there, using the latest online PR techniques.

PUTTING YOURSELF "IN THE LOOP"

Although the primary reason most of our clients sign on for online PR is to stimulate traffic and sales growth, a very valuable side effect is that they become perceived as authorities in their field – and actually become sought out by the traditional media that they're ignoring!

A recent study shows that about 91% of all journalists use Google and other search engines to research their stories. 65% use social media to do further research. Frankly, the ranks of journalism have been decimated because of shrinking traditional news budgets – and reporters have to use internet shortcuts as much as the average person. You can use that fact to your advantage.

The more you put yourself out there as an authority in your area of expertise through online PR, the bigger the chance you have of being recognized by traditional media outlets such as television, radio, newspapers and magazines. And the more you're recognized by those outlets...well, if you haven't guessed yet, it means the more online PR you can do about those traditional media stories!

It all ends up becoming a very lucrative loop that boosts your website, draws the attention of potential prospects and creates a demand for you and your services.

For example, let's say you're a dentist who's just launched an innovative new practice that's the subject of a "Business Week" profile. You go ahead and use online PR to maximize the impact of that profile in the ways we've described above.

Meanwhile, a different journalist at a different business magazine needs more material for a piece they're writing about how dentists are adapting to the new economy. Through a Google search, because you've put in the effort, your name and the "Business Week" article comes up all over the place. That journalist will probably contact you and make your practice a significant part of the story.

Which means you can put your new online PR skills to work to promote that *new* article that prominently features you!

Online PR, when fully utilized, can indeed be an incredible "Game Changer" for anyone willing to follow through with it. You can:

- Boost your online traffic and increase your internet sales
- Make it easier for journalists who need an expert in your field for a story to find *you*
- Make it easier for potential customers to find you through high SEO-fueled Google search results rankings
- Expand your branding footprint all across the internet

The internet has made a lot of things in our lives easier – and PR is no exception. It's opened up the whole world to anyone who knows how to use the tools that are readily available with just a few keystrokes.

For anyone serious about becoming a presence on the web, online PR is not an option – it's a necessity! The next time something interesting is happening to you or your business, consider giving it a try. You might be surprised at the results!

ABOUT LINDSAY

Lindsay Dicks helps her clients tell their stories in the online world. Being brought up around a family of marketers, but a product of Generation Y, Lindsay naturally gravitated to the new world of online marketing. Lindsay began freelance writing in 2000 and soon after launched her own PR firm that thrived by offering an in-your-face "Guaranteed PR" that was one of the first of its type in the nation.

Lindsay's new media career is centered on her philosophy that "people buy people." Her goal is to help her clients build a relationship with their prospects and customers. Once that relationship is built and they learn to trust them as the expert in their field then they will do business with them. Using Social Media and Search Engine Optimization, Lindsay takes that concept and builds upon it by working with her clients to create online "buzz" about them to convey their business and personal story. Lindsay's clientele span the entire business map and range from doctors and small business owners to Inc 500 CEOs.

Lindsay is a graduate of the University of Florida with a Bachelors Degree in Marketing. She is the CEO of CelebritySites™, an online marketing company specializing in social media and online personal branding. Lindsay is also co-author of the best-selling books, "Big Ideas for Your Business" and "Shift Happens," as well as the best-selling book "Power Principles for Success" with Brian Tracy. She was also selected as one of America's PremierExperts™ and has been quoted in Newsweek, the Wall Street Journal and USA Today, as well as featured on NBC, ABC, FOX and CBS television affiliates speaking on social media, search engine optimization and making more money online.

You can connect with Lindsay at:

Lindsay@CelebritySites.com
www.twitter.com/LindsayMDicks
www.facebook.com/LindsayDicks

CHAPTER 9

PROTECT YOUR ASS(ETS) FOR A CHANGE OF OWNERSHIP

BY MARTHA FOUTS

I hate playing games. My sisters constantly changed the rules on me. As the youngest child in the family I could never win. Even as a kid I figured that nothing could feel as good as winning. My family lived in Africa. The schools in Dessie, Ethiopia taught basic reading, writing and arithmetic, but not much more and all of it in Amharic. My parents decided it was time to send me to boarding school in Europe. I could choose a French or an English school. At 10, I had no idea what French was, but my sisters were attending English schools and I wanted nothing to do with anything they were doing.

My parents chose my 15 year old sister to chaperone me. (!?!?!) We flew to Geneva and took a train up the Rhone Valley to Ollon where she bundled me onto a funicular and took off. She left me with a little note pinned to my sweater that probably said "Do not return to sender". The director of the school met me at the station. He ONLY spoke French.

Talk about a game change. This was it. I couldn't ask for water, explain that my luggage was lost or that I had changed my mind about boarding school and wanted to go home. My gig was up. It was do or die. I was scared. I missed my parents. I cried a lot and the kids teased me constantly. I'd ask, "How do I say... 'Excuse me, sir? Can I pet your dog?' They would say, "Excrement, Monsieur? Es que je pourai petté votre chien?" Translation: "Shit, sir? May I fart your dog?" But then, little by little, I learned the ropes. I learned their game and once I did, I thrived.

My comprehension changed from zero to ninety in no time at all. My friends realized this and used me as their talking puppet. Anything they were afraid to say, I would say for them. The teachers were slow to catch on. I got punished a lot, but my status improved dramatically. I developed a fearless and dependable reputation. I never snitched on anyone.

Seeing my sisters again provided me sweet satisfaction. In three months I could speak better French than both of them put together. For the first time in my life I excelled at something they didn't. Adversity builds character and it can strengthen businesses too. It is not until you are put to a test that you realize what you're capable of.

Running a business in a down economy is hard. But let's not fool ourselves, it's hard in good times too. I had a business that pretty much doubled revenues every year for ten years. Great, right? Not really. Unless you have a bundle of money set aside to fund rapid growth or a business model that allows you to collect full upfront payment for your services or products your business is going to be cash strapped. That's exactly what happened in my company. We maxed out our credit lines. We went into debt up to our eyeballs. We never knew if we were going to make it through another payroll. Inventory and A/R grew right in tandem with sales. On paper we looked great, but there was never, EVER any money in the bank account. We had to constantly discount Peter's invoices for cash payment to pay Paul. I'm not saying, "Hurray! Let the bad times roll!" but it's in bad times that 'business gets tough and the tough get going'.

I sold my apparel licensing business almost 20 years ago. Today, I own a company called Trademark Mergers & Acquisitions. We help business owners protect their personal wealth and unleash the equity tied up in their private companies. In other words, we sell companies. Transactions are not always outright sales. Sometimes transactions are done through family succession, management buyout, recapitalization, mezzanine financing, or even through an employee stock option plans. It all depends on the business owners' goals.

Ideally, business owners should work on their exit strategy at the same time they are developing their "start-up" business plan. Why? Because some business models just don't transfer well. They're not good resale models. If you choose one of these models, you need to focus on building your wealth while you still own the business. Taking money out on a regular basis should be part of your business strategy. Don't wait for 20 years for some 'smart-ass' business broker to tell you this.

Why do you want to exit your business in the first place? If you can't answer this question with absolute clarity; if you can't imagine yourself passionately engaged in a new activity outside of your business --- you're probably not ready to sell. Even if you are planning on retiring, you need to be passionate about it. Otherwise, it's probably not going to stick. Is selling your only option? What other alternatives are there? Are your value expectations in line with the market? Is a sale in the next six months likely to net sufficient funds after closing costs and taxes to meet your post transaction goals? My job as an intermediary is to help clients answer these questions. If the business needs to be improved in order to accomplish your objectives, we concentrate on that first.

It is NEVER too early to plan your exit. Even if you are a teenager, you don't want to exit 'feet first in a box'. Life happens. We all do dumb stuff. Not planning for an exit is one of them. You need to know what your post-transaction lifestyle is going to cost you before you exit. Entrepreneurs are busy people. I know. I'm busy too. I used to own 3 companies at once; a retail store, a design and manufacturing facility and an apparel licensing company. I also had two small children. Dancing backwards in high heels? Ginger Rogers had nothing on me ---- but planning for my post-exit lifestyle? Shoot! I didn't have time for THAT!

Don't be embarrassed. You are not alone. The vast majority of business owners haven't done this work either. Most tell me they want $5 million dollars for their business and they will be ready to sell in 5 years. To a business intermediary, this is code for "I have no idea what my businesses is worth, what my future financial needs will be or any of the costs associated with a transaction. And, I can't talk to you right now. My pants are on fire!" Even if you were lucky enough to get $5M for your business 5 years from now, $5M can turn into $2M in the bat of an eye if you don't have your facts straight. We all like surprises but the last place you want to be handed one is at the closing table. And, by the way, there are no "do overs" in a business transaction.

Here are a dozen tips that will help you begin planning for an exit, help increase the value and marketability of your company and hopefully take some of the stress and uncertainty out of the process.

1. **Develop a Contingency Plan.** Entrepreneurs know all about Murphy's Law, but surprisingly few plan for a disability or their own demise. I hate to be the bearer of bad news but we're all going to 'get it' in the end. Unless you want your heirs fighting over your coffin, you've got to face your mortality and let your wishes be known. A contingency plan is to an exit plan what a 'prenup' is to a marriage.

   Four critical elements of a contingency plan are:-

   a. Put your wishes in writing. You already know your spouse doesn't listen to you and your children are worse. Appoint an advisor to consult with them should the worst happen. Specify in writing whether the business should be sold, continued or liquidated. Your family will be stressed out. The more often you go over these instructions, the easier it will be for them. My parents used to force my sisters and I to listen to "the death talk" when we were still teenagers. We used to sigh, shrug our shoulders, poke each other and roll our eyes. But I can tell you this; when my father died, I was grateful. We knew all the steps by rote.

   b. Life Insurance. Work with a competent insurance professional to make certain that proper insurance is purchased by the proper entity, for the right reason and for the right amount.

   c. Communicate. Make sure that all your advisors know about the contingency plan especially your lenders and bankers. Make sure they support your plan. If they aren't 'on board', find out what it is going to take to get them 'on board'.

d. Stay bonuses. Stay bonuses are bonuses paid to key employees to keep them in place after an owner's death or disability. The last thing you want is your key people 'jumping ship' while your company is in transition.

2. **Get Your Company Appraised.** Have an appraiser prepare a detailed base-line valuation. An appraisal is like a physical for the business. Good or bad, it's best to know. An appraisal will tell you the fair market value of your company as well as how marketable the company is, given current market conditions.

3. **Work With a Wealth Management Advisor.** Choose an advisor that has done significant business transaction work. Get recommendations. Check references. Try not to rely on your golfing buddies for this one. It's too important. Seek professionals who have done a multitude of transactions. Make sure the advisor is also knowledgeable about mitigating risk with insurance products.

4. **Commit to a Written Growth Plan.** Entrepreneurs have reputations of 'flying by the seat of their pants', but that doesn't mean they don't have a blue-printed plan etched in blood, sweat and tears inside their heads. Write it down. Teach your vision to your people. Buyers want to see written growth plans and proven track records.

5. **Sit Down With a Tax Planner.** Don't wait for an offer to speak to a tax advisor. When I say "tax advisor", I do not mean your friendly CPA. You need a professional who specializes in liquidity tax planning. Most CPA's focus on income tax reduction strategies for ongoing enterprises. The game changes significantly when you start planning for a transition. This is your last hurrah and possibly the largest, single transaction of your lifetime. You don't want Uncle Sam to have the last laugh.

   Seek tax advice early. Lack of tax planning can cost you a bundle at the closing table. Tax rules are such that most strategies require time to implement. I am **not** a tax expert and I **do not** give tax advice but I know you need to seek counsel early. It can take up to ten years to fully convert a C Corporation to an S Corporation. You may not have that long.

6. **Don't Be a 'One-Trick Pony'**. Diversify your product and service lines. If your company only makes wooden buckets, you're going to be in a world of hurt when a competitor turns up with a plastic pail. Buyers don't like companies that have all their revenue in one bucket. They like companies with multiple products and services and little concentration in any one area. I learned this lesson the hard way. When I sold my company 80% of the revenue came from Spuds McKenzie licensed product. When Budweiser retired Spuds McKenzie we were forced into selling the company. We couldn't replace $30 million dollars of sales and we couldn't hold onto the company unless we did. 'I'm sadder now Budweiser' (Apologies to Tom Robbins – Jitterbug Perfume).

7. **Differentiate Your Business.** Identify what you do differently and better than your competitors. Avoid generic differentiators like "superior customer service" and make sure the differentiator is transferable. If you are the only PhD scientist on the globe with unique expertise you have a great non-replicatable differentiator -- but how are you going to transfer this intangible asset when you leave the company?

8. **Diversify Your Customer Base.** No one customer should contribute more than 10% of your annual revenue. Buyers fear concentration because the loss of one key account could impact future revenue in a significant way. Seasoned buyers will try to mitigate this risk by lowering the purchase price or with an earn-out.

9. **Create Barriers to Entry.** Your company should have one or more factors making it difficult for competitors to enter your space. This could be a secret formula, patented technology, licensed product, blue-chip patrons, intellectual property or advertising clout. Vertically-integrated companies, government regulations, licensing and permitting requirements can also create barriers.

10. **Focus on the Bottom Line.** Business owners like to focus on top line revenue. It sounds better to say that you have a 10 million dollar company rather than a company with a million dollars of net income. Besides which, accountants bend over backwards trying to shrink this number down to zero and you are not going to tell ANYONE that your company actually lost money, even if the

loss is only on paper. As long as the company is growing the top line, turning a small profit and the owner is decently compensated, everyone is happy. Private equity calls these kinds of companies "lifestyle" companies. And guess what? They don't like them. Companies are typically bought and sold on a multiple of earnings. If you decrease your earnings by running up your expenses you will undoubtedly pay less to Uncle Sam, but you are also quite possibly killing the goose before she lays the golden egg.

Consider these two examples.

Example A		**Example B**	
Gross Revenue	$5,000,000	Gross Revenue	$5,000,000
Cost of Goods	$350,000	Cost of Goods	$350,000
Gross Profit	$4,650,000	Gross Profit	$4,650,000
Expenses	$3,650,000	Expenses	$2,650,000
Net Income	$1,000,000	Net Income	$2,000,000

In these examples, both companies are C Corps and pay a corporate tax rate of 35% and both companies sell for a 5 times multiple of earnings.

Example A: Business pays $350,000 in corporate taxes and the company sells for $5 Million dollars.

Example B: Business pays $700,000 in corporate taxes and the company sells for $10 Million dollars.

In these examples, both companies pay a corporate tax rate of 35% and both companies sell for a 5 times multiple of earnings.

Example A: Business pays $350,000 in corporate taxes. The company sells for a 5 X multiple and the seller nets $5 Million dollars.

Example B: Business pays $700,000 in corporate taxes. The company sells for a 5 X multiple and the seller nets $10 Million dollars.

Which company would you rather own? If you recast the discretionary expenses in example B in theory both companies would sell at the same price. But theory and practice are two different things. Clean books are a sign of a clean company. Premium buyers want to see no more than five items on the recasting sheet; interest, taxes, depreciation, amortization and excess owner's comp. Anything else and it had better be extraordinary with an equally extraordinary story to back it up. If you are not concerned about 'monkeying around' with the IRS, buyers have to wonder what would stop you from 'monkeying around' with them. Buyers will pay more for companies with 'squeaky clean' books, more still for companies with reviewed books and most of all for companies with audited books. Small companies typically can't afford audits so keeping clean books is the next best defense.

11. **Build Recurring Revenue Streams.** Recurring revenue attracts buyers like bumble bees to dandelions. Whether you manufacture widgets or provide professional services, try to figure out how to create recurring revenue in your business. Telephone service, garbage collection, insurance, subscriptions, licensing agreements, cable service and sports club memberships are all examples of recurring revenue models.

12. **Empower Your Management Team.** Are you the Pied Piper of your industry? Good for you, but don't let this hard-earned distinction turn into a liability. If your plan is to retire from the business, you need to start transferring your intellectual capital to your management team. Empower them. Let your management team become the face of your business. Encourage them to distinguish themselves as industry knowledge experts, build relationships with your customers and speak at industry events. Help them get published. Unlike you, (unless you plan to stay) your employees are an asset that will transfer with the sale.

Times are tough. There's no doubt about it. The market is down. Financing is still tight. Fewer deals are getting done. But do not despair. There will always be buyers for great companies. Companies that excel in a down economy or just simply stay afloat are going to command decent multiples when the market returns. But don't just sit there. Now is the time to spruce up your company and prepare yourself emotionally, psychologically and financially for an eventual exit. It is forecasted that nine out of ten privately held companies will change hands in the next ten years. There are going to be winners and losers.

Let's hope your company will be one of the winners!

ABOUT MARTHA

Martha Fouts, M&AMI, is a highly successful Mergers & Acquisitions Master Intermediary who is frequently sought after as an entertaining speaker on topics relating to exit strategies, industry trends, and creative ways to maximize corporate value. Less than 100 M&A intermediaries worldwide have completed the rigorous educational and deal closing requirements earning them the right to use the M&AMI designation.

Fouts began her entrepreneurial career straight out of college but not in the rarified air of investment banking and mergers and acquisitions. "I earned my deal making skills from the bottom up selling secondhand American sportswear in outdoor flea markets in England in the early 1970's."

She has applied her 'street savvy' sales and negotiation skills in every business she has owned from retail clothing, to apparel manufacturing, to T-shirt licensing, to sales and marketing and distribution companies. Ten years of corporate sales experience in venture capital and private equity-backed early stage healthcare technology companies added additional finesse. She continues to hone these skills today in her current role as an exit planning specialist and M&A advisor. She has survived no less than three recessions with her quirky sense of humor still intact.

Becoming a Mergers & Acquisitions advisor was a natural progression for Fouts. The sale of her own company exposed Fouts to just how complicated, confusing and emotionally daunting the whole process can be. Running a business day to day, year in and year out requires all kinds of stamina, skill and 'brute force' determination. You can get into business by yourself, but it often requires a team of trained professionals to properly plan a succesful exit. Fouts does not pretend that exiting a business is cardiac surgery but it isn't a simple financial transaction either. Just like a heart surgeon has to consider his whole patient not just his patient's heart muscle, a good exit planning strategist needs to consider the personal, emotional, tax, succession and charitable gifting interests etc., of his clients, not just the purchase price of the transaction. Exit planning is not for the faint of heart or for advisors that don't play well with others. A successful Trademark exit is more than a simple marriage between a willing buyer and a willing seller. Careful advanced planning with an experienced multiple-disciplinary advisory team and determined execution are the keys to a successful exit.

For more information on Trademark Mergers & Acquisitions or for a FREE copy of "How to Avoid Death and Taxes"* (*How to Get Out Alive Without Paying It All to Uncle Sam). Please go to www.trademarkmergers.com

CHAPTER 10

WHY CHAOS IS KILLING SMALL BUSINESS AND WHAT YOU CAN DO ABOUT IT

BY CLATE MASK & SCOTT MARTINEAU

600,000 new small businesses will be created in the next 12 months. By the end of the year, half of them will have shut their doors forever.

That is not okay.

Although to some this may be nothing more than a statistical reality, it's time we start to view this as an unacceptable pattern.

Until the underlying culprit of small business failure is addressed, businesses will continue to close unnecessarily; and small business owners will continue to feel the emotional sting and financial impact of their failed ventures.

So why do so many businesses dry up before they've even had a chance to truly succeed? It has nothing to do with a lack of customers, the economy, the competition, or bad business ideas. With a little bit of determination, each of these obstacles can be easily overcome. The real challenge is an invisible culprit that plagues small business owners through every stage of their existence – chaos.

The moment an entrepreneur opens her doors for business, chaos (the greatest antagonist to any company) creeps in through the entrance and takes up permanent residence. No matter how much experience, education, resourcefulness or outside assistance a new small business owner possesses, she is going to experience chaos.

No one is exempt from chaos. It's an inevitable part of owning and running a company. Perhaps that is why so few business owners do anything about it. In most situations, chaos goes entirely unchecked and is free to lead small business owners down an unstable, treacherous path that ultimately ends in devastation.

CHAOS TURNS THE DREAM OF SMALL BUSINESS OWNERSHIP INTO A NIGHTMARE

Proponents of entrepreneurship love to celebrate the freedom and adventure of owning and running a company. Established business owners put on a smile, perfect their elevator speech about "being their own boss," and proceed to sell you their product or service. The media tells us story after story about the multi-million dollar opportunities grown out of a garage or dorm room.

But few people tell the true story of entrepreneurship -- the story of long hours, sleepless nights, endless worry, mental and physical stress, strained family relationships and non-existent social life.

Instead, would-be entrepreneurs buy into a dream that few will ever achieve. Believing in a promise of more money, more time, and freedom from the corporate world, entrepreneurs ignore the less-than-encouraging small business statistics and take the plunge into ownership.

That's when chaos moves in.

Whether you've owned a small business or not, you can imagine the effort required to keep a company up and running. Every week the small business owner must make sales, fulfill on products or services, pay the bills, manage employees, deal with angry customers, update inventory, meet with clients, find vendors, market their business, collect outstanding balances, and read and respond to emails. In addition to all that, somehow you've got to stay organized.

In a single day, the business owner plays every role from salesperson to IT specialist to plumber (like when the toilets overflow).

Rather than finding more time, money, and freedom as they had hoped, small business owners end up committing everything they've got to their companies—becoming shackled to it. In other words, what they find is a life of chaos—a life that is ruled by unfinished to-do lists and a growing list of new projects to be tackled.

Eventually, organization fails, plans for improvement are forgotten, and the small business owner is forced to run a day-to-day gauntlet. At this point, chaos has conquered the business and enslaved the business owner. Then it's simply a matter of time before the tired small business owner succumbs completely to the chaos.

TO SURVIVE THE CHAOS, YOU MUST TAKE THE OFFENSIVE

With chaos wreaking havoc, it's uncertain how long a company will last. Some fold within a few short months. Others last years before finally giving up. But in every situation, the small business owner is being raked over the coals. They're doing everything they can to keep their dream alive. Unless the chaos is subdued, they are fighting a useless battle.

Sure, they might experience little wins—a major sale, adding a new employee—but these accomplishments are often buried by a laundry list of other things waiting to be done. As long as the business owner is racing to play "catch-up", they will never score any real points. They will always be playing *defense*.

If a small business owner wants to survive, they must learn to take the *offensive*.

Most entrepreneurs are so busy with day-to-day "stuff", they have no time to create strategies, improve processes, or actually grow their businesses. So, the growth and success of a company is limited to what the business owner can manage herself. Then, when there are no more hours in the day or money in the bank account, the business comes to an abrupt and painful halt; a halt that could mean the difference between staying in business and throwing in the towel.

To survive in the small business world, you must continue to improve and grow. It's not a choice. The world is moving too fast to stand still. Just to be competitive, a business must have a dynamic website. They should engage in social media. They need to follow up with their contacts, and they ought to be actively marketing their business.

These are all things you know and want to be doing, but meanwhile, there is always another customer who needs your attention. Your competitors will always move in on *your* prospects and customers. And there will always be another "fire" to put out.

With so much to handle, it's far too easy to lose sight of your goals. Small business owners get stuck in a rut of merely pressing their noses to the grindstone.

Without the tools and strategies to oppose it, chaos alone will determine your actions. And once you lose your focus and ambition…the business will come crashing down. Intentional growth, coupled with a few powerful strategies, is the only way to gain and keep control of your business. It may not be easy, but neither is accepting defeat.

It's time to take control again…it's time to conquer the chaos once and for all.

3 CRITICAL STEPS TO OVERCOMING CHAOS

To the overwhelmed, downtrodden business owner, overcoming chaos may be the furthest thing from their mind. All they want is to make it through another day. But even the most defeated business owner will experience random moments when they remember why they became an entrepreneur. If those moments happen often enough, the entrepreneur will find the strength to make changes in their business. The problem is that most don't know where to start.

But the strategy is simple.

Prepare Mentally

Change is never easy—even when it leads to the dream of more money, more time, and more freedom from your business. Breaking out of your daily routine can be just as difficult as battling the chaos, because it takes effort. When your business is already draining your energy level, the thought of doing more can lead to mental devastation.

That is why the first step to conquering chaos is mental preparation. If you want to improve and grow your business, you must be committed to change. You must be willing to give up the coping mechanisms you've put into place. You must be ready to uproot everything you've been doing and replace it with better, more productive processes.

Understand, however, that this is going to be tough. It may mean more work… temporarily. It's definitely going to take faith. But just like a new diet or starting a family, this is not a one-time deal. It's a lifestyle change. If you're not willing to shift your mental focus, you'll never break free from chaos.

So how do you work past the exhaustion to make that mental preparation? Easy. Just realize you're not living the dream.

- Take a few minutes and write down all the reasons you became an entrepreneur.
- Be sure to include the desire for more time, more money, more freedom to be with your family and the chance to be your own boss.
- Once you've got your list, start another one.
- In the second list, write down all the goals you've managed to achieve as an entrepreneur.

Once you see the chasm between where you are and where you want to be, it's a lot easier to tackle new strategies. With that motivation driving you, you'll be able to refocus your attention on the things that matter most. When the big picture (and not the immediate crisis) is the predominant thought, you'll take action with a purpose instead of simply being reactionary.

When it comes right down to it, that project you're scrambling to get done will still be there tomorrow. So is there something *more* important to be doing today? With the right mental attitude, you'll be in a position to make those decisions.

Improve Your Processes

Whether you realize it or not, you've already put processes in place. You have a process for how you open and read your mail. When you sit down at your computer, you have a process for what you look at and do first. Every sale that takes place goes through a process that you (perhaps unknowingly) created.

But simply having processes in place doesn't mean your business is organized. Having processes in place is no guarantee you will be able to fight the chaos. Only the *right* processes will effectively combat the chaos.

We would be willing to bet that the processes most small business owners have put in place lack timeliness or efficiency. After working with thousands of individuals, we've discovered that small business owners spend an awful lot time doing the wrong kinds of things—things that don't contribute to the growth and success of a company.

For example, a company might create a process for dealing with angry customers after the fourth or fifth customer complaint. They formulate a plan for appeasing the customer, write down the process in a memo, and quickly train employees on the "Customer Complaint Process."

Although creating a process for a critical issue is the right thing to do, the approach could have been better planned. Before launching into another fire-fighting process, why not take the time to discover the source of the fire? Perhaps all five customers had the same complaint. Resolving the issue at the point of conflict will do far more to help the business than pacifying angry customers after the fact.

Again, this idea is going to take time. It will take dedication. But having the right processes in place is well worth the extra time and effort it may take to create them. If you're serious about regaining control about your business, then:

1. Schedule some time *every* week to work on improving your processes
2. Chart all the processes that currently exist in your business

(starting with customer-facing interactions)
3. Determine which processes are working and which are not
4. Stop doing things that are not contributing to your growth
5. Document all new business processes

With the right plans in place, you can minimize the number of "fires" in your business, easily cope with stressful situations as they occur, maximize your personal efforts, and improve the efficiency of your business as a whole. You will turn the tables on chaos and regain control of your business.

Use Technology

Chaos exists, in part, because technology is driving the speed of business even faster. Years ago, when phone calls and letters were the only way to communicate, a business owner had time to respond to customer and prospect concerns. Now, with email being the predominant form of communication, business owners have 24 hours (or less) to take care of issues and questions.

Documents can be faxed in a matter of minutes. If you disagree with a customer, an entire blog post—dedicated to slandering your business—could immediately pop up on the internet. Money and other business transactions can all be done without any face-to-face interaction. Yet somehow, the small business owner is expected to keep up with all of it.

Technology is most definitely a major driver of business chaos. But the same thing that is creating this chaos can be used as a tool to conquer it.

If you haven't done so already, it's time to look at a few small business solutions. You see, you're not the only person struggling to stay afloat. Millions of business owners are dealing with the same challenges, and multiple technological solutions have been created just for you.

With the right tools, small business owners can easily and automatically:

- Keep in touch with contacts
- Manage billing processes
- Store and retrieve contact data
- Market their products and services
- Move prospects through the sales cycle

- Monitor employee efforts
- Track comments about your business on the Internet

You cannot fight (or conquer) chaos without attacking the source of chaos. In this case, you must fight fire with fire. Use technology. It's there. It works. What's more, several companies have created their solution with *your* needs in mind.

A NEW FACE FOR SMALL BUSINESS OWNERSHIP

No small business is immune to chaos. When a single individual takes on the responsibilities of an entire company, they're getting in over their heads. Large corporations hire hundreds of employees to do what this one person is trying to accomplish alone. That doesn't mean the entrepreneur will fail. But it's certainly going to be a struggle.

Millions of small businesses are successfully contributing to the health of the economy. There could and should be more, however. Success should be the general rule for new small businesses, not the exception. The dream of more money, more time, and more freedom should be more achievable.

The era of failed business ventures has run its course. It's not okay with us. And this era must come to a close now. Across the board, entrepreneurs need to recognize and accept chaos as a necessary evil. They need to embrace it and then put the strategies in place to defeat it. Because every door that closes is another attack on the small business world. This is a battle we can't lose. And if we can conquer the chaos, we won't lose it.

ABOUT CLATE

Clate Mask is the co-founder and CEO of Infusionsoft, the leading provider of Email Marketing 2.0 software for small businesses. Clate loves to help small businesses grow. His passion for entrepreneurship is infectious and obvious from the moment he begins speaking. His dream is to revolutionize small business growth through smart automation.

ABOUT SCOTT

Scott Martineau is the co-founder and VP of Customer Service at Infusionsoft. Scott is a serial entrepreneur who can't imagine ever working a "regular job." He is a technologist at heart, driven by his vision: to create an easier way for entrepreneurs to run their small businesses.

CHAPTER 11

TAKE THE LUMPS, TAKE THE LEAD, CHANGE THE GAME, …AND SAVOR THE SPOILS

BY CHRISTOPHER J. COLLOCA, D.C.

TAKING THE LUMPS

As I sat in the law firm's conference room, I knew something just wasn't quite right. I had been here before on two occasions. The first, when I signed my contract to become the Vice President and future owner (successor) of the company, and the second at a board meeting where we reorganized the corporate structure of the company to avoid tax problems. This high rise office in downtown Phoenix overlooking Camelback Mountain and Pinnacle Peak is what you visualize corporate law looking like in the dictionary. I wasn't in Oswego, New York (population 17,351) anymore. This was the big leagues. The conference room table alone could seat 20 people, all with fine leather high back chairs. Only four of us sat there that day - the attorneys and us.

It was June 27, 2000, a day that would change the course of my life. My boss, the owner and President of the Company, had arrived there ahead of me and was waiting with his attorneys in the board room. The board meeting was called to order. The first order of business was an addendum to the corporate bylaws. The second, my employment was terminated without cause, which triggered a cross-termination of my stock purchase agreement. I was sacked. The four years of work that I had sacrificed in building this brand would not be my company in the future.

I had moved to Phoenix to learn this business and buy the company. My financial goal in my twenties was to earn $100,000 per year. I had achieved this goal and in the process, my life had eroded into an unbalanced life dominated by work (sound familiar guys?). I cared for patients Monday through Friday (with half days on Tuesdays and Fridays), traveled on Friday afternoons to most major US cities to teach weekend seminars, only to return on Sunday evening to repeat the same. Thirty-five weekends a year of travel makes for a second full-time job. Needless to say, I was committed to this company and it had all been taken away in an instant.

I had always worked two jobs. It was how I was raised. "The harder you work, the luckier you get," was the motto echoed in my ear as a kid. As the legendary Coach, John Wooden puts it, *"luck travels in the company of those that work hard."*

Through high school and college, I worked each summer and vacation in construction for my brother-in-law, Richard Burger. He taught me to "moonlight", by taking on night and weekend projects where I could earn the equivalent of a week's pay in half the time by doing the small side jobs he gave me or didn't want. If we built a new front porch, I would paint it at night. If we built a house, I would build the deck on the weekend. Moonlighting proved to be a very time-efficient way of earning additional income. Not only did I think the pay was great, it was also absolutely incredible as it gave me my first taste of being an entrepreneur just like Rich, but on a smaller scale – calling the shots and being my own boss!

Through eight years of college and chiropractic school, job one was my studies, and job two was *anything I could get*. From bouncing at local bars, to selling newspaper subscriptions for the Atlanta-Journal and Constitution in front of Wal-Mart's and Piggly Wiggly supermarkets – I learned that work brought financial reward – and the financial gain that made things happen.

There I sat in the law office. Fired. I decided to fight back. (*Note to readers – before you enter a battle like this, please consider the costs – and not just monetary.)*

I hired a high-powered legal firm, and filed a lawsuit. I also focused on building my practice, and formed a new seminar business to continue my passion for teaching. It was a good thing that I did, because I was about to learn quickly about legal fees.

Litigation ensued over three-and-a-half-years. The legal bills began modestly at $3,000-$5,000/month. As time crept on, each month when the bill arrived on my desk, I would play a game and guess what this month's bill would be before opening the envelope judging by its thickness. $9,000? $11,500 this month? As trial approached, the bills were too large to fold and fit in regular standard sized envelopes and they began to come in 9x12 envelopes to accommodate the 15-20 page bill. One month during trial, the legal bill was $39,000 and the forensic accounting bill was $53,000. That was a new record. Ninety-two thousand in less than one month! I told my attorney that most chiropractors earn only $92,000 in a year. How could I possibly afford a bill of $92,000 for one month? This was of course *my problem.*

Despite our success in seven summary judgment motions, after a month in trial, we were handed a directed verdict on three of our major counts - causing us to accept a walk-away settlement agreement. As is the case in many legal battles, the only winners are the attorneys. By the age of 32, I had spent over a half a million dollars in legal fees. This equated to spending every dollar I had earned in both jobs - my practice and 35 seminars each year. I had taken a second mortgage on my home, and a loan from my parents and sister to pay the bill. I had invested all of myself in my work and in building my new seminar business at the expense of my marriage. Soon after the lawsuit ended, so did my marriage of eleven years. I found myself in a small apartment with a futon couch as my only piece of furniture. It was time to take charge and change the game.

Taking the lumps along the way are unfortunately - *not uncommon* - on the pathway or journey to success. I love the quote that I learned from my life balance coach, Dr. Frank Corbo, creator of Habitology, who shared with me, "Never trust a man without a limp." Limps and lumps show transparency, they make you real, and they are never wasted. If you're experiencing some of them today, remember you're in good company. You just may be in the process of 'learning" the experiences you will use to grow you into the person you were meant to be. Please remember: *Never, ever, waste your lumps!*

TAKING THE LEAD

Taking the lumps is part of life. It's just not a pleasant part of life that people like to disclose and talk about openly. Sports are probably the place where I took the most lumps. The circle of life in sports is being the all-star at one level and the benchwarmer at the next. Tony DeRose, one of my football coaches in high-school always said, "the cream rises to the top." I remembered that when I joined all of the other "All-everything" high school athletes at the college level. Day one, I was fifth string on the depth chart at inside linebacker on the JV squad. By season's end, I was the starter. The transition happened gradually. One practice and one game at a time. "You play like you practice," said legendary Ithaca College football coach, Jim Butterfield. Ithaca's football stadium bears his name. *You have to earn the right to be the starter.*

Sophomore year, at the varsity level, I was back to third string behind the upperclassmen and an All-American. By junior year, I earned a starting position. I picked off a pass and began running it back when my knee went out. The pop was audible. It was a full ACL tear requiring reconstructive surgery. I was out for the season. We won the Division III National Championship that year. Our season motto: "Champions Meet Challenges Head On." We lived this motto in everything we did both on and off the field. Having to watch the National Championship from the sidelines put things in perspective for me and made me realize how badly I wanted to be back in the game. This was my relentless motivation to get it back.

I decided to work out twice a day instead of once. One workout would be specifically dedicated to my injured knee and the other, to my entire routine strength and conditioning. At camp the following August, my

40 yard dash time was my fastest in history. The hard work in the off-season had paid off. I was back in the game, earning the starting spot again. The following year, I was elected co-captain of the team by my peers and earned All-America honors – the ultimate goal of my football career. Going above and beyond and perseverance in the face of adversity is what is required to reach your goals – no matter what they are. Napoleon Hill, the father of positive thinking puts it this way, "Persistency is to the character of a man, as carbon is to steel – inseparable."

With the new challenge of losing everything financially as well as my marriage, I needed to dig deep and meet this new challenge head on. The only place to look was within. I set a new financial goal. Not to make $100,000 per year, but to make $100,000 per month. To find success again, I had to apply the 'over the top' work ethic from my football years to business. I had to channel my passion for chiropractic, teaching, and helping others into a business strategy that I could build my life around. While private practice was rewarding, I had witnessed first-hand the feeling of accomplishment in helping other chiropractors care for the masses of humanity. This is where I wanted to focus on being a game-changer.

CHANGING THE GAME

Business growth expert and legend, Jay Abraham says, "There are three kinds of people in this world. Those who make things happen, those who watch things happen, and those that things happen to." In other words, there are the players, the spectators, and the victims. In order to change the game, I had to make things happen. First, I had to carve my niche in the chiropractic market. To carve your niche, you first have to solve a problem in the market.

Hallmark to every chiropractor is the chiropractic adjustment, the manual maneuver delivered by chiropractors that aims to reposition vertebrae and restore the lost mobility that is responsible for patients' pain and other health problems. Chiropractic adjustments are associated with twisting and turning of the patient and a popping sound as the joint is taken to end range and gas leaves the solution when opening a soda can. These two characteristics are not generally accepted by the public, and market data has shown that the number one reason that patients in pain didn't see a chiropractor was because they didn't want to be twisted and turned, and didn't like the cracking that was associated with it. A solution to this problem would be very valuable!

From my previous employment, I had been teaching seminars in the use of a hand-held instrument that chiropractors could use to perform adjustments. It was a rudimentary design of an adapted dental tool used to split impacted wisdom teeth. The scalpel was removed from the end of the device and a rubber door stop added to adapt it to the chiropractic market. Not much had changed in this technology through the company's 35 year history. I had been involved in the research that attempted to validate this tool and well knew its shortcomings. It hurt the doctor's hands and wrists from squeezing it to treat patients throughout the day. It broke down frequently as its internal springs wore out, and it's waveform of the force it delivered didn't make for the most efficient treatment. Many times, when patients were treated with this device, they didn't feel any better after the treatment – another real downside of these spring-loaded adjusting instruments. I identified these problems as inputs to the creation of a new chiropractic adjusting instrument.

I knew that to compete against my former company, my new instrument would have to be *far superior*. Instead of finding something off the shelf to private label and sell, I decided to take the long road and do the research that was necessary to really understand how the vertebrae move during a chiropractic adjustment and how we can best change the muscles to work better from a treatment. From the relationships I had built through the years, I enlisted the 'help experts' in the fields of orthopaedics, anatomy, and biomechanics and conducted research experiments in live human subjects and animal models, to learn how to best treat the spine. We published this research over the course of five years in some of the best scientific journals to report our findings.

Next, I hired a team of engineers to design an adjusting instrument that solved the problems of the competition, while incorporating our research findings. We incorporated the latest technology in circuit board design and miniature microprocessors to create the optimum chiropractic adjustment waveform. I risked it all. I invested all of the money that I earned in my private practice and all of my spare time into this new venture. There was no Plan B. In other words, failure was not an option. I had to lay it all on the line. Starbucks' CEO Howard Schultz says it like this, and I couldn't agree more with this point, "Excellence is the result of caring more than others think is wise, *risking more than others think is safe (emphasis mine).* Dreaming more than others think is practical and expecting more than others think is possible."Passion, persistency, dedication and devotion, along with the proverbial blood, sweat and tears, and the Impulse Adjusting Instrument was born. Now, I needed to introduce the instrument to the market place. Once again I hired experts to (are you seeing the trend here?) – marketing experts. They helped me create the advertising campaign, headlines, subheads and copy. We conducted marketing research and learned that seventy percent of chiropractors already had an adjusting instrument. We also learned that what they didn't like the most about their instrument was that it hurt their hands and wrists. So, on the cover of our brochure, we put a picture of a person rubbing their hurting hands with the headline, "Is Your Adjusting Instrument Doing You More Harm Than Good?" It was an immediate hit.

We conducted Impulse Adjusting Technique training seminars in most major US cities to showcase the product and provide the chiropractors with continuing education license renewal credits at the same time. We launched our campaign and over the course of two years, we sold 2,000 units. Within four years of our product release, our instruments were in use in over 5,000 chiropractic offices in every state in the USA, all Australian States and Canadian provinces and 42 countries around the world. I had reached my goal of $100,000 per month. It was time for a new goal.

In the research we conducted to understand chiropractic adjustments, we used a gold-standard biomechanical technique to measure spinal motions by placing a nail into the spine and mounting a motion sensor to the nail. This way, we could measure precise motions of the vertebrae to the accuracy of a tenth of a millimeter. We found that stuck areas in the spine moved slower and at a different frequency than normal areas. We also found that if we put the sensor inside of the adjusting instrument itself we could use it in clinical practice and provide both the doctor and the patient feedback on the success of the treatment. Because this instrument is intelligent, we named it Impulse iQ.

Impulse iQ had all of the research and validation behind it from publications in the medical literature that chiropractors craved. One adjustment with the Impulse iQ and chiropractors have to have this instrument in their practice. The results speak for themselves. I remember the first time that we did $100,000 in a week of sales. All I could do was smile when I thought back to my time of trial. We're currently finishing the programming on a touchscreen version of Impulse iQ that will enable greater patient education about the treatments and documentation of the before and after results of chiropractic treatments. I have changed my goal to $100,000 in sales in a day.

SAVORING THE SPOILS

The spoils of victory aren't simply in the obvious financial rewards, meaning the things that only money can buy, *but rather in the things that money can't buy*. I am now married again with two beautiful children. Savoring the spoils of your success is having more time to spend with the ones you love. I have placed this as a priority in my life. Because the majority of my relatives live in New York, and I am in Phoenix, I purchased a 75 acre estate where I have started a vineyard. Of course, I've enlisted the help of Cornell University oenology experts to assist in vineyard and winery establishment. This will provide us the opportunity to spend summers in New York as a family.

Finding the balance in life between family, business, and relationships among the other areas of your life, is a challenge and takes a concentrated effort. Remember, life truly is short. Need proof? Do you have children? It seems as though they are growing right before our eyes. I'm learning every day the importance of life balance, and my responsibility to give my family, those that I love most, the same passion and devotion as I do my business. I want to look back on my life with *no regrets*, meaning that I've learned the key to fulfillment, and that is to share time, the most precious commodity in life, with those that mean the most to me.

TAKE HOME MESSAGE

- **Take the lumps, and learn to be cool with your limp.** We all get them. It's not what happens to you in life that defines you. It's how you respond to what happens to you that creates your future.
- **Take the lead.** No one will do it for you and nothing in life is free. Take charge of your life. Make the decisions that are necessary for the change you want and take specific action

steps towards your goals.

- **Embrace the team.** There is no "I" in team. Enlist experts with skill sets that you don't possess to help you create your vision. Surround yourself with positive influences in your team members - who all work toward a common goal.
- **Change the game.** Use market data to define a problem in your industry and create the solution. Invest in yourself and your future. Risk more than others think is safe. Care more than others think is wise. Dream more than others think is practical, and expect more than others think is possible.
- **Savor the spoils.** Find balance in your life from a personal, spiritual, business, and relationship standpoint so your life becomes filled with all you imagined it could be.

ABOUT CHRIS

Dr. Christopher J. Colloca is a world-renowned chiropractic researcher, educator, and inventor. The CEO and Founder of Neuromechanical Innovations, a research-based medical device manufacturer and postgraduate education company with its headquarters in Chandler, Arizona, Dr. Colloca has given hundreds of lectures to thousands of chiropractors and medical physicians on six of the seven continents. His patented works include his invention of the Impulse Adjusting Instrument®, a chiropractic treatment device in use in thousands of chiropractic offices around the world, and Impulse IQ®, a computerized instrument for dynamic spinal analysis and treatment. Dr. Colloca's inventions have revolutionized chiropractic practice, changing the game from traditional manual methods to technologically advanced techniques that are easier on doctors and patients alike. His products and techniques (in use in chiropractic practices in all 50 states and 43 countries around the world), providing treatment to millions of patients annually, are testimony to how he has changed the game.

Prior to graduating *cum laude* from ***Life College School of Chiropractic*** (Marietta, GA) in 1995, he received his B.S. degree from ***Ithaca College*** (Ithaca, NY) in 1990, where he was an All-American football player and co-captained the team. His award-winning original research has been presented at numerous international scientific conferences - resulting in over fifty scientific journal publications. A distinguished scientist, Dr. Colloca has multi-disciplinary research collaborations around the world. He is a reviewer for the ***Journal of Biomechanics***, ***Spine***, and ***European Spine Journal,*** among others. Entrepreneurially, Dr. Colloca has created a multi-million dollar business from ground zero from his core values in innovation, leadership and vision.

CHAPTER 12

MARKETING WITH AUTHORITY

BY JOSEPH LAM, REAL ESTATE BROKER

There's a reason politicians don't just make speeches on television and only put videos on YouTube when they're running for office. There's a reason they actually drag themselves on flights, travel all across the country, state or district and show up in rooms to actually, physically talk to voters and donors.

Because they need to make *the face-to-face connection.*

It helps to establish their authority, to bond with the people and…well, it's not a big secret, but it also helps them to raise an awful lot of money. Money they wouldn't raise if they weren't in the same room asking people to open up their wallets.

Whether someone's running for president of the United States or for city councilman, they *themselves* are the product they are selling. And if you are a service-oriented professional or an entrepreneur, *the same rule applies.*

This is why I believe in "Marketing with Authority" - using in-person seminars to sell yourself and your product or service. Seminars elevate you to a higher status in your field and they also excel at 'bringing in the bucks'.

SEMINARS STIMULATE SUCCESS

40% of all my business comes from my seminars – directly and, through referrals from seminar attendees, indirectly. By consistently holding one seminar a month, I grossed between $11,000,000 to $17,000,000 annually between 2003 and 2006. During the past nine months, I've returned to my seminar business model – and have generated over $5,000,000 in gross sales over the past nine months.

Clearly, the seminar system is still a "Game Changer" in our new economy – but you have to market it correctly and effectively to make sure people show up for it. And a great deal has changed in the past few years in terms of which marketing works – and, in my opinion - what no longer does.

As I mentioned, seminars work best for service-oriented professionals; some categories I would recommend for seminars include:

- real estate agent
- loan officer or mortgage broker
- insurance agent
- CPA's (accountants)
- CFP's (financial planners)
- Lawyers
- Entrepreneurs with a specific product or service to sell

What I've really found to be incredibly valuable about seminars is that they're not just about trying to make a short-term sale – they're about raising your profile in the long-term.

Seminars boost your reputation, establish you as an expert and give you "celebrity" status in your field – all of which help put you "top-of-mind" when someone needs services in your area of expertise. People buy *people*, as most of you already know – people they know, people they like and people they trust.

What better way to enable people to get to know you personally, so they can make those positive judgment calls, than through a seminar-styled presentation? Not only do you demonstrate your knowledge and your skills, but you also create the conditions for that all-important *face-to-face connection.*

If you successfully make that connection, your audience members will have no reservations about calling you – or recommending you to family and friends – when they have a need for someone who does what you do.

You must keep in mind, however, you are marketing yourself *first* - and your product or service *second.* You are building a network of people by "Marketing with Authority" – which *then* ends up resulting in sales.

How many people must attend for you to have a successful seminar? An average number for mine is usually 15 to 25 people. Anything over that number I consider good – and even when hardly any people are in the audience, it can still pay off for you.

For example, I only had 2 people show up for one seminar! But one of the people gave me a $1.2 million home listing to sell. That's what I consider a great return for giving a performance to an audience of only two. So don't 'abandon ship' just because hardly anyone shows up – it still might be more than worth your while to continue with the seminar.

MARKETING SEMINARS ... *THEN*

You obviously don't want just 2 people showing up for your seminar – the more in attendance, the more word will spread about you and the better your chances of making sales. That's why *pre-marketing* your seminar in the right way is so important. You have to do "reputation marketing" – publicizing your seminar to a defined list of prospects that might be interested in what you have to sell.

What are the best methods of pre-marketing your seminar?

Well, in the old days (all the way back in 2006), I used the traditional marketing/advertising venues - such as direct mail, display ads, mailers and newspaper inserts. Now I find that they are incredibly expensive and much less effective – not a good combination for anything you pay for!

Plus, when you step into a disaster when dealing with these "old media," it's very hard to step out of it. I once had 20,000 copies of a flyer printed up for insertion into a local newspaper. Somehow…the printer managed to lose them. *All 20,000.*

I'm not sure how you lose 20,000 of *anything,* but supposedly, some employee had stuck them in the back of a warehouse and no one could find them. The result? There wasn't time to get enough inserts printed up and I missed the newspaper deadline, which severely impacted my seminar marketing.

Which brings up two more gripes of mine about direct mail and print advertising – they take too much lead time to prepare and their success is very difficult to track.

MARKETING SEMINARS ... *NOW*

When I returned to seminar marketing last year, I discovered that online was now definitely the best place to put out the word. No question about it – it's been a real Game Changer.

As technology continues to advance – and more free goodies are generated through the internet – a whole new and incredibly powerful arena for business marketing and promotion has been created.

If you still haven't really given online marketing and social media a try, you're way overdue (and I have a great recommendation to get you started – read the book, "Webify Your Business—Internet Marketing Secrets for the Self-Employed" by Patrick Schwerdtfeger. It provides a comprehensive and detailed marketing roadmap for a business person and gets the coveted 5-star rating on Amazon.com. You can also get his eBook in the form of a free 52-week e-course at: www.WebifyBook.com).

Here are ten online social media resources I consider key to marketing your seminars (and your business in general) in the internet age.

1. Email Marketing

Email marketing is still very popular, fast, easy, and cheap. So cheap, it's free, which is the best price I can think of.

I recently worked with a local builder to help him present a "First Time Home Buyer Seminar." We only sent out one email blast, plus a reminder two days before the presentation – and we attracted over 30 attendees (which, as I noted, is a great number to have in your audience).

Having a quality list to send out your emails to helps your success here.

2. Blog Marketing

A blog is short for "web log" – and writing your own blogs on your own user-generated website helps deliver more traffic to your site. Search engines such as Google favor blog sites over static websites, as they have more content and new content is always being added.

Your blogs also help you "Market with Authority." By offering advice and reflecting your experience in your profession, you will further establish your expert credentials and stand out from the crowd.

3. Facebook

With over 300 million users worldwide, Facebook is, by far, the hottest social media site – and the number two site in terms of most traffic overall, second only to Google. It offers you an incredible opportunity to market yourself.

Start by creating either a Facebook Group or Facebook Page for your specific seminar topic – then invite prospects to "like" your page. Once that happens, you can regularly update them on seminar dates and content.

If you want to learn more about Facebook Group and Facebook Page, go to: www.facebook.com/help and search for "create a group or a page." By the way, if you have the budget for it, you can even use the Facebook PPC (Pay-Per-Click) advertising program to promote your seminar, as well as your business.

4. Twitter

Twitter.com is another amazingly popular social media tool that has seen explosive growth in the short time it's been in existence. As of this writing, Twitter has over 105 million users – and is signing up 300,000+ new users every day. Those users send out 55 million "tweets" per day – and 37% do it by cell phone or PDA, creating instant communication.

After you open your account, you want to gather as many "followers" as possible (other Twitter users who monitor your messages). You can then send out messages of under 140 characters whenever you want. Depending on who you follow, and who follows you, you'll be creating a viral message that goes out instantly to hundreds and possibly thousands of prospects – absolutely free.

5. YouTube

Founded in February of 2005, the YouTube.com site has quickly become the leader in online video. Every day millions visit the site, or view YouTube videos through links on other sites.

This is where you can do some very effective seminar video marketing. You can create a video blog sharing some of the content you'll be offering at the seminar – and embed that video on your own website. You can also have videos of your actual seminars shot and offer edited snippets of your actual presentation as a "coming attractions" trailer.

(Incidentally, you should market these videos, as well as written blogs if you do them, through Facebook, Twitter and other social media sites in your status updates. Include the links in those status updates so your prospects only have to click through to view them.)

The best and easiest way to shoot and upload your web videos is with a FLIP video camera, which is specifically designed for the process.

6. Myspace

Myspace.com was the big forerunner to Facebook and, while it isn't as popular as it used to be, it's still another good social media tool that's effective and free to use. It is, however, more social and more oriented to younger people, whereas Facebook does attract a broader-based crowd and offers more business marketing tools.

7. LinkedIn

LinkedIn.com is exclusively used for building business networks. It will help you make better use of your professional network and you can help the people you trust in return. Currently, the site has over 65 million members, and is signing up a new member about every second of the day. Executives in Fortune 500 companies are all LinkedIn members.

Obviously, this is an important resource for B2B marketing, which you can use to connect with people both above and below you on the business chain to help your own company and market your seminars to other professionals.

8. ActiveRain

If you're a real estate professional as I am, ActiveRain.com is designed especially for your usage. There are over 180,000 members on this site, which contains the world's largest real estate network, and, again, it's totally free. You can also blog on this site.

ActiveRain helps buyers and sellers connect with real estate agents. "Long tail" search terms, such as "First Time Home Buyers" in a specific location, or "senior citizen for a retirement community" are used to help connect with agents in a specific market and/or specialization. Obviously, this is a great resource to again establish your expert status and market yourself.

9. Meetup

Meetup.com features the world's largest network of local groups. It is designed to help organize people to get together in their communities to do something, to share something, to learn something, etc. **It boasts over 6 million members located all over the world and generates over 180,000 monthly "meetups." You can find out more details about the site at** http://meetupblog.meetup.com.

While it's free to join, Meetup does charge around $12 to set up a meeting. Obviously you can see how this would be ideal to help put your seminar together, however. You can pre-schedule several "meetups" ahead of time, which means everyone can see when the seminars will be and where they will be located.

I've found that, if you provide good content and value in your seminar presentations, word spreads virally on this site – and provides some of the best audiences for your seminars. One of my friends has consistently drawn over 30 attendees for his Meetup group every month.

10. Full Calendar

FullCalender.com is the site listed here that will charge you the most for their services - $19.95. And that's still a lot cheaper than printing up 20,000 insert ads for a newspaper, believe me!

FullCalendar.com is yet another social media platform and, like the others, you can set up an account for free. You use FullCalender to publicize your seminar or other event – it will send the details to local papers, websites, radio stations and email lists. It mainly serves major metro areas, such as the San Francisco Bay Area, Los Angeles, New York, Boston, Washington D.C., Chicago, etc. The charge, again, is $19.95 per event.

For under $20, I find this to be an incredibly economical and effective service that will save you hours of work on the computer trying to do this yourself.

When you're using all of the various social media platforms I've discussed above, you should have two common goals in mind with all of them – first, to "Market with Authority" and build relationships, and second, to capture names and contact information for all the prospects you interact with online. It's easy (and important) to build your database from these sites – but your first priority is to sell *yourself* and your expertise. Become their trusted advisor – someone they know, like and trust – and you can count on the sales to come later.

Social media requires an investment of your time, not money. It's easily the best place to start Marketing with Authority. When you build your reputation, both online and at your in-person seminars, you earn your income.

To learn more about seminar marketing, I would also suggest you visit http://www.seminarmarketingpro.com/ to get a free subscription to "Seminar Success Secrets" from seminar consultant Jenny Hamby.

Good luck and here's wishing you success in all your endeavors.

ABOUT JOE

Joseph Lam is a licensed Real Estate Broker, with a background as a business analyst, computer database specialist, information technology consultant and entrepreneur.

In 1990, Joseph founded Adtech Realty & Financial Corporation and served as the president until 2003. Mr. Lam operated a National Real Estate Franchise from 2003 – 2006. Currently, he is a Broker-Associate with Keller Williams Realty.

Joseph was the President for the California Association of Mortgage Brokers—San Jose Chapter. He was a member of the Board of Directors for the Willow Glen Business and Professional Association. He is also a member of the Education Committee for the Santa Clara County Association of REALTORS® (SCCAOR).

Mr. Lam was a volunteer for "Project Banking" with the San Jose Unified School District on teaching fifth graders "How to Balance Your Check Book." He was a Facilitator of Hugh O'Brian Youth Leadership (HOBY). Joseph is also a certified Facilitator of 'Ninja Selling,' and a Faculty Member of Keller Williams University.

Mr. Lam holds a BS from Oregon State University, and a MS & MBA from Binghamton University (SUNY.)

Among the many designations he possesses are: the Accredited Buyer Representative (ABR), the Accredited Staging Professional (ASP), the Certified Distressed Property Expert (CDPE), the Certified Foreclosure Specialist (CFS), the Certified Residential Specialist (CRS), the Certified Short Sales & Foreclosure Resource (SFR), the Seniors Real Estate Specialist (SRES), the Certified Computing Professional (CCP) and the Certified Home Affordable Foreclosures Alternatives Specialist (HAFA).

Mr. Lam is a Co-Author of the book: 'Short Sale 911 Manual.' A Homeowner's Guide on How To Survive The Worst Real Estate Market in History.

Joseph enjoys reading, travel, cooking and good foods, horseback riding, swimming and a game of Chinese 'mahjong.' You may also find him frequently heading up a Meetup group, or giving a seminar on business development and how to invest in real estate.

Joseph speaks Chinese – Cantonese & Mandarin, and some Spanish.

For more information find Joe at: www.JoeLamHomes.com

Or call him at: 800-399-9577

CHAPTER 13

THE DOWNFALL OF THE INSTITUTION, THE RISE OF THE PERSONAL BRAND AND HOW IT'S CHANGING THE GAME

BY J.W. DICKS ESQ. & NICK NANTON ESQ.

I (Nick) was sitting in a sushi bar in Los Angeles, thousands of miles away from my hometown of Orlando, FL. Having found a table, I asked the waiter to assemble my usual selections which included one order of Maguro, one order of Yellowtail, and one Steamed Shrimp, Cucumber and Cream cheese roll with a drizzle of eel sauce (the Nick Roll, as my friends have come to call it), and then I began to do what I do most of the time when I'm alone - I took out my iPHONE to occupy myself.

I checked emails, read and posted a few tweets, and checked my newsfeed on Facebook to see what my friends were up to. I also engaged in a newer activity, "checking in" via geotargeted apps and games like Loopt and Foursquare (If you don't know what these are, you should! Just Google them!). This particular meal was during a period of time several months ago, before Foursquare had been brought to the iPHONE, so I checked-in via Loopt. Much to my surprise, I noticed that a friend that I went to law school with and who also lives in Orlando, had also checked in on Loopt and was just a few miles away from me in Los Angeles. I immediately sent him a text to say 'hi!' and to tell him I was just a few miles away. This prompted us to try and coordinate a chance to meet; the meeting would be for the sake of novelty, if nothing else.

This occurrence prompted us to take stock of what many of us do to bide our time (check-in, tweet, post on Facebook), and how it was not only becoming second nature, but what that means for the way we are going to conduct business in the future. Based on these hyper-connected, entertaining, and informative ways of passing information from person to person, we are really leaving behind a trail of everything we've ever done, everywhere we've ever gone, every opinion we've ever had, and, thanks to some less than scrupulous folks who tend to overshare and take pictures with their phones, everything we've ever eaten. You might be wondering where this trend is headed and what it all means.

Well, in the context of "The New Economy", this trail is essentially a "Personal Brand Map". It's a record of our thoughts, feelings, and experiences, all mapped out in chronological order, from which anyone in our networks (or increasingly, even someone who we haven't allowed in our networks yet) can review and form an opinion about us.

IN THE NEW ECONOMY, SOME MIGHT SAY THAT OUR PERSONAL BRANDS ARE INCREASINGLY IMPORTANT. WE'D GO FURTHER, SAYING THEY'RE ALL WE'VE GOT LEFT.

Think about it. The internet and technology have brought about the following changes:

- Removed the barriers of information flow, allowing us to find anything we want, anytime we want it.
- Made transparency a way of life, allowing the general public to piece together a story even if you aren't telling it yourself - you can't hide most things anymore even if you wanted to!
- Leveled the playing field by giving everyone on Earth an instant platform to publish anything you can think of,

including thoughts, muses, obsessions, hobbies, photos, videos, business ideas, invitations to social events, collaborative efforts, and more.

We've seen this technology bring about the rise of the Personal Brand, while we have simultaneously witnessed the downfall of the institutions that we grew up believing in. This is a total game changer.

We've seen the banking industry fail us through credit crises and mortgage meltdowns. We've seen over-inflated real estate prices which are due, in large part, to the previous bottleneck on real-time information flow. In the past, we'd have to wait for all the data from real estate sales to drip down from title companies and city and county records in order to get a gauge on what was happening. Even worse, we might have to go to a physical location to view the records. Now you can find that all online, from anywhere in the world, with the click of a mouse. Simply revolutionary!

We've witnessed many a corporate meltdown due to lowered barriers to entry. For instance, it is now a very acceptable practice for any business person to schedule a meeting at a Panera Bread or Starbucks location. No formal office is needed, just a place to meet. We've also seen the increase in shared spaces replacing the more traditional executive suites and even some less traditional solutions like existing businesses renting out offices that aren't being used to house new businesses. We have seen increased international competition from countries like China and India, who are in a venerable race to bring their high-talent, low-cost human capital to America, with no plane tickets needed, using nothing but Skype and email. And, finally, we've witnessed those willing to compete and incur lower overhead in order to gain market share that previously would have seemed untouchable. This accumulation of corporate meltdowns has left many unemployed and without the pensions, retirements, or the security we always thought would be there.

This is a major shake up. In spite of the fact that many are calling it a "lost decade" (2000-2009), we instead look back and see a time of painful discovery and major shifts in the way information is shared, received, and processed. No longer do we look to journalists in last Friday's newspaper to determine what movies we want to watch or what restaurants we should try out; rather, we look to social networks to see what our friends think and where they are right now.

THERE HAS BEEN A SHIFT OF POWER. POWER IS NOW AT OUR FINGERTIPS - IN THE HANDS OF THE MANY, NOT IN THE HANDS OF THE FEW.

So, how do all of these powerful cultural and economic shifts affect you? You, as an individual, have become your own brand, whether you like it or not. You can control your brand to your own advantage or you can let your personal brand be run by others who comment on what you are doing. In fact, whether you choose to document your life and your business or not, chances are someone around you is going to document it for you. You don't have to post photos of yourself on Facebook or videos of yourself on YouTube for such photos and videos to end up there. You don't have to post your thoughts on a particular concept or issue online, for them to end up on Twitter, as those around you are doing it for you whether you like it or not. So, the real choice you need to make (before someone does it for you), is to control your personal brand.

THE GOOD NEWS IS, IF YOU LEARN HOW TO EFFECTIVELY CONTROL YOUR BRAND, YOU CAN ALSO CONTROL YOUR LIFE IN WAYS THAT WERE NEVER BEFORE POSSIBLE.

Think about it this way: in the past, if you were a superstar employee, you still got paid what your employer thought you were worth. Now, you can take your brand as a superstar employee to the internet, sharing your knowledge and building a following of people who are interested in your ideas and the projects you are working on. You can become an "internal evangelist" and a thought leader for your industry - all while working for someone else. This buzz about you in turn raises your profile and credibility, which then gives rise to the notion that no longer will you be an employee with limited options. You will now be a free agent operating no differently than the sports stars who are able to offer their skill(s) to the highest bidder.

This new 'free agent' marketplace is already occurring in limited scope through the use of social media sites like LinkedIn that are dedicated to connecting people for business, as well as through sites like Facebook that allow you to share text, video, audio, and even create custom apps to let people know what you do. Not to mention, we are just now in the early stages of internet platforms and tools to make those kinds of connections work to your advantage. The future will give rise to more of what one of our clients, Chuck Boyce, calls the "Independent Executive". This label applies to someone who takes their knowledge from previous employment and sets out to create their own destiny, lifestyle, and income on their own terms. This philosophy takes personal branding to the next level, because it is not just important for the professional or the entrepreneur, but it is now very important for employees who are happy to work in someone else's environment but who want to be recognized, both financially and emotionally, for their very real contributions.

In the past, an unhappy employee had limited choices:

- Do nothing but complain (with increasing disgruntlement)
- Quit and go look for a new job (which has no guarantee of being any different)
- Beg the boss for a change in circumstances (power, money, responsibility) without having any real say in the process

Now, in the new "Branded Economy", you are all allowed to play the role you want in building your brand and building your value. If you don't take control, you will risk becoming irrelevant and relegated to the position of a cog in someone else's wheel. You will be at the mercy of a third party whose self-interest will always outweigh your own - just like the players in the sitcom *The Office* and the comic strip "Dilbert".

Now that the game has changed, what will you do to control your own destiny? As we have gotten known for telling our clients, we'll now tell you the same: *You have the choice, to Brand or Die!*

ABOUT NICK

Nick Nanton, Esq. is known as "The Celebrity Lawyer" for his role in developing and marketing business and professional experts into Celebrity Experts in their field, through personal branding, to help them gain credibility and recognition for their accomplishments. Nick is recognized as the nation's leading expert on personal branding as Fast Company Magazine's Expert Blogger on the subject and lectures regularly on the topic at the University of Central Florida. His book *Celebrity Branding You®* has been selected as the textbook on personal branding at the University.

Nick serves as the Producer of America's PremierExperts® television show and The Next Big Thing® radio show, both designed to recognize the top Experts in their field and bring their solutions to consumers.

Nick is an award winning songwriter and television producer and has worked on everything from large scale events to reality tv pitches with the likes of Bill Cosby, President George H.W. Bush, Superbowl Champion Don Shula, Legendary Basketball Coach Bobby Knight, Rock 'n Roll Hall of Famer, Stan Lynch (Tom Petty & The Heartbreakers) and many more. Nick is recognized as one of the top thought leaders in the business world and has co-authored the best-selling books, *Celebrity Branding You!®, Big Ideas for Your Business, Shift Happens* and *Power Principles for Success* and has interviewed the top business leaders in the world, including Donald Trump, Richard Branson and Tony Hsieh, CEO of Zappos.com . Nick also serves as editor and publisher of Celebrity Press™, a publishing company that produces and releases books by top Business Experts. CelebrityPress has published books by Brian Tracy, Mari Smith, Ron Legrand and many other celebrity experts and has published books for more than 60 best-selling authors. Nick has been featured in USA Today, The Wall St. Journal, Newsweek, The New York Times, Entrepreneur® Magazine, FastCompany.com and has appeared on ABC, NBC, CBS, and FOX television affiliates speaking on subjects ranging from branding, marketing and law, to American Idol.

Nick is a member of the Florida Bar, holds a JD from the University of Florida Levin College of Law, as well as a BSBA in Finance from the University of Florida's prestigious Warrington College of Business. Nick is a voting member of The National Academy of Recording Arts & Sciences (NARAS, Home to The GRAMMYs), a 4-time Telly Award winner, and spends his spare time working with Young Life, Florida Hospital and rooting for the Florida Gators with his wife Kristina, and their two sons, Brock and Bowen.

To connect with Nick:
800-980-1626
Nick@CelebrityBrandingAgency.com
Twitter.com/NickNanton
Facebook.com/NickNanton

ABOUT J.W.

J.W. Dicks, Esq. is America's foremost authority on using personal branding for business development. He has created some of the most successful brand and marketing campaigns for business and professional clients to make them the Credible Celebrity Expert in their field and build multi-million dollar businesses using their recognized status.

J.W. has started, bought, built, and sold a large number of businesses over his 39 year career and developed a loyal international following as a business attorney, author, speaker, consultant, and business expert's coach. He not only practices what he preaches by using his strategies to build his own businesses he also applies those same concepts to help clients grow their business or professional practice the ways he does.

J.W. has been extensively quoted in such national media as USA Today, The Wall Street Journal, Newsweek, Inc. Magazine, Forbes.com, CNBC.Com, and Fortune Small business. His television appearances include ABC, NBC, CBS and FOX affiliate stations around the country. He is the resident branding expert for Fast Company's internationally syndicated blog and is the publisher of Celebrity Expert Insider, a monthly newsletter targeting business and brand building strategies.

J.W. has written over 15 books, including numerous best sellers, and has been inducted into the National Academy of Best Selling Authors.

J.W. is married to Linda, his wife of 38 years and they have two daughters, a granddaughter and two Yorkies. J.W. is a 6th generation Floridian and splits time between his home in Orlando and beach house on the Florida west coast.

CHAPTER 14

PUT YOUR OFFICE ON "CLOUD NINE"

BY TONY GRECO

"CLOUD NINE."

We've all heard the expression – it means a state of complete happiness. Bliss. So let me ask you, is that what you imagine when you picture your company's computing infrastructure?

Didn't think so.

Instead, maybe you picture unexplained crashes. Expensive, time-consuming software updates. Freezes. Viruses. Firewall problems. An employee whose answer to a computer problem is to smash every key on the keyboard with his fist.

Or you might picture traveling on the road or being unexpectedly stuck at home and suddenly realizing you don't have the files, or worse, the programs you need to finish a critical project. Bliss would be the ability to do anything, anywhere, without the need or assistance of a staff of IT professionals.

Maybe the IT guy pops into your head. You know – the one who talks to you like you're a five year-old, then takes about 5 times as long to fix something as he says it'll take… if he can fix it at all… if you can understand anything he's saying… which you don't.

So, instead of being up on Cloud Nine, it feels like your system can send your operation straight to hell at any moment – costing you valuable hours or even days of productivity.

And you probably think, in the words of Bob Dylan, "There must be some kind of way out of here…"

Well, I'd like to think we've found that way. And no, it doesn't involve going back to IBM Selectrics. Or pencil and paper. Or cave drawings. But it does involve some technology that was introduced back in the 80's. Remember those room-sized mainframes and dumb terminals? Well, they're back in a new and unique set-up

But mostly, it involves a Cloud – Cloud Computing, or Virtual Enterprise as we like to call it.

Whatever you may have heard about Cloud Computing, you haven't heard about *our* system -- because we created it, or at least the engineering behind it. We made it work like it should have when it was first introduced. And we've already successfully implemented it at several large corporations with enormous success. We know we can revolutionize any workplace with ten or more employees with our innovative Cloud Computing (Virtual Enterprise) structure.

And if you don't know what Cloud Computing is all about…well, we'll explain the whole thing to you. And we won't treat you like a five year-old.

But first, a little background, to explain how we ended up in the Clouds.

A NEW ERA OF I.T.

I know first-hand the frustrations and the irritation that I.T. brings to any business owner – because I've been in the I.T. support and consulting business for over 7 years. I started out wanting to be a lawyer, took a detour through the financial services industry and ended up getting a masters' degree in Computer Engineering (financed, fortunately, by that financial services detour). I ultimately realized that I.T. was my calling – I was always a big gadget guy and whenever anyone in the family needed a computer fixed, I was the person who got the call.

I also saw a place in the market for someone with my combination of communication skills, technical knowledge and my entrepreneurial ways. Yes, I took a few shots at I.T. guys a little earlier, and maybe I was a little harsh. But the fact is, I saw far too many I.T. "professionals" who were so introverted, they could barely carry on an adult conversation – and usually resorted to spouting computer gibberish so they could feel superior.

Most of the I.T. guys who I came in contact with also couldn't run a business to save their lives. For the most part, they were also far from friendly, both in how they dressed and in their overall demeanor. I couldn't help feeling that a different, more polished and professional approach would be successful. And if I offended you because I just described you...well I apologize. But you and I both know the truth.

I started tekGIANTS in 2003 to offer a professional and advanced approach of integrating technology with business to help a client become more successful. I knew there would be success in combining a consultative approach to managed IT services.

tekGIANTS wasn't so giant at first – it was mainly just me, knocking on doors trying to get something going. But I was fortunate, two years later, to have my brother-in-law, Dana Dearth join the company – his knowledge and experience gained from working as a programmer for Microsoft for almost a decade enabled us to really start gaining a foothold in the I.T. sector.

Slowly, we began to see that there was a place for an entirely new approach to the way businesses looked at I.T. We didn't want to just be computer repairmen – we wanted to be able to offer exciting new technology solutions that would enable companies to run more efficiently, and be more successful with the integration of our services and by utilizing the latest in technology - without all the normal day-to-day computer headaches, jargon and other B.S. a CEO does not want to have to deal with.

And so, just as I worked on changing up the personal side of the I.T. business, we now went to work on an exciting new way to take the usual company I.T. infrastructure up to a whole new level.

CLIMBING UP TO THE CLOUD

We saw an amazing solution in Cloud Computing – which was catching on in the I.T. industry. If you're not familiar with Cloud Computing, basically the "Cloud" in question refers to the internet. There are 3 types of Cloud computing; Private, Public and Hybrid.

Almost all companies have some sort of Private Cloud at this point – that's just about allowing users to access your network outside of the confines of your building. Public Cloud is the hot new kid on the block – that means your company has the ability to host your infrastructure in a data center located wherever you choose.

Hybrid Cloud computing is just what its name implies: a combination of the two, where you have a failover of your in-house servers over to a Public Cloud environment and some sort of replication happening. Although some companies cut corners and have inadequate staff to do this properly, Hybrid in the preferred method of many large corporations.

This is a concept that's been around since the early days of the internet – and, frankly, it hasn't worked that well for a lot of people until the last few years. Now, its time has finally come – and the overwhelming advantages that it provides to businesses just can't be ignored.

Cloud Computing is the new trend because of the simple fact you can have a new server up and running in minutes, instead of days. In addition, it cuts down on cost, power, and bandwidth. We have now taken Cloud Computing a step further and have engineered the solution to eliminate the desktop altogether and operate completely from the Cloud. We call our solution HIVE Virtual Enterprise.

The most important fact is this: we've done a great deal of testing and trial-and-error on building the perfect Cloud Computing set-up. We guarantee that *the user experience is the same* as if the client still had that complete PC system sitting on their desk.

Now, your next question might be…well, what *is* sitting on their desk then? And that's a fair question.

The answer is something that's called a "thin client." Not much more than a monitor, mouse and keyboard – with a total cost of $150. No moving parts. Uses less power than a light bulb. But it still does everything a PC does – plus *no one has to deal with any maintenance headaches*. We take care of firewalls, the software updates, and any other day-to-day issues, because everything is on our server at our offices. I know some of you remember those dumb terminals from the 80's. Well that is what a thin client is...greatly updated, of course.

The fact is, there are many Cloud companies out there. Many are just hosting their own servers, in an insecure environment. So take this advice from one business owner to another; do your homework before you pick a Cloud computing provider. Make sure that the datacenter is SAS70 Certified, and has redundant power and bandwidth. And ask your would-be Cloud provider the following questions:

1. Are your servers replicated?
2. Do you offer Virtual Private Networking (VPN)?
3. Are you checking security? (This is the most critical piece of the puzzle. Many Cloud companies are hacked DAILY.)
4. What is the Disaster Recovery Plan of your Cloud provider? *Always* ask this question.
5. Are you in compliance with HIPAA, FINRA, and other government regulations?
6. Are domains (company.com) being shared or partitioned on the same server?
7. Does your Service Level Agreement state all your procedures including, but not limited to, how fast you will put them into place?
8. Where are your data centers? If your company has 3 data centers all in Florida, for example, that could be an issue.
9. Can you offer restricted accounts?

Rest assured, our company can answer all these questions the way they should be answered.

In addition to the above queries, you can also search the internet for what users are saying about the company you're considering, and do a few trial accounts with several providers to "test the waters".

Please don't let me scare you away from Cloud Computing – you just want to make sure you're dealing with a completely professional company and minimize the risks involved in using any technology, old or new.

The bottom line, however, is that you should be embracing Cloud Computing with open arms, because of its tremendous benefits. My clients find that it:

1. Reduces Costs.
2. Reduces Staff.
3. Increases Scalability.
4. Increases Storage Capacity.
5. Automates business processes.
6. Creates a more mobile work environment.
7. Requires less maintenance and downtime.
8. Allows instant data and application delivery (at least with our solution).
9. Rapidly deploys new resources.

HIVE VIRTUAL ENTERPRISE

Now, this may make you a little nervous – *your* entire office data is on *a* server you cannot see, touch, and hear humming in a back room somewhere offsite? What if something happens at our offices? Well, the answer is…*it doesn't matter*. We have the server replicated on four other servers at other locations. Which means all of your data is totally safe and secure.

Another huge advantage is that with HIVE Virtual Enterprise, your complete office computer set-up – meaning all your applications and data -- can travel with you anywhere you go. You can log in to your "desktop" through an iPad, iPHONE, laptop or any other mobile device, anywhere in the world. No more worries about being without critical data when you're at home or on the road, and best of all, no more desktop computer.

The overall savings to any operation can be incredible. As I mentioned, the thin client that employees use at the office is incredibly inexpensive. You also save on I.T. services, servers, routers, and, best of all, power bills – making HIVE a great way to start "going green."

Of course, all Cloud Computing is not created equal. Most companies only provide limited services – like what Google does with internet-based applications such as Google Docs. We, however, believe we are the only company providing Infrastructure-as-a-Service through our particular method utilizing highly engineered servers, load balancing and high-end servers and infrastructure.

The fact is that most business owners are not computer experts – they learn what they have to in order to run their companies as best as they can. But as computing has become more and more complex, as well as more and more vital to a business operation, it's also becoming more and more of a headache to both the people running the companies and to the people who work at those companies. Not to mention that more and more companies have an inadequate level of I.T. personnel, due to the poor economy.

We believe HIVE Virtual Enterprise is the ultimate Headache Reliever for everyone in business today.

THE CLOUD ADVANTAGE

I'm certain Cloud Computing will become more and more the norm as time goes on. Internet speeds are increasing pretty much across the board now - and everyday computer users are already becoming more accustomed to working with the Cloud Computing concept (even if they may not *know* they're engaging in Cloud Computing). By 2013, almost 90% of all companies will be utilizing some type of Cloud Computing.

Increasingly, large enterprises are seeing the major advantages of switching over to some form of Cloud Computing. Some of the many business benefits include:

- A Lower TCO (Total Cost of Ownership): You avoid a large capital investment in I.T. equipment as well as the ongoing costs of software, support and upgrades. If you're interested in seeing just how much your business can save with its particular computing needs, we've created an easy-to-use calculator at http://hiveve.com/new_site/pricing.php.
- One-Stop Shopping: Most Cloud companies have made it their mantra to include everything (or as close to it as possible) in their services.
- Simple Scalability: If you need to quickly grow or cut back, you can add or remove servers in a second.

- Complete Mobility Becomes Your New Reality: Whether it's telecommuting, working on the road, or simply getting some stuff done on your iPad at the beach, Cloud Computing liberates you from the brick-and-mortar confines of your business. Almost half of all U.S. workers are expected to telecommute at least occasionally by 2016 – and more than any other factor, Cloud Computing will enable that to happen.
- Disaster Recovery: With your information/software stored elsewhere, firewall-protected and replicated in another location, you have several layers of security to prevent any disruption to your ongoing business.

Clients that switch over to our HIVE Virtual Enterprise system enjoy all these benefits and more. One multi-million dollar company, Lightpath Technologies Inc., has 275 users and is still growing at the time of this writing. They managed to cut I.T. costs by over 50% and streamlined operations both in their Orlando, Florida office and at their facility in China, where we have 65 users on our thin clients, working off our Orlando server. They've boosted efficiency, productivity and reduced expenses – and that, of course, is every business owner's dream!

SELECTING A CLOUD PROVIDER

A lot of I.T. companies, besides ourselves, are now beginning to offer Cloud Computing services. How do you know which one is a good fit for your business?

It's obviously important to do your research – this is a critical decision that affects your basic business operation and you want to make sure you're in good hands. In addition to what I've already discussed, you need to take a hard look at:

- How many clients are using this company's Cloud.
- How happy those clients are.
- How well the company can meet your particular needs.

In addition, you should:

- Research the company thoroughly.
- Get an accurate picture of the company's viability.
- Make sure their Service Level Agreement (SLA) includes a

failover (the ability to switch over to a back-up server) and disaster timeframe with accountability included. Make sure their failover sequence has been tested.

- Ascertain that the company has multiple data centers/ locations. A single location easily leads to an unstable Cloud.
- Get a copy of and read the company's policies and guarantees thoroughly.

Finally, you should test their system yourself and make sure the speed and access are up to standards. Don't accept that they're having "a bad day." You don't want that bad day to spill over into an important work day on your end.

We believe that we are currently the only company offering a true "Infrastructure-as-a-Cloud (IaaS)" Cloud Computing offering at this time, in the innovative way that we've structured it. HIVE Virtual Enterprise was designed to be both traditional (so users aren't thrown by having to learn a completely new system - they still have direct access to a "desktop" they're used to), *and* revolutionary (so that cost savings and productivity are maximized to a new and incredible level).

So forget about continually patching and repairing your own aging I.T. system. Forget about dealing with the dreaded I.T. tech. And forget about being anchored to your desktop at the office.

Float away from the enormous cost, responsibility and inconvenience with Cloud Computing. You'll find that "Cloud Nine" is a nice place to hang out.

Feel free to find out more about us at www.HiveVE.com.

ABOUT TONY

Since graduating with Honors from Regis University in Denver, Colorado with a Master's Degree in Computer Engineering, Tony Greco has innovated several cloud based technologies. One of which is a patent-pending system called HIVE Virtual Enterprise, a revolutionary way to operate your business, in the cloud, from any mobile device or terminal/PC. Tony is also the founder of tekGIANTS, Inc., a full-service IT firm with hundreds of clients spanning the globe.

Tony has extensive experience in the realm of cloud computing, virtualization and SaaS-based development. He has successfully helped several large enterprises take the plunge into the cloud, and recognize a significant cost-reduction within those companies.

CHAPTER 15

GO BEYOND YOUR WALLS

BY ALEC DAY, CO-FOUNDER, CLAIMTHEWEB.COM

To increase sales, improve efficiency, bring down costs and send the convenience factor through the roof for consumers, there's one giant "Game Changer" that can make all the difference for a business – selling online.

If that sounds like an obvious statement in 2010, it depends on what part of the merchant market you're talking about. For the big national chains, the answer is yes – years ago, they discovered they needed to create online accessibility to their products and services and it's made a big difference to their overall operations. That retailer revolution is mostly history.

But for many, many smaller mom-and-pop sized businesses in communities all across the country, the big leap to cyberspace hasn't been made yet. Why? They either don't see the tremendous benefit eCommerce could make to their bottom line, or they're intimidated by the technology. Or, in a lot of cases, it's both reasons.

At Claim The Web, we've worked hard to help these smaller businesses go beyond their walls and expand to an online store – with powerful turnkey shopping cart solutions that we've made as easy to use as possible. We've also customized the process as much as possible, so we do as much or as little of the work as our clients need to have done. So far, our clients' success stories have been completely rewarding.

I'd like to share in this chapter just how we work with our clients to meet their individual needs, and also how Claim The Web can help any business transition to a strong online presence. But first, let's look at a textbook example of how one business went from a neighborhood store to an incredible countrywide presence – and really demonstrated the amazing potential of eCommerce and internet marketing.

FROM NEW JERSEY TO NATIONAL SENSATION

Shoppers' Discount Liquor, located in Central New Jersey was a successful area business, grossing about $5 million a year. The store was begun and built up by a husband and wife who had emigrated from Russia.

Their son began working in the store when he was old enough – and began thinking beyond the simple brick-and-mortar business model that his parents adhered to. First, he trained himself in wine-tasting until he felt he was enough of an authority on the subject to begin advising his customers on what was a good buy. He then rebranded the store as "Wine Library" (which had a much better ring than "Shoppers' Discount Liquor") to appeal to a more upscale crowd.

The reboot of his business was incredibly successful. Store traffic began to increase as did the sales – some of it due to the simple fact that people were now seeking out the son's advice and buying what he recommended. But, again, there was only so far the son could take the store's revenues since he was limited to just selling at the one physical location. So he turned to the internet and found renewed inspiration.

He began selling wine online and also began recording a wine video blog, called "Winelibrary TV" in 2006. And he rode the new popularity of social media to promote the video blog and his website endlessly through YouTube, Facebook and Twitter.

Now, instead of the store making only 5 million a year through its brick-and-mortar sales, it's now generating 60 million in gross sales – over ten times its original revenues. At the same time, he's built his online presence to the point where, today, he has close to 90,000 visitors to his website on a daily basis, as well as almost 900,000 followers on Twitter.

As a side development, the son – whose name is Gary Vaynerchuk – has also transformed himself into an incredibly successful self-help and business advice guru. He just signed a seven-figure deal with a publishing house for a book series and has been profiled in "The New York Times," and on CBS and ABC news. He's appeared on the Conan O'Brien and Ellen DeGeneres shows and has become a national figure.

Gary's drive and sales smarts are clearly not the norm – and his level of success is incredible. But the lesson of his story is that he saw the limits of being bound inside the walls of a physical store – and that the easiest, best way to go beyond those walls was to take his business online.

THE SECRET TO OUR ONLINE SUCCESS

Our clients have also found a welcome level of increased success from working with us to create a robust eCommerce website and online presence. For example, Mrs. Cavanaugh's, a chocolate store chain, realized customers really only came to buy chocolates from them a couple of times a year, mostly for special occasions – most people pick up their sweet treats at a supermarket and don't make regular trips to a candy store.

Well, within two weeks of switching to our shopping cart software with our URL structure and customized design, they saw a 73% increase in sales. And within 4 months, their sales were up 160% over last year. Clearly, www.MrsCavanaughs.com has turbocharged their profit picture thanks to going online.

We've had a number of other companies who have dramatically boosted their bottom line by working with our eCommerce tools. Donna Bella Hair Extensions (www.donnabellahairextensions.com) added close to $30,000 in sales within 3 months of adding our custom store and utilizing a Google AdWords campaign. Pest Products Online (http://www.pestproductsonline.com) saw a revenue increase of 64.9% within one year of working with us.

There's a reason we're uniquely qualified to help these smaller companies find online success – and we think that reason is another real Game

Changer for any business. That reason is we make it a point to use our eCommerce tools *ourselves* to create *our own* moneymaking websites. That means if our software doesn't work – we *don't* make money.

And that's what you call a powerful impetus to get it right.

By using our own product, we see firsthand what works – and what *doesn't* work – when it comes to selling online. Since our own profits are at stake, you can bet we pay attention when any adjustments results in higher sales – or, for that matter, lower ones.

A lot of companies do what we do – but there aren't very many of them that actually use their own software to try and make money. They view that as an expensive experiment but we see it as necessary research. We think so because it's one of most important elements of our business approach; one that helps us connect with other merchants who we help with online sales operation set ups.

By owning and operating our own online stores, which generate millions in revenues, we not only continue to improve and refine our services and software, but we bring that firsthand knowledge to our clients when they're looking for practical advice that will help them increase efficiency and raise their revenues.

It's a win-win for us and for them.

TAKING YOUR BUSINESS ONLINE

If you currently run a store that only has a brick and mortar location, there are a lot of compelling reasons why going online with your products and/or services can be an incredible Game Changer for your business. You may already have a profitable enterprise and don't feel the need to make the jump. Why bother? Well, here are a few of reasons why we think you should:

- **YOU CAN SELL TO THE WORLD**

Your potential customers are no longer limited to just your surrounding geographical area. You can now literally sell *to the entire world*. That alone means that, if you create an effective online presence, your sales have to see a substantial increase.

Going online really benefits a store that primarily caters to tourists. You may sell a local product line that reflects your area – for example, maybe you own a surf shop with your own unique line of beach apparel that's in great demand from tourists. Those tourists go home, and their friends might see the stuff they bought from you and go wild for it. Unless you offer an online option for buying, however, they have no way to purchase it themselves. This holds true for any local business with products that would appeal to people outside the area.

- **YOU CAN BUILD A BETTER RELATIONSHIP WITH YOUR CUSTOMERS**

Once you've established your online "identity," you can use your website and social media tools to build a relationship with your customers and prospects, as Gary Vaynerchuk did. People like to connect with people, not with companies – so putting a face on your online business is a great way to inspire customer loyalty. That's easy to do these days through personalized emails, as well as Twitter and Facebook updates from the owner of the store.

One of our online stores is www.wire-sculpture.com, selling jewelry-making supplies and education. Brandon, our marketer and primary email contact for wire-sculpture, quickly began to develop a following. People would contact him directly with questions about products and customer service inquiries. This quickly grew to a whole other level as people developed a personal connection to Brandon. They started to send him pictures of themselves, their pets and other parts of their lives, as well as samples of the jewelry they made from the supplies they purchased on the site.

The demand proved to be too much for Brandon, already busy programming and marketing the site – so we had to have one of his personal assistants transition to responding nearly full-time on Brandon's behalf, replying to customers' personal emails and helping them solve jewelry problems. It's a connection that's paid off, as the site tripled sales in the first four months of 2009, partly because of the personal email campaign authored by Brandon that created a real relationship with our customers—not just a corporate face. Your customers want to do business with a person, not a corporation.

- **YOU CAN MAKE MONEY AUTOMATICALLY**

Just like the online marketers promise, you **can** make money while you sleep – because almost everything on an online store is automated. Email responses, order placement and fulfillment, payments…all of it for the most part gets handled by our software without you having to worry about a thing. Obviously, some customer service-oriented issues need to be dealt with personally, but, for the most part, our shopping cart packages, once they're set up, run by themselves.

- **YOU CAN TARGET YOUR IDEAL MARKET(S)**

It's incredibly easy, once you're online, to target the ideal market for your goods. With so many people on the internet, almost any niche group is online on one place or another – it's just a matter of finding them and marketing to them.

You do that through such online selling tools as Google AdWords and SEO (Search Engine Optimization) methods. We help our online merchants to use these techniques in the most cost-effective way. In particular, the search engine capability of our software helps our clients, once they put their products online, rank incredibly high on Google results page – often the number one, two or three positions.

We also specialize in helping our clients push their products out to bigger sites such as Amazon, to drive more traffic to their store and expose more potential buyers to their merchandise.

In conclusion, it's pretty clear that the benefits of taking a store online are powerful. You expand your potential customer base to an almost unbelievable degree, you have a vast array of new and affordable marketing methods to deliver your marketing message and most of the day-to-day work is automated.

If you work with the right eCommerce company, it also doesn't matter if you have a great deal of computer skills. We pride ourselves on helping clients with the process from start to finish if need be – and, again, since we run our own stores with our own software, we know all the challenges and problems they either are facing or will face inside and out. And we know the best ways to tackle them.

Going online is the ultimate Game Changer for a business – especially if you've already built a solid physical store with a lot of satisfied loyal customers (who can hopefully provide you with video testimonials!). Selling to the world has a great deal more potential than just selling to the neighborhood.

ABOUT ALEC

Alec Day, is the co-founder of Claim the Web, INC, a leading e-commerce solutions provider. The Claim the Web group of companies own and operate several successful online properties that generate millions of dollars a year in revenue. Alec's extensive background in marketing and advertising brought huge success to the table when he and co-founder Mark Ryan started Claim the Web in 2001 as some of the internet's pioneers in online commerce. Still a pivotal force behind the software, Alec spends much of his time today driving huge growth in his own online properties; he also travels the country training and speaking to groups from around the world on how to make money on the internet. Alec enjoys spending time outdoors in his hometown of Ogden, Utah; his hobbies include traveling and starting and nurturing businesses. He resides in Ogden with his lovely wife Krystal and newborn son AJ.

CHAPTER 16

CREATING REAL WEALTH THROUGH ENTREPRENEURSHIP

THE 8 ESSENTIAL DISCIPLINES TO GROW YOUR SMALL BUSINESS

BY CLIFFORD JONES, FOUNDER AND CEO OF WEALTHNET PARTNERS, LLC

August 17, 2002 was a day that would forever change my life. I had resigned my position as vice president of investments with a major Wall Street firm. For the prior twelve years I had been building my own business under the brand of several big firms.

The public doesn't really get the fact that most financial advisors are commission-only, trained sales professionals who manage and grow their own "books" of business. By building a client base with millions in assets under management, big firms pay big advisors millions every year to capture new market share.

Even though the financial services industry enabled me to make a great living, sell my book of business three times, develop a financial mindset and hone my sales and marketing skills, it was time to move on. That fateful day in August, I had decided to break my contract with the firm. It would cost me almost everything I owned. And it was worth it.

Despite the tinge of fear lodged in my gut, I knew it was time to start a new business. I wasn't quite sure how I was going to pull it off. My wife and I had two young children and money was tight. But I desperately wanted to do more with my life and serve people in a more meaningful way. And the prospect of getting a job was not an option for me. I am an entrepreneur.

I learned several essential lessons while starting and growing my financial consulting business. Each of these lessons reinforced my desire to be a more successful entrepreneur and to serve others in a more meaningful way. The first lesson was that the wealthiest of my clients had all created their wealth by starting, funding, marketing and growing successful businesses. While some of my clients were executives, doctors and lawyers, the happiest and the wealthiest of my clients were entrepreneurs. They loved what they did for work every day.

The second lesson I learned was that my clients who owned businesses made a far better return on their capital than they could achieve through the stock market over time. Their best investment had always been their own business. Most business owners scoffed at typical stock market returns and the loss of control of their working capital.

The third lesson I learned is the power of creating an "infinite" return on capital. Picture a small business owner starting her business with a few thousand dollars borrowed on credit cards and turning it into $15 million. Now that's a home run in my book. That's an example of creating an "infinite" return on capital.

While many small businesses fail, many more succeed. Being an entrepreneur is about more than the money itself. As a financial advisor, I noticed my clients had purpose and meaning through their work. They loved their work. They could control their time. They could take nice vacations. They could coach their kids in sports. They could be home every night for dinner -unlike their corporate executive friends who were slaves to airports, long business trips, and the uncertain job security of Corporate America. This is how I define real wealth today.

I too had learned the power of creating an "infinite" return on investment. I started with no capital and sold my book of business three times over twelve years. The fundamentals for creating real wealth through entrepreneurship are the typically the same, as I will address shortly. You need to leverage your strengths, be willing to jump in and work hard, and never give up.

Most people think you need big bucks to start, fund, market, grow and sell a successful business. For businesses that need lots of equipment, buildings and people, it's essential to have more capital up front. Yet look around you today. Millions of people leaving Corporate America have started their own small businesses with little or borrowed capital.

While making my plan to leave financial planning and investment consulting, I had interviewed many of my clients to understand their biggest problems in business. I learned that people, sales and marketing were the biggest issues. I set out to create a new consulting business that would help my clients sell more, work less, and leverage Internet-based technologies. I wanted to leverage my unique abilities in marketing and sales. I love learning about and testing new Internet-based technologies as they emerged in the 1990's. I knew I could make a business out of helping others learn how to sell more, work less and create real wealth.

Almost anyone can grow a business if they know how to manage relationships, market effectively, sell, leverage technology and manage people. Fear is what holds most people back. If you have a dream to position yourself properly, market well and sell effectively, you can grow your business over time. You just need the guts to put your neck on the line and find out if you have what it takes to be successful.

What does it take to succeed in building your own business? In his best-selling book, *Outliers*, Malcolm Gladwell reveals that timing, innate ability or talent, blended with lots of hard work over time, is the proper formula for determining success in business, sports and life. Mr. Gladwell suggests that people who have committed more than 10,000 hours to their discipline are people with incredible wealth. He cites Bill Gates as a primary example of someone who invested many thousands of hours programming computers. Right time. Right place. And thousands of hours invested in doing what he loved to do.

Of all the skills required to succeed in business, marketing and sales are at the top of the list. I decided to leverage my unique abilities in marketing, sales, and Internet-based technologies when I started my current company, WealthNet Partners, LLC in 2002. As of this writing, I have accumulated more than 54,000 hours working as a sales and marketing professional. By conservative measure, that's 40 hours a week, 50 weeks a year for 27 years, learning how to market, sell and leverage the Internet.

How do you find your life's purpose and the perfect business? What's the best business for you? The simple answer is: 'Put in your time', ... Pay your dues, … Learn and adapt as you go, … Be willing to take risks, … Hire a coach. Focus on helping other people get what they want by solving their problems with your product or service.

There is a revolution taking place in America today. In fact, it's a global revolution driven by entrepreneurs. While millions of jobs have been eliminated in recent years, millions of people are taking control of their lives and financial future by starting, funding, marketing and growing small businesses. This is how real wealth is created for most people.

Despite the well-documented failure rate of small businesses, the simple truth is that millions of businesses do succeed over time. Success is manifested through vision, hard work, skill, and luck. If you have the guts to be in business for yourself, you can create real wealth. Where's the proof? Look at the simple fact that small businesses provide the vast majority of jobs in America. Look around you at the people who run their own businesses and ask them how they feel about their lives, their bank accounts and their future.

Is it easy to start, fund, market and grow a successful business? No way. But for me and millions of others, the alternative of finding a JOB (Just Over Broke) is painful. Here are the 8 essential disciplines for creating real wealth through entrepreneurship. These disciplines apply to start ups as well as established small businesses.

1. Dream big. I have yet to meet a successful entrepreneur who doesn't 'dream big'. Your dream must translate to a clear vision, proper funding and a solid plan. If you have purpose and a deep connection to achieving your dream, it's much easier to execute through the tough times.

2. Identify and attract your ideal customer. You must be crystal clear about your ideal customer. If you're not completely clear about this you will scatter your marketing, sales and service resources in too many directions. Focus your sales and marketing capital and be highly targeted.

3. Craft your Unique Positioning Statement (UPS). Forget the typical elevator speech. What problem do you solve for your customer and how can you articulate this clearly to your market? What makes you special or different from your competition? It is critical to be crystal clear and communicate this well to your prospective customers.

4. Organize and manage your relationships. Leveraging the right Customer Relationship Management (CRM) system is critical to communicating with and managing your business relationships. Forget spreadsheets and the pile of business cards sitting on your desk. You need a real system. Commit yourself and your team to learning a system and using it daily. Today's web-based technologies are either free or very affordable "pay-as-you-go" systems. We use Infusionsoft and absolutely love the fact that it integrates our relationship management, email marketing, ecommerce and affiliates.

5. Leverage the right team. You can't do everything yourself even though you may want to try. Whether you are in business for one day or ten years, what is your highest and best use of time? Build a team of employees and independent contractors around you to best leverage your time and unique abilities. Hire the best people and professionals your money can buy for marketing, sales coaching, management, bookkeeping, technology, tax and legal disciplines.

6. Leverage the right technologies. The Internet has changed the rules and enables you to compete with big companies for your share of the market. Your website, Customer Relationship Management (CRM) system, email marketing, search engine optimization, social media and marketing systems must be synchronized for maximum efficiency.

7. Market with education. Marketing is part art and science. We prefer "attraction-based" marketing campaigns to traditional cold calling, direct mail, and trade shows. Traditional marketing disciplines have their place. Marketing with education sets you apart from most small businesses. Craft a website for maximum conversions. Earn permission to market to people. Create and market free eBooks, video, email, White Papers and Webinars to teach your ideal prospect how you can solve their problem.

8. Sell, sell, sell. How much time do you invest every day selling? Selling is a critical "pay time" activity for every business owner. You've heard about location, location, location. But nothing happens before you sell even if you have the best location. As a business and sales coach, I hear people tell me they are not good at selling. That's what I call serious 'head trash'. Get over this quickly. Effective selling is asking intelligent questions, listening, consulting, enrolling, and earning trust. We all get better the more we work at it.

Being in business is the best investment you can make if you are willing to assume the risk and responsibility. Every day provides you the opportunity to learn and improve your skills. Embrace your ability to test, learn and grow. Creating real wealth through entrepreneurship requires a deep connection to your purpose as an entrepreneur, providing value, building a team, and leveraging the right technologies to scale and grow.

I am truly blessed to do what I do every day. It is an honor and privilege to serve other entrepreneurs as they pursue real wealth. We consult and coach business owners, professionals and consultants around the world who work in a wide variety of industries. Our sales, marketing and technology disciplines apply to any business.

My team and I are part of the global revolution of entrepreneurship. We are "trusted advisors" to our clients. We continue to test, develop and leverage new tools, systems and software applications to help our clients. We get to make a difference for people and the global economy by helping to grow small businesses through our consulting and business coaching services.

My goal is to help you understand that if you don't have real wealth, you can achieve it. It is entirely possible for you to find your highest purpose and create real wealth through entrepreneurship. If you are struggling to grow your business, keep working at it. If you fail, start over. Don't let the tough times discourage you. Never give up!

Congratulations if you are one of the fortunate few on this planet to have already achieved real wealth. This puts you in the unique position to give back and help others. The most important thing we can do as entrepreneurs to impact job growth and the expansion of the global economy is start, fund, market and grow successful businesses.

ABOUT CLIFFORD

Clifford Jones is the founder and president of WealthNet Partners, LLC, an Internet marketing and business development consulting firm based in Scottsdale, Arizona. Cliff founded his consulting business in 2002 after selling his financial advisory practice to a major Wall Street firm in 2000. Cliff's greatest passion is teaching entrepreneurs that starting, funding and growing successful businesses is the absolute best investment most people can make.

Cliff was raised in New England among a family of dedicated entrepreneurs. Inspired from a young age to pursue the path of entrepreneurship, he studied International Business and Economics at Ohio Wesleyan University. Following his graduation in 1983, Cliff worked for eight years as a sales and marketing executive in the hotel industry where he learned to manage teams and multi-million dollar marketing budgets for luxury corporate hotels and destination resorts.

In 1991, Cliff decided to pursue a more entrepreneurial path and proceeded to build and sell three books of business as a financial planner and investment advisor. Over the twelve years invested in building and selling his practices, Cliff worked exclusively with high net worth entrepreneurs and professionals. It was an incredible opportunity to learn from highly successful people while continuing to hone his skills in sales, marketing, investment management, business planning and commercial lending.

Cliff is dedicated to working with and inspiring other entrepreneurs to build successful businesses while giving back to the global community of entrepreneurs. Cliff and his wife of twenty-four years have two sons in college. He loves fitness training, cycling, outdoor adventures, playing golf, business blogging, writing and reading tons of books.

CHAPTER 17

GO VIRTUAL BY "DOING IT ONE TIME FOR FREE TIME"

BY BREWA KENNEDY

We are living in rather exciting times. Never before has there been such a plethora of rapidly-emerging technologies, many of which truly deliver (and even sometimes over-deliver) on their promises. From robust web applications, to the rise of the smart phone, the technologies available today have no doubt been instrumental in various entrepreneurial success stories in the last ten years. Now, opportunities abound for expanding your territory by setting up shop, not only in your immediate area, but also elsewhere *virtually*. And this has all been made possible by technology. Thanks to technology, the outsourcing of various business processes is within reach for just about any business--big or small.

I work in the highly-regulated field of property and casualty insurance. My small business helps hundreds of clients to protect their homes, automobiles, and small businesses, as well as the future of their families. Insurance, by its very nature, requires attention to lots of details, and connectivity to lots of resources to get the job done right. In the first days of owning my business, I, like most entrepreneurs, ran my operation much like the veterans in my field-- the old-fashioned way. However, because I have never really been a conformist, I knew that there had to be better ways to do many of the things that were required of me. And so, I set out to change the way that the local agent conducted business. I wanted it to be fresh and new, but I also wanted it to make sense-- all the way around. I needed to create a WOW experience for my clients, as well as to maximize the efficiency of the operation.

Any small business owner undoubtedly has to wear lots of hats. Often times, due to limited financial resources, small business owners must take on the role of the marketing person, the CPA, the customer service contact, the IT guy, and so many others. Other times, small business owners do everything on their own simply because they are afraid that the work won't get done exactly the way *they* would do it. This is a huge mistake that business owners must correct before expecting any sort of return on their overwhelming investments of time, energy, and care that they put into their businesses.

In my field, depending on the type of insurance an agent writes, volume can factor hugely into the steadiness of an agent's income level. I quickly learned that looking for a handful of key niches would enable me to automate many of my business processes, while producing at a high volume. For my bottom line, this meant that I would be able to reduce the number of additional people needed to run my business operation efficiently. After identifying key niches to go after, I set out to find web applications that would complement my operational objectives, and then I did the unthinkable in my industry: I hired a *virtual assistant*. Almost instantaneously, the hiring of a virtual assistant helped me to rid myself of a lot of the lower-level (but still very important) tasks that needed to be done on a daily basis. Even though my assistant was not physically present, both she and the technologies that we used proved they paid me dividends by gaining valuable time. This really makes a difference in your business' bottom line.

Here's how my situation works: my virtual assistant, who lives in another city and state (3 times zones away, to be exact), has access to information that she needs via an online portal. She, along with everyone in my organization, shares a web presence that allows us to collaborate securely within our own web domain. We're able to work on documents together, send one another emails, chat by text, voice and video, and even view one another's calendars. My assistant does all sorts of things for me, like filing (electronic documents, of course), faxing, receiving and returning phone calls and emails, answering general inquiries, data entries, and she even makes appointments for me to visit my barber!

We have a robust phone system that links all of us, wherever we are – and can be changed at a moment's notice via an online portal. Our operation sounds like a really big one when someone calls in, so the perception that our clients have of us is usually that we are a really big operation. We've leveraged the use of phone technology to partner with the insurance carriers with which we do business, so that they provide the bulk of the servicing for our clients' policies. And our client management system is directly interfaced with each company, saving us the hassle of redundant data entry.

You can imagine the ridiculous amount of paperwork that insurance requires, right? Not necessarily. In our operation, we use about 97% less paper than most other insurance agencies. Through the use of dual computer monitors, there's really not much need to ever print anything. "What about all those signatures?" ...you must be asking. I've got an answer for that one, too. Many organizations call themselves 'paperless' by virtue of the fact that they scan all the enormous amount of paper that they generate into a document management system, and then shred the paper files. We take it one step further. We use a secure electronic signature platform that reduces our carbon footprint, and keeps us from having to chase paper in the first place. So, nearly 100% of the paper that we do scan is derived from incoming mail from various sources.

Our operational goals are clearly spelled out, which enables our sales staff to truly operate from their homes, or any remote location. They are never required to come to the office if they don't want to. All that matters is that the work is done, and that it is done correctly. And that's it.

Lots of businesses are doing the same thing nowadays. Successful organizations are being built from the ground-up, in a very organic fashion, through the use of some or many of the techniques discussed here. You can do it, too. The benefits are numerous. You would save by reducing or eliminating the need for physical office space, thereby reducing or eliminating the need for a daily commute. Imagine not having to commute to work (or at least, not every day). Imagine not having to worry so much about gas prices. Isn't this awesome stuff?

You see, for a great deal of businesses, taking at least the bulk of operations to a virtual space really isn't a bad idea – especially if you don't stock any sort of inventory for whatever it is that you sell. There are usually lower-level tasks that business owners can outsource to virtual human help, and even to virtual software applications, which require only a web browser to operate. It is absolutely imperative that you, the business owner, *own* your business. You cannot let your business own you! You should be delegating things that you do poorly, things that others do better, as well as things that aren't being done right now, but should be.

The term 'outsourcing' tends to get a bad rap, since it allegedly takes away job opportunities for other citizens. But, as a business owner, your goal should be making certain that your bottom line is in the **black**, and not in the **red**. Suffice it to say, I have no problems with outsourcing. It's the wave of now--and of the future. Besides, there are tons of outlets to which one can outsource, right on your own country's soil.

HERE'S HOW TO "DO IT ONE TIME FOR FREE TIME"

You can automate all sorts of processes: 'Onboarding' new clients, sending targeted messages to present clients via email, fax, voice, sms, and even 'snail mail', periodic invoicing, bookeeping and mail sorting...the possibilities are nearly endless! Because of the power of the internet, sharing and collaborating on information is extremely easy, and can be done from anywhere with an internet connection. And for pennies on the dollar, you can easily obtain help from others, who don't share your physical presence, for anything from answering calls to just about any repeating task.

1. The key is turning your tasks into documented processes so that they are teachable. I can assure you that this is a great way to free up a lot of your time. If you don't already have documentation, you can even get help doing that! Start by thinking about how you run your business operation. Think of things that you could (or should) delegate to others. Chances are, there's an inexpensive (or free) web application that can make your life easier. Or, at the very least, there's someone, someplace, who is willing to take those tasks off your hands for more than a reasonable or even cheap price.

2. Read up on blogs that focus on emerging web applications that are geared for business development and efficiency.
3. With the onslaught of information overload in this internet age, you must do what it takes to filter out all the noise, so that you can maximize your work hours. The end result is that the more focused time you spend on your business, the more money you will make. Don't let information overload take over your time. (And trust me-- it will!)
4. Tame your cell phone. Tame your office phone. Tame your email. Limit your availability to the masses. Interruptions are what I affectionately call 'derailments', and they should never be taken lightly. Here's why: studies show that it can take as much as 20+ minutes for most workers to regain traction in their productivity after an interruption. There really isn't a good reason that you shouldn't have a laser focus on your workday. No reason at all.
5. Use currently available tools and maximize their fullest potential. If you use Outlook, learn how to user filters to automatically process emails. Gmail is another awesome email program that has many powerful features to help you maximize one of the most commonly used forms of communication. Of course, what I like most about Gmail is that it requires only a web browser.
6. Surround yourself with great people, and empower them to make decisions. First demonstrate to them your goodwill when it comes to doing the right thing by your clients and customers, and then empower them to do the same. This strategy alone will score you huge returns. It will free up some of your valuable time to do what it is you do best in your business. And it will make them better at supporting your efforts.

There's a lot more that I can tell you about automation and outsourcing. I have even created an instantly downloadable e-book on this very topic. The book is yours for the asking, and you can download your copy today at www.brewakennedy.com, where you'll find other great information, including my automation blog, and links to some of my favorite resources.

ABOUT BREWA

Brewa Kennedy began his work life at the ripe old age of 19 as an airline professional with Southwest Airlines. Southwest, which is famous for its unique corporate culture and its encouragement of employees to be expressive, helped Brewa to learn that he was truly a maverick and an almost deliberate non-conformist. Brewa was invited to become one of the original Crewmembers of a fresh, new airline that America now knows as JetBlue Airways. The experience of being an integral part of creating a brand new airline from the ground-up was fuel to Brewa's passion for constant innovation and change to do better than the *status quo* in business.

Leaving the airline industry, Brewa's first love, was one of the hardest things he ever did, but it was a crucial step for his destiny's fulfillment to become a serial entrepreneur. Brewa has found tremendous success in various ventures in the real estate, mortgage, and insurance industries. After signing-on to be an Exclusive Agent with Allstate Insurance, Brewa soon saw that being an Independent Agent was a better venue in which he could express his passion for innovation and creativity. With the onset of the growth of technology, he quickly seized opportunities to create new ways to process business and to provide extraordinary service to his clients.

Hugely famous among his followers as a hard worker, Brewa is an expert at automating workflows and business processes, while helping business owners to save money and increasing their efficacy. He has helped dozens of small business owners in regaining valuable time and reducing operational expenditures.

Brewa is an active member of the Florida Association of Insurance Agents, and serves as the Chairman of the Agency Automation & Technology Task Force. He resides in Orlando with his wife and two children.

Brewa is passionate first about people, and then about new technologies to help us be truly more effective. He maintains a blog and resources that can help you in your business. His website is www.brewakennedy.com.

CHAPTER 18

GAME CHANGERS IN TECHNOLOGY

BY COURTNEY BARNETTE – 407-963-0095

"Can technology be a game changer, or is it the person that uses the technology, that changes the game?"......CommXperts

Few things in this world change faster than technology. New products are introduced daily that are better, faster and smaller than the previous models. However, only a handful of products such as the Apple iPHONE and the Microvision ShowWX can truly be labeled as game changers. See how Small/Medium business, and Enterprises too, are trying to keep up with technology, and devoting time and resources, to stay ahead of the curve.

iPHONE

Just a few short years ago, it was a challenge to find unlocked GSM devices with dual-mode capabilities for international travel. An Unlocked GSM (Global System for Mobile communications) is one that can be used on multiple networks and has the ability to do many things that a regular phone could not. These early generation smartphones had VoIP (Voice over Internet Protocol) capabilities as well as interchangeable SIM cards allowing for both international and local calling and came with a price tag of $400-$500 each. However consumers balked at the stiff price tag, and wireless companies had to offer them at a lower price with a two year minimum contract commitment to subsidize the sale.

Then, Apple introduced the iPHONE and revolutionized smartphones as we knew them. Suddenly the consumer began to embrace texting, instant messaging, VoIP over wireless (such as Skype) and the benefits of having an unlocked device which would work on the network they chose. Customers readily paid the $499 price tag in order to get the device capabilities without being locked into a contract, or decided on the iPHONE at a Subsidized price and commitment to AT&T.

When talking about wireless networks, bandwidth refers to the amount of data that can be transferred from one point to another and is usually measured in bits per second (bps). This speed is produced by national carriers with wireless networks (such as Sprint or AT&T). 2G refers to the 2nd generation networks (1G was the original analog system) and typical bandwidth speeds were 300-600 Kbps. Most people had not even heard of a 2G model until wireless carriers launched the 3G (or 3rd Generation) which runs at speeds of 600 Kbps – 1.7 Mbps. Soon, 4G networks will run ten times faster with incredible speeds of 3-6 Mbps with bursts up to 10 Mbps. Imagine how customers and business alike can conduct business with even faster speeds?

In our instant gratification world, consumers want their information better, faster and right now. The increased speed of connectivity introduced by the iPHONE satisfies this need and more. With this launch, Apple's marketing exploded. The iPHONE was the first device that enabled the consumer to connect to the internet with great speed and EASILY search the internet at any given moment. This put the iPHONE in a category all its own! It also created a challenge for businesses to stay connected, and allowed employees the freedom of using the iPHONE for personal use too.

Furthermore, content is king. While today's devices allow for instant connectivity, not all handsets are capable of social connections. With applications, Apple and the iPHONE are allowing smartphones to connect to social media and keep the consumer connected in optimal ways. There are more than 1 billion apps that have been downloaded from Apples iTunes, and many more on the way. There are also two other smartphone platforms on the rise as well, RIM's BlackBerry and Google's Android platforms. Developers are in high demand to create the total wireless experience, as well as continuing to develop the apps that keep customers connected and productive.

PICO PROJECTOR

As technology evolves, consumers are utilizing video more and more. (There is a reason YouTube has over 100 million videos and continues to grow daily.) We love to watch videos and SHOW our stories. As a busy society, we do not stop to read anymore. We want to watch.

Microvision recently introduced a game changer in their SHOWX pico projector. This projector utilizes 3RGB (Red, Green and Blue) laser technology allowing an image to wrap around whatever it is projected upon. In addition, it literally fits in your pocket making it the most easily transported projector on the market. Approximately the size of an iPHONE or a Blackberry device, this tiny projector can display an image of up to 200 inches. Now that's impressive!

Not only does this projector make presentation delivery easy, but its cutting edge technology creates a buzz all its own. Whether you are using this for entertainment, business, or simply to impress, this device is a game changer. This device has people everywhere asking, "Have you seen my Pico?"

COMMXPERTS

If you haven't heard of Courtney with CommXperts yet, you soon will. In a market flooded with companies pushing any and all electronic devices they can to make money, Courtney at CommXperts stands apart. As President, his mission is to help consumers navigate the overwhelming, confusing and technical world of electronic products in order to make the best informed decisions for their personal and professional lives.

Courtney lives and operates CommXperts using four main business principles.

- **Confidence:** Courtney KNOWS that they are the experts in their field. In the past couple of years, technology and communication have exploded 'beyond the box'. By staying flexible, CommXperts has kept up with the changes and is able to educate and advise their customers about what is the best fit for each situation.

- **Intrigue:** Courtney believes that CommXperts can learn something from every conversation. Thus, there is a genuine interest in every person they help. CommXperts listens to their customers, learns their needs and finds the best solution.
- **Passion:** Courtney loves technology! He is passionate about helping others. Nothing beats seeing the joy in the customer's eyes when they are paired with the right products that will solve their problems and enrich their lives.
- **Respect:** Courtney also understands that while CommXperts are the 'Xperts' in their technology field, many of their clients possess limited knowledge in this area. Furthermore, Courtney knows that no one knows the business and personal needs of each customer better than the customer. Therefore, CommXperts treats each client with respect and works hard to communicate in a language the customer understands in order to determine which products are the best fit.

6 UPCOMING MOBILE TECHNOLOGIES TO WATCH FOR:

1. **Bluetooth 3 and 4 -** As broadband continues to grow, so does connectivity. The next series of Bluetooth explores the way we connect through this type of technology. Bluetooth 3 will allow for WiFi type connections and speeds, allowing customers more control of how they share their content.
2. **Expansion of the Mobile Web -** With the growth of HTML type sites, future smartphones will be able to render the web in a much better way. Advancements in web platforms will continue to grow for smartphone-capable handsets, and grow the overall share of web browsers embedded-in-device to 85% by the end of 2011.
3. **App Stores and Widgets -** Need we say more. If you haven't heard of an APP yet, this is surprising. You might have heard about it, but don't know how to use them effectively. As businesses continue to expand their mobile footprint, customers will as well. This will give consumers and business alike that advantage to create connection type services to the

data worlds they need.

4. **M2M** - This might be viewed as the previous acronym that you have seen on your wireless phone bill, but this doesn't stand for Mobile to Mobile. This M2M stands for Machine to Machine. As Apps and the business world expand, think about the flexibility customers will have with imbedded connectivity such as copy machines, table top computers – such as Menu's at your favorite restaurant, or even Security Systems at your residence. This technology will grow at a slower rate, but customers continued control, will help push the market as we currently know it.
5. **Touchscreens** - As we have seen since the launch of Apple's iPHONE, touchscreens are becoming more relevant in everyday life. The simple touch and flick capabilities are going to continue to grow in the smartphone market, but what about the M2M market as well. Our previous example of restaurant ordering 'ring a bell'? How about the rental options for business travelers when they pick out their favorite rental car? This technology will grow to upwards of 50% of all smartphone shipments by the end of 2011.
6. **Security** - Last but not least, we continue to connect in this mobile world, freely and quickly. But one struggle customers are going to have to take notice of is what information they are making available to others? If you thought your computer could be at risk, so can your smartphone. In today's 'always connected' world, businesses and consumers alike are going to implement additional security features to keep private portions of our life safe and secure.

Communication is always going to be the key. Yet how we communicate is constantly changing. The more connected we become, the more we communicate through technology. We text, email and instant message each other from our smartphones, netbooks and iPads. In fact, mobile marketing is the wave of the future. Over 1.8 billion wireless handsets are in use today. 74% of them utilize text messaging and 95% of all messages (and emails) sent to a wireless device are opened within minutes of delivery. Everyone is connected and communicating in new ways.

As technology becomes more confusing, consumers need help making sense of it all. Here is where CommXperts is a game changer. With a unique ability to help individuals 'wade through the murky waters of technology' and explain changes in a language that a non-techie person can understand, CommXperts is fast becoming the "go to" company for all things technical.

As technology continues to evolve with increasing speed and we shift from traditional communicators to those dependent on that technology, how does one keep up with the changes? With their busy lives, consumers don't have time to research every new device. Who can they trust to steer them in the right direction? CommXperts.

CommXperts' services include current business technology analysis, sync services (between smart phones and computer systems), business applications, PPT conversions to video, business card scanning, wireless phone activations (Major Carriers), wireless mobile broadband connectivity, WiFi hotspots, Set up of 'fail-over' networks and 4G services.

In addition to helping consumers communicate better, CommXperts specializes in helping companies increase ROI (return on investment) on current technologies, implement new technologies, and plan for future innovations.

ABOUT COURTNEY

Courtney started in the Wireless Industry in 1997, quickly becoming one of the Top Performers in Florida and the Southeast region leading each area to top sales performances, winning President's Awards and Region of the Year honors. Courtney next moved through a variety of management positions before becoming the Southeast Indirect Regional Manager for a large wireless provider. By 2006, Courtney had moved from wireless activations into distribution, marketing and enterprise where he worked with Fortune 100 and 500 companies with Wireless Product Placement, Mobile Applications and Device Management Solutions.

During the time he was working with the wireless carriers and distributors, Courtney found his niche in the wireless industry and marketing technology as a whole. With a vision for the expertise, service and experience that he could offer, Courtney contacted former Verizon Wireless Manager and longtime friend, Shawn Rowell. In 2007, they launched Communication Xperts (dba: CommXPERTS.com) with a mission to bring unparalleled customer service, technology sourcing, customized mobile services and marketing expertise to SMB and consumer markets. Looking beyond the wireless products they could offer, Courtney saw that they could help consumers and business owners with everything involving their mobile communications.

In three short years, CommXPERTS has become a value-added distributor of innovative consumer electronic products designed to increase productivity for both businesses and consumers. CommXPERTS provides distribution and customized services to over 5,000 B2B customers in Canada, Latin America and the United States. Their customized services include strategic planning along with distribution of cutting-edge products such as bar code scanners, solar chargers, Wireless Internet (WiFi) and Wireless "Mobile" Event Equipment. Helping entrepreneurs launch, source, market, advertise and distribute their products is just one example of the customized services that CommXPERTS provides. The CommXPERTS staff has over 30 years experience in electronic sales and distribution as well as event production.

Always on the lookout for revolutionary new products that will offer their customers the best return on investment, Courtney is excited about the newest phase of CommXPERTS' products and services - Mobile Event Marketing. This new branch of CommXPERTS will give their business clients more options for creating a marketing presence by offering trade show expertise and set-up, mobile WiFi hotspot capabilities, data capture options, unique mobile advertising equipment and more. This will increase ROI and communications with any client. CommXPERTS will offer virtual branding and a mobile marketing division for companies who want to have a presence in Florida and the Southeast.

The one constant in today's world of technology is that it's always changing. To navigate it successfully and utilize technology requires extensive knowledge and continued learning. Most consumers don't have the time or the ability to keep up which is exactly why Courtney created CommXPERTS. With CommXPERTS, consumers now have a trusted resource for all things techie and business owners have a technology and branding department. Together, everyone succeeds.

CHAPTER 19

MAKING YOUR PRACTICE PERFECT

BY DR. SCOTT SCHUMANN

"…if your business is to change - as it must to continually thrive - you must change first. If you are unwilling to change, your business will never be capable of giving you what you want."
~ Michael Gerber, *"The E-Myth Revisited"*

If you think the practice of dentistry hasn't changed much over the years, consider this: before World War II, most Americans didn't even brush their teeth on a regular basis. That became more of a habit after the war when soldiers returned home, having been forced to include brushing their teeth as part of their daily regimen.

Later, in the 50's and 60's, flossing was still a pretty new idea – and putting fluoride in the drinking water was considered to be a Communist plot by many. Preventative education was minimal and dental implants were just a wacky idea being attempted by some scientist in Sweden.

That meant people had a lot more ongoing dental problems that required visits to their friendly neighborhood dentists. And, frankly, there was a sense of inevitability people had about their teeth. They expected to lose them – leading to the traditional visual joke of someone's dentures in a glass by the side of their bed.

A lot of today's technology just wasn't available – and dental practices were much simpler to run. A dentist hung out his shingle, and mainly just drilled and filled – pulling a bad tooth or two when it was necessary. It was easy and cheap to open a practice – and there were a lot more patients than dentists available. You could run a dental business like a traditional mom and pop shop and do very well.

In recent times, however, dentistry has undergone incredible "Game Changers" that affect both patient and dentist in key areas. Rather than merely *reacting* to these changes, I firmly believe today's dentist has to *act*. That's how you progress from survival mode to actually being able to prosper and grow, even in difficult economic times.

THE FIVE BIG DENTAL DILEMMAS

Let's look a little more closely at the changes that have come our way in every dental office across America.

First of all, most patients are much savvier about how to properly take care of their teeth. People are taught to brush and floss from an early age – and they drink fluoridated water. For the dentist, this is great news. Yes, we still see startling cases of dental neglect, but people's teeth are in much better shape. Still, this unfortunately impacts our fees and our profits in a negative way.

Second, increased competition from other dentists has also cut into everyone's profits. I've had a lot more practices open up in our area – and we're all marketing aggressively for the same patient base. Luckily we haven't had any "turf wars" that erupted with gunfire – but it can get a little tense!

Third, the Great Recession hit everyone pretty hard – and it's still an uneasy recovery. That means many see a visit to the dentist as an unnecessary luxury – when tough times hit, it's one of the first things they cross off the list. On the practice side, it can be harder for us to find financing for patients whose insurance won't cover a certain treatment, or for the uninsured who can't afford to pay for the full cost of dental care at one time. It's a two-edged sword.

And speaking of dental insurance, that's number four on my list. Originally, dental insurance plans meant more people would visit the dentist, because the majority of the costs would be covered. Unfortunately, since many of those insurance firms wanted to control our fees and lower the quality of care, it also meant a reduction in our profits, unless we cut corners – not a pleasant scenario.

Finally, marketing has become more difficult and expensive. As I mentioned, there's a lot more competition selling themselves in an effort to get new patients. Not only that, *everyone* is marketing 24/7 these days in an effort to break through the clutter – which, of course, only creates more clutter.

CHANGING YOURSELF – CHANGING YOUR PRACTICE

All five of these areas represent substantial challenges – and yes, they have been Game Changers, in the sense of working against us scoring a win! But they're not insurmountable, by any means. Let's take them on, in order.

#1 – MAKING TREATMENT PAY OFF FOR YOU AND YOUR PATIENT

Yes, people are taking better care of their teeth, but, thanks to today's 24/7 media, they're also incredibly conscious of how people in public life, both celebrities and politicians, are sporting beautiful smiles due to cosmetic dentistry.

And they want the same kind of dazzling grins as the Kardashians. That's why cosmetic dentistry has become a big profit center for many practices – veneers, crowns, whitening treatments are all sought-after treatments.

Not only that, but people are living longer – and they don't want to have to deal with dentures. Dental implants are the next best thing to keeping your real teeth – and, again, they are a relatively new source of income for today's dentist. With the graying of the massive baby boomer generation, concentrating on this market can definitely make a difference for any dental practice.

Finally, preventative dental treatments are becoming more and more sophisticated and commonplace. A new generation of dental procedures is on the way that includes vaccines that prevent the onset of cavities and gum disease, medical therapies that eliminate drills and needles, and the ability to regrow damaged tooth tissue and bone. All of these promise big benefits to patients' overall oral health and continued work for today's dentist.

#2 GROWING IN THE FACE OF INCREASED COMPETITION

How do you handle more dentists in your area? Unless you can afford to buy them out, you simply must become better – better at customer service, better at running an efficient operation, better at marketing, better at your systems and better at offering your patients the latest and best treatment techniques.

Serve your customers' needs – anticipate them – and don't disappoint them. Train your staff to do the same – and make sure you're all working towards the same goals. By creating systems that hold everyone – including yourself – accountable, and by setting revenue and patient goals that everyone is aware of, you can measure progress and make certain you're growing the way you need to grow – despite three other dentists opening their doors down the block.

Offering and promoting the extras can also really help differentiate you from the others. For example, sedation dentistry can actually make visiting the dentist a pleasure! We'll send a patient to la-la land, they'll be totally comfortable and not even be aware of how time is flying by. A new trend, the dental spa, takes patient comfort to new levels – and also attracts a higher class of patient.

#3 BUCKING TOUGH ECONOMIC TIMES

Nowadays, dentists are not only competing with tight money, but they're also competing with the price of satellite TV's, computers, iPads and all the other expensive toys that are almost a requirement for most people to have (I know they are for me!).

We, of course, use all those expensive toys ourselves to make the patient experience more comfortable – with TV's and computers in our patient rooms. But we go beyond that to aggressively find financing for those patients who can't afford to pay everything up front. We offer ways, if they qualify, that they can pay for treatments over a 5 to 7 year period if need be.

The most important thing is to be incredibly benefit-oriented in your approach to patients – so they can appreciate the value of what you can do to improve their smile or just attend to their oral health. A visit to the dentist is no longer a routine every-six-month occasion in many homes – so selling other services, such as cosmetic treatments and implants, has to be front and center in dental marketing.

The point is not to rely on tried-and-true dentistry - and not just look for more cavities to fill. By offering the most modern cutting-edge services and treatments, you attract more patients with higher incomes that can help pay for those who might be having trouble paying for the basics. Working the combination helps a practice grow and prosper, by keeping all patients happy with your service.

#4 THE DENTAL INSURANCE EFFECT

As I said, the rise of dental insurance plans meant more patient visits – but lower fees. This meant you either had to increase your volume or cut corners. I saw how this really ended up killing some practices – and I vowed not to change the level of my treatment and my service.

The only way to accomplish that was to only join a select few insurance plans that covered my costs adequately – and also to increase my marketing to those prospects who had the *good* dental plans in place.

The big problem with most dental insurance is that it hasn't kept pace with actual dental practice costs – many benefits are still locked into the same numbers they were in the 1960's, around a half-century ago. Policies don't cover enough – but the people paying for them still let their payment structures be the determining factor in how they approach their oral health. Not a good situation.

Through the right marketing and the right insurance alliances, I've managed to continue to grow my profits and my patient base – without compromising the level of quality of care. That's a great win/win.

#5 TAKING MARKETING TO THE NEXT LEVEL

Dentists, like all businesspeople, have to be smarter about every facet of their business today – most importantly, the aspect of marketing.

Just mailing out a coupon or placing a newspaper ad isn't enough anymore. You have to measure your marketing ROI (Return on Investment) and know what's working and what's not, so you can spend your limited marketing dollars the most effectively.

And you have to automate as much as possible. Installing software such as InfusionSoft to capture lead information, and using it for future marketing programs, means you don't have to rely on a staff that's busy running your office to remember to take down the contact info of everyone who calls.

That doesn't mean you don't train your staff to take advantage of all marketing opportunities with both existing and potential patients. They should always be ready to suggest a treatment or service that someone might need, and to discuss that treatment or service in a friendly and knowledgeable way.

Finally, marketing *yourself* has become incredibly crucial – let's face it, a dentist is the most important product at a dental practice. You're selling *your* expertise, *your* experience and who *you* are.

That's why participating in Celebrity Marketing in recent years has done wonders for my profile and my credibility. Patients see articles and interviews with me in venues like "USA Today" and on television, as well as chapters such as these in business books That, in turn, makes them think more highly of me. They know I go the extra mile to know my business and my field and that I'm confident enough to share that information with the public. Now I'm no longer just another dentist, but I'm an *authorit*y on dentistry. That, in turn, boosts my recognition with potential patients in my area.

BE YOUR OWN CEO

Although I've addressed some important specifics in running a successful dental practice in today's market, I'd like to close with one important "broad stroke" – dentists today have to run their practices as if they were a CEO of a larger business. They have to know marketing, they have to set up systems, they have to deal with staff issues and they have to do all this effectively. We can no longer just think of ourselves as merely dentists. The business side has become 'way too important' for that.

I made that mental shift in my head a few years ago after I almost lost my life in a botched operation. I recommitted myself to excellence, and participated in invaluable coaching and masterminding programs – that helped me complete the transition to looking at my practice with completely different eyes. Working with incredible experts and coaches such as Dan Kennedy, Brian Tracy, Tom Orent and Ed O'Keefe took me to a new level that I never even knew existed!

The great thing is I'm now able to help other dentists work on their businesses by helping them develop the same kind of systems that have brought me phenomenal success. Here are a few of the websites I've created to do just that:

- dentalscriptsmadeeasy.com – helping dentists train their staff to help patients make good dental decisions
- dentalpersonality.com and dentalpersonalities.com – showing dentists how to personally connect with patients as a "real" person, not just some rich doctor out to use their money to buy himself a fancy new car
- dentalofficesystemsmadeeasy.com – helping practices develop efficient office systems and enabling the easy training of their staff to learn these systems
- ravingfanprogram.com – a new referral program for dental practices or businesses, which utilizes current patients or clients to recommend businesses to friends and family members

I'm happy to have achieved all that I have achieved and eager to share my secrets with those who want to experience the success I've had. I would say that I was lucky to surpass the goals I set for myself, but I know that it wasn't just luck – it was hard work and the willingness to change my way of thinking both about myself and my dental practice.

Changing yourself? That's the ultimate Game Changer.

Dr. Scott Schumann, a native of Columbus, Ohio, grew up loving the Buckeyes, playing sports, and collecting rocks. Dr. Schumann and his wife Robin live in downtown Columbus with their dog, Bourbon, the boxer. Dr. Schumann loves supporting the local arts, sponsoring little league teams, golfing, fishing and attending concerts as well as NASCAR events.

Dr. Schumann graduated from Ohio State University Dental School in 1989 and then completed his residency training at University of Texas Health Science Center at San Antonio in 1991, with training and certification in advanced dental techniques, dental implants and sedation dentistry. He also received a fellowship in Hospital Dentistry, helping him to excel in assisting his medically compromised patients. After returning to Columbus Ohio, Dr. Schumann started his career and began teaching in the Advanced Dentistry Clinic at the Ohio State University, teaching dental residents advanced cosmetic, implant, hospital, and sedation dentistry for ten years.

An active member in the Columbus Dental Society, Ohio Dental Association, American Dental Association, Academy of General Dentists, American Academy of Cosmetic Dentists and the American Dental Society of Anesthesiology, Dr. Schumann and his team have kept up to date on the latest developments in dentistry.

Dr. Scott Schumann's office in Grove City, a suburb 8 minutes south of downtown Columbus, Ohio, is often referred to by clients as "fun" and "cool"—2 words not often associated with dentistry. Dr. Schumann and his staff are well known for their love of helping their patients achieve the smile they always dreamed of. Now through his innovative systems, Dr. Schuman is helping dentists around the country achieve the lifestyle and success they always dreamed of while helping patients change their lives. His professional team and his facility, with amazing new technological advancements, makes each patient visit as 'fun' as possible without guilt or embarrassment while allowing him to leverage his time and experience to grow his dental practice.

Dr. Scott Schumann has been published in multiple research journals, as well as featured in *21 Principles of Smile Design* and *Shift Happens*. He has presented at various conferences and events and has been quoted in the Wall Street Journal, USA Today, and Newsweek and well as appeared on America's PremierExperts® TV show on NBC, CBS, ABC and FOX.

To learn more about Dr. Schumann and how he helps to grow dental practices visit www.dentalofficesystemsmadeeasy.com

Or call toll-free 888-496-1250

CHAPTER 20

GREAT COMMUNICATION WILL KEEP YOUR RELATION-*SHIPS* FROM SINKING

BY AMY REMMELE

Real life examples of communication errors are plentiful. (1). Dr. Smith received feedback from several of his colleagues that Dr. Jones was making mistakes in reading test results. Dr. Smith decided not to tell Dr. Jones and ultimately Dr. Jones was sued for malpractice. When it was found that Dr. Smith knew about the problem, he was also named in the suit. (2). A patient in a hospital "crashed," but the crash cart was missing some life-saving items. Nurse John had restocked the cart without looking at the checklist of items that needed to go on it, reasoning "I've done this hundreds of times before." The patient lived, but had clearly been endangered. (3). Jenna was unloading groceries from her trunk when a man approached her and offered to help her carry them in. Jenna sheepishly agreed and was raped once the "helper" was inside her apartment. (4). Sam monopolized most of the talk time at the owners meeting of his business, raising his voice whenever anyone disagreed with him. The only task that was accomplished after two hours was the one that Sam brought to the table. (5). Myra knew the solution to the shipping problem that everyone in the department was talking about. The last time she had put in her "two cents," however, the supervisor had said her idea was ridiculous and would not work. So this time her two cents -- actually worth more like $150,000 -- remained unvoiced. (6). A rookie line worker told his supervisor, Tom, that the machine he operated was making a "funny noise." Tom smirked at the line worker, thought "He's a newbie, he probably just wants a break," and walked away. Three days later, another worker's hand was crushed in the machine. (7). Jane quickly backed out of the conference room and vowed to herself to say nothing when she walked in on Dave groping Sally. Sally, an excellent worker, left the company when nobody believed that she was being harassed.

None of these communication failures were due to people not knowing the HOWs of communication. We can give people lists of SHOULDS about good communication and yes, they are necessary. We can teach people the HOWs of good communication and yes, they are crucial. This is where most trainers and consultants stop. They have a tool box filled with SHOULDs and HOWs that are rote and well-rehearsed. But when it comes to fixing communication problems, only covering the SHOULDs and the HOWs will cause us to fail miserably. It is really the WHYs that are important. Understanding human behavior and motivation is the key to people problems, and communication reflects these inner workings of people.

The overriding premise is that nobody does anything that they are not "paid" to do. Think of payment as anything that motivates. It can be money, material goods, attention, sex, or good feelings - such as general happiness and well-being, the warm feelings one gets from helping others, or pride in a job well done. Other motivating, "payoff" feelings, for many people, include status among peers, the power to dominate or intimidate others, being right, winning, seeing someone else suffer, and gloating. Payment can also come in the form of avoidance of a negative consequence or feeling. Examples include avoiding fear-provoking objects, like storms or people with weapons, or situations, such as crowded rooms where escape is difficult, public speaking or any situation involving evaluation. Avoiding physical or emotional pain can also be a drive. Communication becomes much clearer once the "payment" idea is understood and accepted.

Let's look at some of the payments in the communication failure examples above. Dr. Smith either over-valued his status as a "nice guy" or he feared confrontation more than he cared about patient safety and best practices. Nurse John felt too important or too convinced of his accuracy to check a list when restocking the crash cart. Jenna wanted to be polite and would not risk feeling embarrassed by rejecting a "helpful" man. Sam wanted to "win," cared only about his own agenda, and was willing to sacrifice relationships with his co-owners to achieve his goals. Myra's fear of another rebuff outweighed her need to contribute, and her supervisor clearly valued being dominant over any greater good. Tom's beliefs that new people are ignorant and that workers just want to slack off cost an employee the use of a hand. Jane, concerned about her own position, would not tell the truth about Dave's harassment of Sally.

These examples make it very clear why the National Center for Patient Safety puts the following quote on their website: "Communication failure is a leading cause of adverse events." Adverse events include errors, accidents, and even death. So, listen carefully! Your life may depend on it.

The *Rules of Engagement*, or the HOW-TOs of good communication, are straightforward. First, there is the Golden Rule. All people want to be treated with respect and keep their dignity. Everyone wants to be heard and understood. Nobody can be satisfied if they have no power in a relationship. Because these are universal rules, knowing how you want to be treated informs you greatly about how to treat others.

Second is the Rule of Empathic Listening. Empathy is understanding the meaning, feelings, thoughts and/or overall experience of another as if from the "inside out," and conveying that understanding in a language suitable to that other person, including nonverbal language. Good Accurate Empathy expands the speaker's self-exploration and self-understanding by adding depth, meaning or feeling to what has already been conveyed. In other words, listen, understand, then prove you understand by reflecting back what you hear and see. Accurate Empathy can be scored on a scale from whether a listener's response to a speaker adds to, detracts from, or simply matches the meaning and significance of what a speaker has said. The main drive behind empathy, however, should be to listen carefully and really care that the communication moves to another, deeper level. Empathy is not sympathy, judgment, criticism, advice or "fixing" the problem. It is just understanding and helping the other person to express his or her inner experience. And when we are trying to sell or provide service to another person, it is the most important skill we can have. Selling and customer service are about providing solutions to people's problems, which cannot begin until you really understand the customer's or client's perspective.

The third rule is Assertive Communication. Assertiveness falls on a continuum between Unassertiveness and Aggression. Much of the time, the level of assertiveness in our communication is a function of what our history showed us about results or payoffs. People whose experience showed them that subjugation gets them what they need will tend to subjugate their rights to those of others and be very unassertive. People who have benefited from going in with "both guns blazing" will tend to continue this aggressiveness and violate the rights of others. And those who have learned that there can be a satisfying middle ground will tend to affirm and respect both their own and others' rights, and communicate assertively.

The Fourth rule is the Platinum Rule, which is about meeting others in the zone they find comfortable. It is about individual interaction styles. Some people like to get right down to business while some like to chat a bit first. Some people are introverts and others are extroverts. Communication is much smoother and more efficient when everyone involved respects individual styles and gives each person a little of what makes them comfortable.

Finally, a motion picture is worth a thousand words. Circling all the other rules is the Body Language Rule. Be mindful of your own and others' bodies, which tell the truth even when the words are lies. And be mindful to put your body and your words in sync. Some universal guidelines are to make comfortable eye contact, talk facing each other close to squarely, respect personal space, use hand gestures that are open and inviting, and use facial expressions congruent with the present-moment feelings. If your tone is growl-like and accompanied by a shaking finger, expect the other person to fight back or run away, regardless of your words. If you are looking at the ground and mumbling nervously, do not expect to be taken seriously. Another universal law is to never express disgust or condescension to anyone with whom you want to have a relationship. Expressing these emotions is pure power- and intimidation-mongering, and an ultimate relationship deal breaker.

But I promised that the HOWs would not override the WHYs here. While knowing the HOWs is important and I am always happy to teach them, it is the WHYs, the motives and attitudes behind the communication, that will save the day. Symphonic and symbiotic communication occurs when the conditions are met that all of the people involved genuinely care about the big picture, each wants to hear what the others have to say, and each respects the others' views even if they disagree with them. Even when a person wants to "win," that person will not do it at the cost of destroying the relationships involved.

When communication failure occurs, look for the payment that the person or people causing the failure are receiving. It can come in many different forms. The listening part of communication may not occur because the non-listener believes he or she is so right that there is no need to hear anyone else's opinions or even the facts. After all, what is the point of hearing more information if you have already made the "right" judgment or conclusion? Closely related is the "I want to win at any cost" type. This person thinks, "Who cares who is right or wrong, so long as I come out on top?" A third relative of these two is the personality that says, "I am so busy that I do not have time for this babble." All three of these cousins spend most of their "listening" time thinking of what they are going to say, or whom they are going to silence, next. They just do not see any point in listening to anyone else. Another group of people who are busy with what they are going to say next have the trademark of interrupting others or never pausing enough to allow others to speak. These people were probably never listened to by others and feel desperate to be heard and understood. It is difficult for this type to have the faith that they will get a turn to be heard, so they just talk through everyone else's turns. Some people are stuck in deep-seated, maladaptive belief systems (like "you can't trust anyone" or "being involved with people just gets you hurt"). For these people, listening to others would challenge their beliefs and cause them discomfort.

Empathy is more challenging than simple listening, so avoiding it often blocks communication. One simple factor leading to empathy avoidance may be lack of skill. Empathy is not taught in school and very few families provide good models, so many people grow to adulthood without the know-how. Some people believe that empathy is too passive and/or that empathy can look like agreement. Sometimes when I demonstrate empathy to clients, and urge them to try it, they immediately shut me down with "I cannot just sit and listen and understand. I need to be fixing the problem." Empathy does not fit these people's task-oriented framework. Some people feel very uncomfortable with allowing others to talk, process and figure out on their own how to fix problems. These individuals want to grab jobs out of the hands of others and fix everything right away. Being Mr. or Ms. Fix-it of course inhibits others' development. The "fixer" puts the "fixed" in a position of feeling dependent, "one down" and inadequate. The best managers and owners see the error of this thinking.

The "empathy as agreement" argument is more difficult to overcome. People who are used to conflict and to winning argue that empathy is "wimpy" and a way of giving in. "Empathy is too touchy-feely" is a common argument from business clients. These people are used to pushing aside feelings or other "soft" things that they believe will interfere with decisions, processes and finding solutions. They equate empathizing and real communication with too much feeling. For these people, emotions are uncomfortable because they feel too much like unproductive time-wasting. Finally, some people cannot bring themselves to empathize because they have *affect intolerance* and cannot manage their own emotions. It is difficult for them to "be in the room" with any feelings, so they tune out or create a distraction.

Irrational beliefs and wrong thinking can also disrupt communication on the speaking side. Some people have biases and stereotypes that prevent them from fully communicating with certain groups. Some people believe that communication just leads to conflict, put-downs and abuse. With a person who has a history that supports this belief, it may be very challenging to convince them to try expressing themselves. To such people, avoiding conflict is the strongest motive, perhaps even signifying survival, so their motto is "the less said the better." The other side of this is the bully, who insists on striving to win, has an inflated sense of self-importance, and has power. While his rhetoric may sound like concern for the greater good, he really just wants to rule. This type of dishonesty is a great contributor to communication failure. But it is easily unmasked by watching the actions. When actions and words are different, the cliché "actions speak louder than words" tells us which to listen to.

Everyone has flaws and finding solutions to communication failure starts with honesty. Imagine a bully who says, "I have a tendency to be pushy and want to win." That would put the communication on a new plane. Imagine the physician who comes to admit to himself that the importance of his status or image is leading him to sacrifice best practices or patient safety. He would probably re-think his position and change his ways, or stretch his comfort zone to confront a careless or incompetent colleague. If we admit that we believe we are "so right" we don't have to listen, or that the topic is making us uncomfortable, we are then more likely to listen or communicate more directly.

Another communication problem occurs with ambiguous messages. Because our ancestors were more likely to survive if they erred on the safe side, messages that are not clear are almost always interpreted negatively. So when someone hears the ambiguous statement, "The boss wants to see you in her office," that person will probably experience anticipatory anxiety. To avoid becoming associated with such aversive emotions, be clear. Even if the end result is negative, upfront clarity will help avoid unnecessary anxiety.

The main lesson I teach people about behaviors, including communications and its "payments," is to do cost-benefit analyses on each of them. You cannot say "yes" to something without saying "yes" to its collateral effects and without saying "no" to some other options. We can make any choice but we must be willing to live with the consequences, all of them.

When it comes to cost-benefit analyses of communications, keep them in mind anytime you want to break one of the Rules Of Engagement. There will most likely be a cost. Sometimes it will be minor, and sometimes it will be life-and-death. The rub is that you cannot always tell beforehand how serious the consequence will be. The man who left the ferry door open in England many years ago had probably failed to check his list of duties on many occasions, but on that fateful day, over 500 lives were lost when the ferry went down.

A business owner may be able to dismiss communication failure, saying that at the level many of us operate, it does not cause the type of adverse events that result in accidents and injuries and death. Can he or she, however, dismiss the thousands of dollars that even minor communication failure costs? Anytime you are going to communicate to "win" or "just make a point" or "be right," pause for a moment. "Taking shots" at another person may be shooting holes in a relation-***SHIP*** you are standing in. You may even sink!

ABOUT AMY

Amy Remmele, owner of Peak of Success, is known as the Psych-cess coach, because she balances sound **Psych**ological lessons with business suc**cess** principles. As a coach, Amy works with women who are in difficult or challenging relationships, with professionals who want to stand out and make a mark, and with couples. As a consultant, trainer and speaker, Amy works with business owners who want all of their relation-***SHIPs*** to be smooth sailing and who want everyone in the organization to internalize the company's sales and marketing strategies to create the best image. After years of counseling and coaching people in their personal and professional lives, Amy knows that great communication creates unsinkable relation-***SHIPs*** and is the foundational skill for all of life's successes.

In her book, ***Chief Life Officer: Your Life Is The Most Important Business You'll Ever Own (CLO)***, Amy uses business as a metaphor of life, outlining people's inner "departments" and how they function best through an authentic, shared mission. From mapping out a "business plan" and goals for life, through communication and relationship creation, to maintaining and accessing support systems, ***CLO*** enables the reader to ask, and answer, life's vital questions. Amy also co-authored, with Dr. Kent Bath, the book, ***Re-Phrase It: Adding Empathy and Emotional Intelligence to Your Everyday Life***, and the relationship workbook, ***Empathy, Communication and Conflict Resolution Home Study Program***.

To learn more about Amy Remmele, The Psych-cess Coach, and to receive valuable life lessons through ebooks and the Peak Of Success newsletter, visit www.PeakOfSuccess.com or call 716-626-5977.

CHAPTER 21

TOTAL WELLNESS = ABUNDANCE

BY ANOLIA O. FACUN

Life is not all about money or making money.

TIME is gold. HEALTH is wealth. KNOWLEDGE is treasure. You may have all the money in the world, but if you are not healthy to enjoy your fortune, what good is it?

Marianne was a successful entrepreneur and real estate investor. She was preparing to retire and fulfill travel and philanthropic goals. Then, the real estate crash occurred. She lost everything. After making an all-out effort to salvage what she worked so hard for and watching her dreams fade away before her eyes, she thought of ending her life… However, she came back instead even more determined! Now, she's once again a very successful entrepreneur, and a stronger person. What helped her cope? What is the best lesson she said she learned? She's now on a mission to share with others how to survive and still thrive, even during tough times.

Today we face mounting challenges: staggering numbers of foreclosures, homelessness, unemployment, economic meltdown, health care crisis, deteriorating moral compass, and the greatest disaster of all time

- many people living their lives without realizing their full potential. It's time we wake up and face the root of our problems and deal with real solutions.

The GOOD NEWS: Life is certainly much more than just getting up each day, going to work, making money, going home tired, eating and sleeping... just to get up the next day to do it all over again. It is reassuring to know that daily survival is not the only game to be played. It is time to think 'out of the box', time to gain insight on how to approach life in its totality – in order to achieve the results that you desire.

The thought of being happy, healthy and living in abundance, although desirable, has become an impossible dream for many. I can relate to this because during periods of personal tough times, I have said, "Don't talk to me about such nonsense!" But is it really nonsense? Is it really impossible?

I would probably still feel that way had I not met people who are actually living that kind of life in spite of what is happening around them. Those special people have been a great discovery to me - like finding a gold mine. It is like discovering the key to life itself: its secrets and answers. With the combination of science, logic, and simple common sense to test the principles' validity, it is my joy to let everyone know that practicing "Total Wellness" truly works wonders!

WHAT IS TOTAL WELLNESS?

To most people, "wellness" only involves the physical. People spend billions of dollars annually in search of that perfect, healthy, beautiful body. They buy expensive machines and gadgets to exercise and stay fit, and attend spas and clinics to stay young and beautiful. But why is it then, that there are countless numbers of successful businessmen, movie stars, athletes, wealthy men and gorgeous women, who supposedly have everything, but are still lonely, empty, and miserable? Some get involved in drugs; some even commit suicide. It is evident that it is not just looks, fame and fortune that matters.

It is quite unfortunate that we now live in a very physically and financially oriented society. If you ask our young students what their basic needs are, their automatic response will be "food, shelter and clothing." Naturally, as these youths grow up, they tend to focus more on these physical aspects. Along with that is the remarkable obsession for a beautiful body or anything else "nice to look at," thinking that these are the things that will make them happy.

Being a former nurse has been a great advantage for me. I learned early what "health" really meant and how it can greatly affect my entire life. It means "being well" or a state of "well-being," simple words with broad meaning. It is certainly more than just about ideal body weight, a good diet plan, or even a terrific fitness program. I learned that when I take care of a patient, I was not only to care for the broken leg, fever or pain. I had to care for an individual's PHYSICAL, MENTAL, EMOTIONAL, SPIRITUAL and SOCIAL needs for his/her TOTAL WELL-BEING."

An example: A star football player comes to a hospital for a serious spinal injury. While the medical staff's initial priority is to stabilize his physical condition, their next immediate consideration is the mental and emotional impact of his condition. Furthermore, there are the social considerations and spiritual counseling if so desired. For someone who is not that strong and who is left alone, the situation can be devastating. At this time, family and friends are usually the best sources of support for him. They are the major factors influencing his speedy recovery.

The secret is learning how to become not only PHYSICALLY *fit,* FINANCIALLY *secure, and* SOCIALLY *adaptable, but equally important is to discover your inner strength or true power by being* EMOTIONALLY *stable,* MENTALLY *equipped and* SPIRITUALLY victorious, *as* a *"healthy* WHOLE-BEING." *Your means of survival, true health and happiness, success and victory in life, depends most on the way you care for and handle your TOTAL WELL-BEING.*

Based on medical information, the inseparable, integrated parts or areas of one's total well-being are:

- PHYSICAL – your body and its desires; what you see.
- MENTAL – centered in your brain; your mind, intellect, reasoning and way of thinking.
- EMOTIONAL – your emotions or feelings; associated with the heart as the center of our emotion because of the way it is affected as it pounds when we are afraid, angry, excited or in love.
- SPIRITUAL – your inner being, your conscience (knowing

what is right and what is wrong).

- SOCIAL – those surrounding you, those you associate with and build relationships with – family, friends, etc.
- FINANCIAL – your pocket book, your checkbook balance, assets and other money matters. (This one is not normally included, but I added it because I see its impact on people.)

Let it be known that an "individual" is made up of integrated parts that cannot be separated, ignored or disregarded. Each part is uniquely important and has specific needs to be met. That is why when we focus on just one or two of those parts, we usually end up feeling that we are missing something. We feel that our life is not complete, or not all-together. This is when we need to realize that we are in need of a self check-up, or if needed, professional help.

There are people who don't even realize their own symptoms, and are likely to deny that they have any health problems at all. When I see someone smoking, I do not just see a person who is a candidate for lung cancer. The main thing that comes to my mind is, "There must be a reason why this person has to smoke."

HOW DO YOU ATTAIN TOTAL WELLNESS?

Let's look at the science-based "Problem Solving Process" to answer this question. This approach is applicable and practical to use in every aspect of our lives: personal, business, job or career-related circumstances.

I. Identify the problems you wish to solve or improve. Write them down. Be specific.

II. Analyze the factors that lead to the problems identified, and the possible means of correction leading to your desired solution or result.

In a physically driven society, it is so easy for anyone to like what is seen and obvious, jump into it, and realize it was a big mistake. If one only gives things some thought, it would *prevent* him/her from unnecessary pain and regrets.

Realize that you have OTHER PARTS that need to be considered. What will be good for every part involved in that ONE BODY? Learn to listen to your WHOLE BEING. All parts must be considered in the decision-making. Otherwise, not just one or two parts suffer, but the whole person is affected and suffers the consequences. Now this is your chance to do some personal analysis or reflection in your life.

III. Plan of Action: Health Balance and Priorities

Here, the mystery of life is disclosed for you and me. It is nothing new. It has been available for ages and generations, but remains undiscovered by many. Happy and victorious people who I observed and interviewed declare the following life's guiding principles as their main source or key for a happy, healthy, abundant life. Through my own personal experiences, I have tested their validity.

Evaluate your priorities. How much time, attention, energy or effort are you putting in these areas of your life right now? This will tell you what level of success, health or happiness you are at. Compare the two sets of priorities:

"Unhealthy Zone" Priorities: vs.	**"Healthy Zone"** Priorities:
Financial (Income Generation, Money)	Spiritual (Spirit)
Physical (Body/Looking Good)	Mental (Mind)
Mental (Mind/Educational Smarts)	Emotional (Feelings)
Emotional (Dwelling on Feelings)	Physical (Body)
Spiritual (Spirit/Relationship with God)	Social (Relationships)
Social (Relationships)	Financial (Income)
Results:	**Results:**
• Worry – Fear	> Happiness – Joy
• Confusion – Insecurity	> Security – Peace of Mind
• Loss – Emptiness	> Purpose – Fulfillment
• Destruction	> Wealth – Abundance

To have a winning team, every player is important. They have to be healthy, present, and prepared to play, to win with the team. *No one should be doing his/her own thing.* Each player is aware of the different members' function(s). It is their collective goal to be able to learn to work together as one. When that goal is accomplished, a great, beautiful performance and result can be expected, as the play of a WINNING TEAM.

Just like for on any team, *leadership* is equally important. That is why we have a "head coach" to direct the team, a "quarterback" to execute a football play, a "team leader" to coordinate and make sure that the job gets done. Can you imagine a team with players just doing their own thing?

Who will take the lead? This point is crucial. It is vital to choose the right leader in order to have a better chance of winning. "We are here (to play) to WIN!" ...That is the goal. Could we not apply the same strategy to our game of LIFE? Shouldn't we treat our whole being also as "a team"?

Amazingly, this also explains why we have so many failures in our society. Our society's condition happens to be a reflection of what is going on with its individual members. Our society should focus on putting each member on a healthy track, so we can once again have a better chance of WINNING TOGETHER. When each individual attains health, it results in a healthier family; which then creates a healthy community and a healthy society.

When one's spirit has a personal relationship with the living God, and becomes the driving force of one's whole being, it is amazing that there is a definite command to the mind to embrace the good things and delete or reject the bad input. When inputs are good and positive, the actions and outcomes are good and positive as well. No longer will the impulsive, self-centered physical being be the driving force, but the responsible and conscientious SPIRIT will now direct the mind and the other parts of one's being.

SECRET OF SUCCESS IN LIFE FORMULA:

Right SPIRIT → Right MIND → Right EMOTION → Great outcome for the other (remaining) three will follow.

The right SPIRIT, MIND and EMOTION automatically direct the physical to behave and take care of itself better, and direct the financial to manage its use of money and resources wisely. Socially, relating and dealing with people becomes no problem when you think well and feel good, are considerate of others, and are doing your best to live your life right. It becomes automatic.

I found it interesting that this is consistent with what was said all along in what is considered God's Word, The Bible: "But seek first the kingdom of God and His righteousness, and all these things shall be added to you." (Matthew 6:33 NKJV)

IV. Implementation: It Is TIME!

We have arrived at a needed "correction time." Instead of focusing on problems, it's time to focus on SOLUTIONS! The TIME has come for us to RISE UP to our true potential… to appreciate and highlight our hidden talents, amazing gifts, and unlimited abilities; and to bring back the dignity of human-kind.

The secret is out! People are becoming more aware that there's such a thing as a 1-3 year plan to move them towards Total Wellness and Financial Freedom… and living an abundant life is realistic. Let this be known and make more people aware, so we all benefit. This is the time that we need each other the most - to work together - joining our hands together to MAKE A DIFFERENCE.

15 WAYS TO MAKE A DIFFERENCE TO YOURSELF AND OTHERS FOR TOTAL WELLNESS:

1. SMILE more often! You'll be amazed at how many others will smile back at you. Besides this is the best facial exercise you can do to delay aging signs!
2. EAT RIGHT! Boost your immune system by eating more natural food, like fresh fruits and vegetables. This alone can significantly reduce your weight and health concerns.
3. EXERCISE regularly. The reason is not just to lose weight, but it's a great habit to maintain good health by improved circulation, elimination of body toxins, etc.
4. DRINK WATER – drink more than "colored drinks" for your health. Water has no sugar or additives.
5. READ and LEARN more. Devote time and money for self-improvement or personal development, the best investment you can make that truly pays off.
6. ACCEPT YOURSELF. You are gifted and blessed more than you know.
7. SPEAK the TRUTH. Seeking the truth can set you free.

8. KEEP BELIEVING. PRAY. Nurture your spirit. This won't cost you anything. Help or answers to your needs can be just a prayer away.
9. For THE PEOPLE YOU LOVE, SAY IT AND SHOW IT! They need to hear and see you care. Spend more quality time with them. It is what they'll remember most.
10. NOTICE and SAY something good or positive to someone, and mean it.
11. BE FORGIVING & UNDERSTANDING as you seek forgiveness and understanding.
12. LOVE, CARE, GIVE and SHARE more. This practice is the very purpose of your life.
13. SING, DANCE, and BE HAPPY - no matter what. Brighter days are yet to come!
14. Learn how to BUDGET or manage your money. Stay away from DEBTS and CREDIT CARDS. Spend only on needs with the money that you actually have.
15. VOLUNTEER and be INVOLVED in your COMMUNITY and make good things happen.

    Simple acts of kindness for our YOUTH, SENIORS, VETERANS, UNEMPLOYED and HOMELESS citizens can mean a lot. The best is yet to come!

Why live life with worries and fears, wasting time and energy on feeling past failures and insecurities, or thoughts of future uncertainties?

There's no point in living in the past. It is done; it is gone. Learn from the lessons and move on. Enjoy and make the most of your *present*. Live TODAY to the FULLEST as if it were your last. Give your best always and that's enough for each day! This way you know your tomorrow, when it comes, is already going to be much better.

When you are HAPPY, have TOTAL WELLNESS and PEACE, you are already experiencing TRUE SUCCESS or ABUNDANCE in LIFE! That is LIVING LIFE to its FULLEST!

For healthier communities, competition is the word of the past. COLLABORATION is the word we can now practice. Social Responsibility. Social Entrepreneurship. Discover your whole new world of unlimited potential and be a part of the SOLUTION!

Together, WE Can Make a World of Difference!

Let's DO IT, let's GO FOR IT!

God bless us all.

ABOUT ANOLIA

Anolia Orfrecio Facun is a lady with a mission: To share and show people, regardless of circumstances, how *abundance* can actually be achieved by simply understanding and applying the **"Total Wellness"** principles. For over thirty years, Anolia dealt with and witnessed thousands of people from all walks of life go through life's complexities in search of happiness, health and prosperity; and drew conclusions based on science, logic and simple common sense. These basic human principles are nothing new, and still apply: People need wellness in all areas of their lives to experience *completeness* or *total well-being* and its naturally occurring abundant result.

Anolia is an active Community Health Advocate, Public Educator, Author, Entrepreneur, Community Volunteer and Avid Traveler. She previously held three licenses: a Registered Nurse's license with Bachelors Degree in Nursing (BSN); an insurance license dealing with insurance and other financial services; and a Real Estate license. She was born in the Philippines, the eldest of six children. She came to America at a tender age of twenty two as a nurse, with a suitcase and a few dollars in hand. She knew nobody and had no address to go home to when she arrived, although asked to report to work the following day of arrival. Her experience as a young recruited nurse in this new land of America was a story by itself. She managed to cope, survive and even thrive through all the learning experiences she'd been through. Thinking of how these experiences and valuable lessons learned over thirty years will all just go to waste if not passed on, she decided to put them in writing through her two books: ***"Today's S.O.S."*** (Secrets of Survival), and ***"Yes! The Secrets Work!"*** - Discover Your Unlimited Potential and Purpose in Life. In both books, she reveals her personal life stories and the health and total wellness teaching she'd been sharing over the years - through parents' classes at schools, workshops and seminars at churches, businesses and others. She also appears as a guest speaker at various functions. Anolia has received numerous awards and recognitions from her business and community involvements. In all these, she acknowledges God to be her ultimate source for everything.

She founded recently what has now become the **"Total Wellness = Abundance"** movement with the purpose of reaching out to individuals, businesses, and communities to go back to *basic human principles* for dealing with, or managing, their daily personal, career, business or social lives. It works!

To learn more about Anolia, and how she can share with your group, visit **www.HappyFamilyShare.com** or call toll free 1-888-873-0511. She will gladly help.

CHAPTER 22

INTRODUCING THE TAX-FREE BUSINESS OWNERS PROTECTED PENSION PLAN

BY CHUCK OLIVER

As business owners, we have learned to maneuver through the choppy waters. But, there is an enormous storm looming on the horizon. It is poised to threaten your retirement, your safety and your well-being. **We can't change the direction of this storm, but we can reset our sails for a safer passage.**

I promise you that I can resolve the threats to your retirement. Let me show you how to leverage to your advantage, a safe and proven retirement plan that will enable you to take advantage of the tax code - with one of the most unique planning tools ever created.

I am going to show you how to start up or catch up on what is needed to guarantee you a comfortable retirement. You'll see how to accomplish this while using someone else's money and doing it all entirely TAX FREE!

We will cover the process and then show you a case study that will enable you to better understand the impact of this design in action. Finally, we will provide a short video that will give you a clear overview.

I have understood business owners concerns as far back as my college days. Then, I honed my entrepreneurial skills by creating my first business with a squeegee, a bucket, and a friend. We made extra spending money by washing windows in the affluent Columbus, Ohio suburb of Bexley - sometimes as much as $1,000.00 on a Saturday!

After college, I formed my own financial planning company. It was then that I really felt the full impact of the challenges faced by employers when they try to design and implement their own secure retirement.

We thought outside the box when we created our businesses and we need to think outside the box again in regard to following this new and non-traditional formula for planning our retirement. **Now is the time. We must adjust our sails!**

Let me point out some of the retirement planning misconceptions we have held in the past. I understand the draw and power of the idea of reducing one's taxes by making the traditional 401K, SEP, or Simple IRA contributions. We have been brain-washed to believe a myth - that you must put money into an account that grows while deferring taxes so that we will retire into a lower tax bracket and therefore, not feel the impact of a higher tax when we retire and withdraw our contributions. Well, let me put that idea to rest right now!

In the twenty years that I have been in the financial retirement planning arena, I have yet to see a single client retire into a lower tax bracket. Today, that fallacy is even more ridiculous because, at this writing, taxes are projected to rise to an astonishing 50% or more!

IMPORTANT POINT:
If I offered you a loan, you should have two questions:

1. What are you going to charge me?
2. When do you want the money repaid?

If the reply was that the money was not needed right now, and I would let you know when the money was needed and what the cost of the loan would be, would you take this loan? Of course you wouldn't! 401K's,

SEP's, AND SIMPLE IRA's are, in effect, variable rate government loans brought to you by our government. A government that has borrowed itself deep into the next four generations. A government that cannot manage the U.S. Postal Service, the banking industry, the health care industry, the auto industry or even its southern borders. The list of failures just goes on and on. If you have a 401k or other qualified plan for yourself and your employees, you are sitting on a tax time bomb.

No. 1. You will pay higher taxes when you go to take money out and so will your employees. You are holding a ticking tax time bomb and the impact of the damage after detonation is growing by the day.

No. 2. You, the employer, have all kinds of rules to follow inside these Government regulated retirement plans; the top heavy rules, the tax reporting requirements, the In-Service Distribution rules, etc… are a distraction.

No. 3. You, the employer, have exposed yourself to litigation by your employees by offering the traditional retirement plans (401K's, SEP's, simple IRA's). You have created a fiduciary relationship responsibility for yourself as the employer. There are suits where employees have sued their employers for losses in these accounts and the employees have actually won! Why take a chance of exposing yourself to such litigation when a better answer exists, a better resolution for you and for the people who serve you and your company?

NOW FOR THE GOOD NEWS:

THERE IS A SOLUTION TO ALL OF THE AFORMENTIONED DRAWBACKS TO A TRADITIONAL APPROACH TO RETIREMENT.

I am also aware that most business owners are not conscious of an alternate pension plan solution, because they have other distractions and mind sets.

FACT ONE: Most business owner make sure their employees, vendors and creditors are paid and that their business is operating smoothly, leaving little time and resources to fund or plan their own retirement.

FACT TWO: Most business owners' retirement expectations are tied to the belief that when the time comes, they will sell their businesses and this sale will fund their retirements.

FACT THREE: Only one in four businesses actually sell. Of the 1.2 million businesses that go up for sale each year, only 25% of those businesses actually sell. Right now, with a serious depression looming on the horizon, that number will crater.

FACT FOUR: Of the 25% of businesses that have sold, few sold for their multiple or paper value.

I have helped to plan, design and create the most Tax Advantaged and Asset Protected Pension Plan in existence. This type of plan has NEVER lost any value for over 200 years. The main characteristics of this plan design are:

- Borrow your own retirement plan funding monies tax-free.
- Deduct the interest paid for the money borrowed from someone else giving you a tax advantage.
- Grow the money in the plan tax free.
- Know that the money in the account is protected from ever losing to a wild market, so your principal is always protected.
- Grow your retirement at 140% of a linked index versus just 100% in a traditional investment.
- Borrow the money from the plan tax-free, at any time because you are not locked out or faced with penalties for removing money before age 59.5 and you are not forced out at age 70.5.
- The money you borrow is from the company's general account, not your accumulation account. So your account value still grows. You are using OPM-Other People's Money from the account as a tax free retirement income source. This strategy allows you to legally use the same money twice.
- Protect your retirement assets from litigation in certain states.

The only vehicle that can offer and perform within these parameters is a **Maximum Funded Life Insurance Contract.** A contract that is designed for living benefits and not death benefits

By doing Business Equity Transfer, you can begin putting your business equity to work for your retirement right now – so no need to gamble everything on being able to complete a business sale down the line. You would be allowed the tax-free use of your business equity-and you would also receive tax-free growth on it.

This isn't a new concept nor is it akin to playing some kind of shell game with the IRS. You are simply using your business equity for your retirement fund, instead of possibly losing that equity altogether if you have a problem selling your business. Why would you not want to take advantage of what you know now to prevent disappointment or frustration later?

Make your business work for you. The threat of business becoming harder with rising taxes, unemployment, health care, etc., makes now the right time to be sure your retirement is designed in the most advantageous way possible.

IT IS NEVER TOO LATE TO TURN THINGS AROUND! We are going to tell you how to plan and prepare your own worry-free and tax-free retirement. I know that you have already read some of this, but it definitely bears repeating. Instead of trying to sell the equity in your business when you are ready to retire, transfer the equity into your own personal retirement account now with minimal tax consequences. This will become your **PERSONAL PROTECTED PENSION PLAN.**

You need to perform a business equity transfer. To do this, you take proof of your cash flow or accounts receivable to a bank or other lending institution and they will lend you, according to your circumstances, between $100,000 and $10 million and you will be required to pay only the interest for the next 20 years. At the same time, in a different transaction, your company or business will lend you personally the same amount of money that the business equity transfer lender did, at a very reasonable rate.

You are approved for a plan of $100,000 to $10 million and have deposited the money that you borrowed into a special account, your own personal retirement savings account. This will allow the money to grow tax-free linked to a market index such as the S&P 500. You are only responsible for paying the interest on the borrowed business funds for the amount borrowed in that year. Your interest earnings continue to accumulate tax-free and at a guaranteed rate of return. When you do retire, your tax-free retirement income can pay off the loan or you can satisfy this loan from the sale of your company and/or the disbursement of its business assets.

Once your loan is paid off, the business will pay you a bonus to cover the income tax on the money transfer. For the rest of your life, you can withdraw the interest earnings on the account annually to fund your rather handsome retirement. The money from this vehicle comes out tax-free, continues to grow tax-free and upon your demise, transfers tax-free. Remember, your account is never subjected to market losses; it participates in only the upside of the market and never in the down side because protection from market downturns is built into the plan. Upside potential with downside protection is the perfect world!

Case Study One: (My own case)

My case is funded with OPM in 5 years. This enables a Max Funded Insurance Contract (not for death benefits, but for living retirement benefits). This provides lifestyle income protection, so I never run out of money before I run out of life.

Because you should never recommend something that you have not done for yourself and being so intrigued by this strategy, I implemented this unique non-qualified plan for myself. Here's how my plan looks:

The money for my retirement is leveraged from a commercial lending source (OPM). By not using my own money, I gain the ability to put in an amount of money over the next 4 to 5 years that would have taken me much longer to make and save. Most people save a total of only $2,000 per year. At this rate, a person would only be able to save between $8,000 to $10,000 over a 4-5 year period, compared with $100,000 to $10 million over the same period using OPM and compound interest. My personal protected pension plan allows the money to grow tax-free, be withdrawn tax-free, and transfered tax-free.

In twenty years, I will have amassed enough tax free cash that I can withdraw the money tax-free, pay off the borrowed monies (OPM) and in ten years, withdraw approximately $100,000 each year, completely tax-free for the rest of my life.

The money in this account is not deemed to be earned, passive or portfolio income and it has no negative tax consequence on social security benefits. The plan money is not off limits before 59.5 or forced out at age 70.5. By taking responsibility, we are rewarded with a tax-favored retirement that very few know about or have taken the time to learn.

In this case study, I used an average rate of return of under 5.5%. The 10-30 year average on this type of plan has been better than 8%. Remember, you never have to make up for losses since you have a principal protection floor. This means that you don't have to make back your losses before new gains are added to your account.

IT DOESN'T MATTER HOW YOUNG YOU ARE OR HOW OLD YOU ARE, THIS STRATEGY WORKS!!!

Case Study Two: (Business Owner Age 48, little saved currently for retirement, beaten up by the market and very concerned about taxes.)

This case study is one of my current clients. He is funding his plan with $125,000 of OPM for the next four years, which gives him a total of $500,000. In approximately 10 years, he will have enough money to pay off the $500,000 loan from his plan and in another 10 years, he will be able to withdraw $145,000 per year *completely tax-free.* If he chooses, he can sell his business or other assets to retire the loan, keeping the $500,000 in the accumulation account of his plan. **But, this is a decision that does not have to be made up-front.**

If he chooses to retire the plan loan with other assets, he would generate over a $215,000 retirement income per year with no tax impact, no tax impact to his social security and have a litigation-proof protected pension (state specific). This pension is safe from taxation, market loss and physical health setbacks. The plan allows him to withdraw these six figures for the rest of his life.

To learn more about how simple this retirement planning solution really is, simply go to: www.personalprotectedpensionplan.com

How great it is to captain our own ship and be able to take advantage of a less stormy, safer passage into the new world of retirement planning!

"I am the captain of my fate; I am the master of my soul."
~ Invictus

ABOUT CHUCK

Charles "Chuck" Oliver, Founder and CEO of The Chuck Oliver Team and creator of The Hidden Wealth System, is an industry-recognized wealth strategist who works with retirees and those who are about to retire and their families, who are uncertain about planning for, and in, retirement. Their concerns center around taxes, market risk, and the possibility of out-living their income.

Chuck helps his clients gain clarity, balance, focus, and confidence about their wealth creation and preservation. Chuck refutes the wisdom of the importance of paying off mortgages and putting the money into IRA's, 403(b)'s, and 401(k)'s.

Chuck and his Team educate clients on how to increase their retirement income by 50% or more with little or no tax, no market risk, and how to establish a tax-free income for the rest of their lives that will transfer tax-free to future generations.

www.thehiddenwealthsystem.com

CHAPTER 23

"REHAB AND GROW RICH®"

BY PAUL DAVEY, RENEGADE REAL ESTATE INVESTOR

Would a Game Changer for your life be having the ability to safely generate 12 to 30% annual returns through purchasing real estate with funds from your retirement account? If so, I invite you to read on.

As a former NYC police sergeant, I thought I'd never unlock my own financial handcuffs. Now I've not only done it for myself, but I'm helping others to do it also. As a real estate investor, broker and general contractor specializing in the purchase, renovation and re-sale of single family homes, I have completed $14,840,000 worth of rehab projects resulting in profits of more than $3,280,000 for myself and my partners.

Today I earn at least $40,000 per month using my proven system of investing in real estate rehab projects for myself and for a small group of private clients. Now I'm working fewer hours, enjoying more time with my family and going on vacation more than ever before. But it wasn't always that way.

I was both a NYC Police Sergeant *and* a contractor working 16 hour days and struggling to support my family. I had the good fortune to meet a retired contractor who had made millions as a real estate investor. He told me his story of how he began as an immigrant laborer and went on to create a net worth of more than *7 million dollars* within 25 years.

I took the exact strategies that he taught me and increased my personal income from $4,000 a month to *$40,000* per month.

THE TRADITIONAL INVESTING TRAGEDY

Now, some experts will tell you that investing IRA funds in real estate is not common – and, to be honest, they're right! Most investors aren't familiar with this strategy – but it's quite common among the world's wealthiest investors. As a matter of fact, it's frequently a key component of their long-term wealth-building strategy.

That's because they're not looking to be common – they're looking to be rich. These days, the conventional rules make long-term wealth building very, very difficult, if not impossible.

The collapse of the stock market in late 2008 devastated millions of people throughout this country. Individuals lost their life savings – and their sense of security as rewards of years of hard work evaporated before their eyes.

These Americans wondered - how could this happen? They followed the rules. They were fiscally responsible, long-term savers and they invested in stocks and mutual funds that seemed to know only one direction – up!

They did what everyone else did - invested their hard-earned money in things they had little knowledge of, and no control over. Most of these investments were made because of the advice given by financial advisors with no personal stake in these peoples' outcomes and with no proven wealth-building ability. The result was financial disaster for too many everyday people who didn't know what hit them.

HOW "REHAB AND GROW RICH®" WORKS

My Rehab and Grow Rich® system provides investors with a safe alternative to the Stock Market and the opportunity to earn high annual rates of return either in their IRA's, their cash accounts or a combination of the two.

By taking the old investment rules and throwing them aside, you safeguard your money from the destructive whims of today's financial markets.

I have created a proven step-by-step system to educate both new and experienced investors on the tremendous opportunities available to them when they use real estate investing correctly, in order to take control of their financial future – but I'll share a few key secrets of how it all works in this chapter.

The basis for the program is purchasing distressed properties at significant discounts. The types of properties we target are: handyman specials, estate sales, bank owned, fire or structurally damaged properties. We are able to make these purchases at a significant discount to the after-repaired value of the home. By having them fixed-up (rehabbed) and putting them back on the block (with a short turnaround time of 30-40 days), you can realize an amazing profit.

Through my own experience, I created "Rehab and Grow Rich" to give my clients information on:

- **Training** on how to find, evaluate and buy distressed properties.
- **Coordinating** the property rehab, and remarketing the property.
- **Sources of Funding** their purchases
- **Short-term Real Estate investing Secrets**; going from initial
- purchase to closing on sale in 4 to 6 months.
- **Self-Directed IRA Investment Strategies**

As I mentioned at the beginning of this chapter, you can realize 12% to 30% annual returns – all tax deferred – on these IRA real estate investments. I've completed over a million dollars worth of real estate transactions within my IRA during the past year myself.

According to *Forbes Magazine*, $4.6 trillion is currently invested in retirement accounts. That money has the potential to reshape lives. It's our duty to inform investors of the opportunities this money holds for them. With the "Rehab and Grow Rich® system, people will have more power to control their future and secure long term wealth."

Currently, as a broker, I have a group of 5 investor/clients that I locate properties for, analyze the profit potential, negotiate the purchase, coordinate the rehabs, and resell their properties. They like to use my services because I offer one-stop shopping - I know how to find them the right distressed properties, how to get them rehabbed quickly and at the lowest possible cost, and how to resell them in the most effective and profitable way. They don't have the time or the necessary experience to accomplish the entire process so they rely on me to make it happen.

Yes, cash is required to purchase rehabs, but the good news is that it doesn't have to be your own. It's not difficult to find opportunities to joint venture with other investors, provide labor for equity or run the actual rehab projects. You can use traditional financing, buy through self-directed IRA investing, as well as a host of other creative and viable options.

Residential rehab projects represent the best opportunities for most investors. Many real estate trainers suggest the practice of wholesaling, which generally yields a small $2,000-$3,000 per property. This involves getting the contract on a property and then 'assigning' your position to another investor. This investment strategy may work for some, but, in order to earn the kind of money we do, an investor would need to complete 6-8 wholesale deals for every rehab project we complete. Frankly, I feel it takes too much time and effort for too little a pay-off.

A typical start-to-finish deal that I do for one of my investor/clients looks something like this:

- $200,000 purchase price with closing costs
- $55,000 rehab costs
- $300,000 net sale price after commission and all carrying costs

This results in a $45,000 net profit for my client; a return of approximately 17%, not bad for 6 months or so of work. The annual ROI would be over 34%.

The best part is that you can realize these kinds of returns without a large time commitment. I handle the real estate investing for myself and for my clients on a part-time basis. It's not incredibly time-consuming to locate and purchase 2 excellent rehab projects every year. These rehab projects could result in $40,000-$120,000 in additional income, while you continue to work a regular job, or even run multiple other businesses, as I do. Several of my retired clients are earning more now than when they worked full time. One group of golfing buddies completes 3-4 large joint venture rehab projects annually – 'keeping their hats in the ring' while making substantial income.

My private clients are so excited about the returns they're getting, both in cash and in their retirement accounts, that I have a waiting list of new clients anxious to work with me. That's why I'm currently training brokers throughout the country on how to get involved in the next big growth field of real estate – self-directed IRA investing.

Let me share with you a case study – a recent "Rehab and Grow Rich®" project I've successfully completed – that will give you an idea of the costs and the potential profits of this system.

- I purchased a fire-damaged single family home as "partners" with my IRA. I paid $184,000 – half paid by me, half paid by my IRA, as "Tenants in Common," each with a 50% undivided interest.

  The property required a $120,000 renovation – and those costs were also split equally by me and my IRA ($60,000 each)

  After renovations, the property sold for $457,000 - resulting in a net profit, after all the expenses, of $137,000. $68,500 profit was returned to my IRA, 100% tax deferred, and $68,500 profit went to me personally (as taxable income).

  The final result ? A **43% return on investment.** Total time from initial purchase to completed renovation and resale? **7 months**. – Annual ROI is approximately 72%.

THE 7 STEPS TO IRA RICHES

Before you begin to work with self-directed IRA Investments, you need to create the proper infrastructure that will ensure your success. To accomplish this, you need to follow what I call "The 7 Steps to IRA Riches." They are as follows:

1. Select an IRA custodian.

You need to work with a company that allows you to make real estate purchases within your IRA. Many traditional IRA companies offer you limited and traditional investment options – individual stocks, mutual funds, CD's, etc. We're about breaking tradition.

My IRA custodian allows investments in all of the above as well as real estate, newly-originated mortgages, judgments and liens, discounted mortgages, options and a host of other opportunities. My experience with them has been outstanding and I highly recommend them. You can find their contact information at:

www.Rehabandgrowrich.com/paulrecommends

2. Select an experienced attorney.

A key member of your team will be an attorney that specializes in real estate transactions. My attorney expertly handles contracts and deed recordings, arranges title insurance, and quickly clears up tax liens and other issues that would result in delayed closings. Ideally, the lawyer you choose will have a good track record of working with other investors that are using their IRA's to purchase real estate and write loans.

3. Select a real estate broker.

It's essential to work with a top real estate broker that specializes in investment properties. They should be able to bring you a steady stream of rehab properties to consider, and provide you with current market data - including Current Market Value (CMV), After Repaired Value (ARV), and the Average Days on Market (DOM) where properties are taken from list date to closed sale - as well as school reports and other information not readily available to the general public. If you would like to work with an agent trained by me with knowledge of the Rehab and Grow Rich® system, go to: www.RehabandGrowrich.com/agent

4. Select a general contractor.

A licensed general contractor is essential for your Rehab projects. They will provide detailed price quotes, timelines for project completion and onsite management while the rehab is underway. Many investors, once they have the proper experience, can serve as their own general contractor. We offer home study programs that cover rehab projects from A-Z, including private coaching and onsite training at both the locations of our current rehabs in progress and also at distressed properties we're considering buying - where we perform field inspections to determine their condition. To access a nationwide directory of Contractors trained in the Rehab and Grow Rich® system go to:

www.RehabandGrowRich.com/contractor

5. Select an insurance broker.

Insurance is an important component of any rehab program – that's why a reliable insurance broker makes a big difference. In some cases, rehab projects won't qualify for traditional homeowners insurance. In that instance, we get what is known as a "Builders' Risk" policy. This type of coverage will protect your investment while the rehab project is being completed and before the property qualifies for standard insurance. The downside is that the cost of this kind of policy can vary wildly – so you must shop for the best price.

My insurance broker writes policies in 48 states and works to get the best insurance quote. You can find his contact info at www.RehabandGrowRich.com/insurance

6. Educate yourself.

Educating yourself about real estate investing and the construction industry will greatly increase your comfort level with the process and help you feel confident about growing your IRA account quickly. You can obtain this kind of valuable knowledge by: purchasing the course, participating in local Real Estate Investment Associations (REIA's), reading books and articles on the subject, and also by working with the Rehab team that you've gathered from steps 1 through 5. View my list of recommended reading here. www.RehabandGrowRich.com/reading

7. Put it all together.

Once you've put your team together, start looking for deals and transferring IRA funds as needed. Start by selecting an area you're interested in, have your broker send you properties in the target area, analyze the properties, choose the best one, get pricing guides from your contractor and start making offers. As I noted earlier, real estate investing within your IRA can provide a great opportunity to grow your account at extremely high rates – with a 15% annual return, your account balance will double every 5 years.

A $100,000 account grows to $201,135 after 5 years of 15% annual returns.

For example, an Investor with a **$1,000,000 self-directed IRA earning 15% returns can pay himself $150,000 annually** - and never touch the principal until required distributions begin at age 70 ½. And if the investor in this scenario was 59 ½ or older, there would be no 10% early withdrawal penalties – just the normal taxes on the withdrawals.

- You can make withdrawals from your IRA at any age. However, prior to age 59 ½ distributions would be subject to a 10% penalty (in most cases) and taxed at your regular income-tax rate. In the example above you could withdraw the $150,000 profit that your account returned every year and never touch the principal balance. Once you turn 59 ½ no early withdrawal penalty would apply.

Please note, that you can truly ***Rehab and Grow Rich***® – grow your retirement account at amazing levels and secure an incredible retirement. However there are **"Prohibited Transactions**" that can void your IRA and make all taxes due immediately. To make sure this doesn't happen to you read our free report on Prohibited Transactions and how to avoid them at: www.RehabandGrowRich.com/prohibitedtransactions .

In conclusion, let me talk about one of my favorite movies – "The Princess Bride." I have watched it countless times over the years with my daughters. In one scene, the hero, Wesley, is captured by one of the villains, but is promised safe passage back to his ship. Realizing they are deceiving him, he replies, "We are men of action; lies do not become us."

Many financial advisors will say that the stock market is a safe bet for the future. I firmly believe that's as much the truth as the bad guys promising Wesley a safe return. Your life and your financial future will not improve until *you take control of your own investments.* All the best hopes, intentions and plans are of no value without the right action to advance us towards our dreams and goals.

Your personal financial path should be one of carefree prosperity, with the ***Rehab and Grow Rich***® system it can be.

ABOUT PAUL

Millionaire Real Estate Investor / Self Directed IRA expert: Over $15,000,000 worth of rehab projects completed.

Real Estate Broker: National Association of Realtors, NYS Realtors Association, Long Island Board of Realtors.

General Contractor / Builder: National Association of Home Builders, Long Island Builders Institute, NYS Builders Association.

Email – Paul@RehabandGrowRich.com

Fax – 631-204-6615

CHAPTER 24

NON-BINDING MEDIATION: THE BEST KEPT SECRET IN ALTERNATIVE DISPUTE RESOLUTIONS

BY GENEVIEVE M. LYNOTT, ESQ.

Disputes happen. How those disputes are handled affect business. Litigation is the traditional manner to have a dispute resolved. However, there are alternative dispute resolutions available, such as arbitration and mediation. Many factors must be analyzed to determine the right process for the parties to resolve their disputes. In these economic times, everyone should consider agreeing to Non-binding Mediation.

A "trial" is a judicial examination and determination of issues between parties to action, whether they be issues of law or of fact, before a court that has jurisdiction. "Arbitration" is a process of dispute resolution in which a neutral third party (arbitrator) renders a decision after a hearing at which both parties have an opportunity to be heard. "Mediation" is a process of dispute resolution in which a third party neutral (mediator) assists the negotiations of two or more parties to achieve a mutually acceptable agreement.

Both litigation and arbitration have a third party making the determination for the parties to resolve their dispute. Litigation is time consuming and extremely expensive. Arbitration and mediation are much faster and less expensive. Mediation is the least expensive and the only form that allows the parties to make their own resolution, yet is the most under-utilized form of dispute resolution.

In a simple, breach of contract case between a general contractor and subcontractor, the dispute and outcome can be very different depending on the process of resolution.

SITUATION A – GOING THROUGH TRIAL

Subcontractor ("Sub") files a straight breach of contract claim against a General Contractor ("General") for failure to pay $100,000 on one project after having 10 years of a good working relationship. General, once served with the Complaint, contacts his attorney and files a motion to dismiss. The Judge sets a briefing schedule and hearing date for the motion to dismiss. Sub wins the hearing and General answers the complaint. Now the case is "at issue" and ready to move into the discovery phase.

Written Discovery called interrogatories and requests for production of documents are issued by each party. Once all the written discovery is responded to and documents are exchanged, it is time to set up oral depositions. Each witness sits down with the opposing sides counsel and answers questions under oath before a court reporter. Once the witnesses are all deposed, it is time to move on to the experts. Experts Discovery including reports and depositions takes time and a lot of money.

General believing he has a strong case, files a motion for summary judgment. The Judge sets a briefing schedule and hearing date for the motion for summary judgment. After the hearing the Judge determines there are still too many disputed issues of material fact and schedules a pre-trial conference with all the parties.

The Judge attempts to force the parties into a settlement at the pre-trial conference to no avail. Sub and General both prepare for trial.

Three long days of testimony and evidence are submitted to a bored jury. Neither party was able to have every exhibit they wanted submitted into evidence over objections from the other side. Both parties feel there was more they wanted to the jury to hear from them, but with the motions *in limine* and objections, some testimony was unable to be heard.

As the jury deliberates for six hours, each party waits. Sub thinks about how he had to borrow money from his mother-in-law to pay his legal fees for this trial. General thinks about how he wishes things never got so bad with this Sub because he would really prefer to work with him again.

Five years after the Sub filed his original complaint, the jury returns a verdict in favor of the Sub in the amount of $35,000.00, and no legal fee award. Both parties are unhappy with the decision. The Sub can not afford to appeal; he does not even have enough money to pay back his mother-in-law for the legal fees he already incurred. The General does not want to appeal because he lost on what he thought was his best argument and does not want to run the risk of winning on appeal and the next jury awarding even more money. Sub and General never work together again.

SITUATION B – GOING THROUGH MEDIATION

The case is at issue and during discovery the General inquires whether the Sub would be willing to Mediate the matter. Sub agrees and the parties pick out a third party neutral.

Sub and General prepare written submissions for the neutral Mediator. Some parts of their written submission they agree to disclose to the other side and other parts are kept confidential with the Mediator. Three days are scheduled for the Mediation within a one month time frame.

On the first day of Mediation, the neutral Mediator allows counsel for the Sub and General to make their opening statements allowing both contractors to hear the factual and legal arguments that will be made for them and against them. The Sub and General are also permitted to present additional points they would like all parties to be aware of during the opening meeting.

After listening to opening statements and positions, the Mediator breaks into caucus. A caucus is simply each party meeting separately with the Mediator. In caucus, parties are free to discuss issues with the mediator they might not be willing to state in front of the other parties. The Mediator is held to the highest standard of confidence, and will never reveal anything stated in caucus to other parties without permission.

Initially in caucus, both the Sub and General are venting and extreme about their legal and factual arguments to the Mediator. On the second day in caucus, the Sub explains to the Mediator that he's going to have to borrow money from his mother-in-law to keep the case going, but really believes he should get paid from the General. The General explains to the Mediator that he would really like to work with this Sub again and is more worried about the prevailing party attorney fee clause in the contract than the amount he believes is actually owed.

The General agrees to allow the Mediator to disclose to the Sub how he would like to have the Sub work on another project with him. Upon learning this, the Sub reveals that another big project would help his business out, but is nervous because he was not paid $100,000 on the last project. Sub then admits to the Mediator after hearing in the General's opening statements he may have some set off issues for the $100,000 he is seeking and is willing to negotiate if there is also a new project as part of the deal.

The Mediator goes back and forth in caucus between the parties attempting to see if the parties can reach an agreement amongst themselves. The General and Sub agree that $45,000 without any attorney fees included is a good amount for the Sub to receive for the disputed amount and to sign a contract together for the next project which will end up benefiting both parties. The agreement reached was created, controlled and determined by both the General and Sub with the help of a neutral third party. Both the General and the Sub leave the Mediation feeling that their issues were heard and a positive resolution was reached.

Once the parties decided to mediate, their dispute was resolved within a month. Both parties felt heard and walked away satisfied with the Agreement they reached with one another.

TOP 7 REASONS WHY MEDIATION SHOULD BE THE LITIGANTS' CHOICE

1. **Control over the outcome**

   When you allow a third party to determine a dispute, there is never a guaranteed result. Non-binding Mediation is successful when the parties reach an agreement. The parties have complete control over what they want to include within that agreement, rather than having a Judge or Arbitrator make their decisions for them. Matters completely outside of the original dispute can be included as part of the solution. Some of the best agreements are creative and meet each parties needs.

2. **Let your voice be heard**

   Parties get to make opening statements at the start of the Mediation. It allows them to explain their factual and legal position to the other side. Additionally, in caucus, parties get to explain the reasoning and thought process involved in each issue within the dispute.

   Most disputes arise through communication breakdowns. It is a rewarding experience for each party to have someone listen to them and their side of a dispute. In Mediation, parties get the opportunity to tell their opposition their side of the dispute and privately tell the Mediator the reasoning behind and within their issues.

3. **Relaxed rules of evidence**

   Mediation is not a court room. The rules of evidence do not apply. Documents can be reviewed and knowledge learned through hearsay can be shared, which might not be permitted to be disclosed at trial.

   This is especially important to parties who want the entire story explained. Often at trial, a party walks away feeling… if only the jury could have heard xyz, it all would have been different. In Mediation, everything can be heard.

4. **Non-binding; your choice**

   No one is forced into an agreement in Mediation. Each party has a choice whether or not to enter into an agreement. If the parties cannot reach an agreement, they are free to proceed with Arbitration and/or Trial.

   Because Mediation is non-binding, it takes the pressure off the parties. A neutral Mediator will never force parties into an agreement. Any agreement has to be determined and agreed upon by the parties themselves.

5. **Interest based**

   There are always outside factors and interests beyond what is stated in a Complaint. The Mediation process allows the neutral Mediator to identify and examine the real interests of the parties involved in order to assist these parties to reach a resolution, sometimes creatively.

   Often the communication breakdown is severe in disputes, and the parties cannot identify the interests or reasoning of the other. Having a neutral listen and identify the interests involved begins the repair process to the broken lines of communication.

6. **Cost efficient**

   The cost of litigation includes more than legal fees, expenses, and collection issues. There are emotional, relationship, and business opportunities that pay a price in every trial.

   Mediation is a less time-consuming process and particularly less expensive. Parties do not have to wait until a complaint is filed to consider mediation. In these economic times, more businesses are writing mediation clauses right into their contracts.

7. **Creating and claiming value for mutual gain**

   When the parties do reach an agreement in Mediation, it is typically more than just a comprised settlement. The Agreement allows each party to create and claim value by generating an Agreement that is mutually beneficial.

> Having control over the outcome allows the parties to create the value.

Keep in mind that mediation does not just benefit parties in contract disputes, it has the ability to benefit almost everyone. Whether you are a business owner having a dispute with a customer, employee or another business owner, mediation is the first step in dispute resolution all parties should look into to solve their dispute. I am a legal professional who assists small businesses and individuals with their legal needs, yet understand there are human needs as well. One of the basic human needs within a dispute is the need to be heard. That is part of the beauty within mediation, parties get to unleash their need to be heard upon the neutral. Then each party can move on and use their ability with the neutral to establish a compromised settlement between themselves. If an agreement is reached it is only because it is what each side desired. The mutually agreed upon settlement is the 'win-win' within each mediation.

Mediation is the wave of the future. It is the only cost efficient, interest-based dispute resolution that leaves the control in the hands of the parties having the dispute. It benefits employers attempting to retain employees after internal disputes, as well as benefiting business professionals in dispute with one another. The retention of employees and business relationships is well worth the minimal cost of mediating. In fact, if mediation is not required as a step only in litigation… it can be utilized at any time within any dispute. Part of its magic is having a third party neutral.

If you have any questions or need additional information, please feel free to contact me Genevieve M. Lynott, Attorney and Certified Commercial Mediator.

ABOUT GENEVIEVE

Ms. Lynott is an accomplished attorney in both state and federal court as well as a certified commercial mediator. Ms. Lynott helps individuals and small businesses with their legal needs. As an advocate or neutral, Ms. Lynott will take her years of experience and put them to work for you.

Ms. Lynott is famous for asking clients how she can help them, listening to their responses and developing an action plan based on the needs of the individual or business. Ms. Lynott has worked for firms in Chicago and the suburbs. She now has her own practice in McHenry, Illinois, which allows her to give the personal service and attention she believes her clients deserve.

To learn more about Genevieve M. Lynott visit
www.mchenrylawyer.com or call (815) 403-6866.

CHAPTER 25

YOUR NEW INDEPENDENT EXECUTIVE LIFESTYLE

BY CHUCK BOYCE

To be successful, you must take charge and take action.

I have often wondered how people can go through the life being tossed around like an unmanned ship at sea, with no one at the helm, no one navigating the waters, and no one taking any positive action to change their course.

They see themselves stuck in a job, or on the 'hamster wheel of doom' running faster and faster, but not making any progress forward towards their goals. They have abdicated responsibility and given up control of their success and security to an employer that can kick them to the curb with little or no notice.

The days of the paternal company are long gone, to be IN the game you have to understand WHAT game you're playing. The key to success and security today is to take responsibility and grab control. Business ownership and entrepreneurship is the only way to guarantee your efforts are rewarded to the fullest. Be warned that this path is not without risk, and many times a little adversity goes a long way to finding prosperity.

This was very evident to me as I held a management position in a rapidly growing, privately-held firm. We had earned a spot on the prestigious Inc 500 list of fastest growing private companies, twice. I poured my time and talent into this organization in the expectation that if the company continued to be successful, I would enjoy more rewards, continued employment, and ultimately security.

This delusion was quickly shattered on a November morning when the owner of the company I was working for called me in to her office. I was accompanied by another manager and while I thought that was odd, I thought I was participating in a routine status meeting. We ran through all of my clients, the status of their projects, and the results I had achieved. The owner closed the meeting by announcing that my services were no longer required by the company, and I had 20 minutes to pack up my stuff and leave the premises. I would be chaperoned by the other manager in the meeting until I was walked out the door. Happy Thanksgiving.

That moment made it perfectly clear to me that unless I was sitting on the other side of the desk, I would always be susceptible to the whims, desires and motivations of someone else. I needed to *change the game.*

Like most entrepreneurs, I had a series of minor successes and a few near-fatal ventures. I was pouring all of my energy and resources into building these businesses, pretty much for the sake of building them. I was never clear on the purpose the business was supposed to serve for me and my family.

After a lot of study of other successful entrepreneurs, I discovered that I was missing a clear picture of what my life was supposed to look like and how my company was to provide the financial security, to achieve those goals. I had taken Michael Gerber's principle in the E-*Myth Revisited* of picturing my company when it was finished to the ultimate extreme. I was looking so far past the horizon, I couldn't see the beach I was standing on.

I had to ask some crucial questions:

1. What do I want my life to look like in the future?
2. What do I need to change in the company today, to achieve my vision of the future?

3. What are the key indicators that will measure this progress?

Through this experience, I discerned that what I really desired was the lifestyle I had enjoyed during my 5 years in corporate America, but on my terms. This vision became the foundation for what I have termed my Independent Executive Lifestyle.

The Independent Executive is a business owner or entrepreneur that understands we are in business to fulfill our personal goals, desires, lifestyle and destiny. We are building our businesses to support and work for us, without becoming a slave to the business. We value relationships and leverage those relationships to achieve our objective.

This point of view is very contrary to what most of us were taught in school. We were told that our success and security is dependent upon getting good grades, working hard in school, and landing a good job. We then needed to pay our dues, and climb the ladder. We were lead to believe that security came from having a good job for a good company. We were taught to go out and find a steady paycheck.

This may have worked for our parents and their generation, but it is unrealistic to believe that a corporate job at any level is the key to security.

In my own family, both my father and grandfather joined General Motors after finishing a military career. For a long time, there was a lot of discussion of me eventually going to work for GM as well. Fortunately, that path never materialized for me. Otherwise, I could have very well have become 'road kill' during the bailout of yet another company that was deemed too big to fail.

America's foremost business philosopher, Jim Rohn said it best, "Profits are better than wages. Wages make you a living; profits make you a fortune."

I agree, knowing that you have created a business that can - through its design, structure and systems - predictably and reliably generate a profit on the dollars invested into it, is the ultimate security. There is no longer any security in getting a paycheck.

If you have determined that business ownership and entrepreneurship are the right choice to fulfill your personal goals, the next step is finding a business that will fulfill your lifestyle design. A few of the important questions you need to consider when determining what type of business you're going to get into include:

- What experiences both personally and professionally can I use in my new business?
- Is someone willing to exchange money for my product or service?
- Can the business by systematized and automated to make the best use of the time invested?

These questions are just a 'jumping off' point. There are probably a hundred or more questions you will need to ask yourself and answer. However, don't fall victim to analysis paralysis. It is better to take action and figuring some stuff out along the way, even if it requires you to make a course correction and clean up a few messes as you go.

There are many roads to success. Start mapping out what your Independent Executive Lifestyle is going to look like for you. Explore the option of entrepreneurship as a vehicle to get you to your lifestyle goals. Commit to taking action today, and everyday to move closer towards your vision. Change the game you are playing from one in which you are a pawn, to the one where you can be the king!

ABOUT CHUCK

One of the top alternatives people are using to create wealth in this tough economy is through development of their own small businesses. Chuck Boyce and his organization are helping people do just that by providing online access to resources while assisting entrepreneurs fight some of the isolation associated with working from home.

"Our goal is to build a community of online resources, so if you find yourself, either by choice or necessity, starting a business of your own, you won't have to figure out everything all by yourself. We have developed a place you can go to get access to the expert information you need. When you have a question you can ask people who have already faced the problems you're trying to overcome today."

"The current unsteady economic situation is what initially inspired us to start this service because we've worked with independent professionals in the past and saw a growing need for this type of online community to be able to connect people with each other and critical resources. We continue to watch the unemployment rate moving higher, and people are finding themselves unemployed. Thousands of skilled laborers are out of work and many of these people just can't find jobs. Their alternative is to start their own businesses in order to secure their financial future."

Many times the first thing to be lost after losing a job is a person's self-esteem and confidence. Chuck says they offer resources to help people develop the self-assurance they need to start moving forward again. "We try to show them that they are not alone by introducing them to others like themselves that have been in the same situation, have made clear decisions and moved forward and experienced success in a relatively short period of time."

Tip for Success

"I urge people to set their course and start something new if that is what the situation calls for. I started my own business, a desktop publishing company, when I was 16 years old and have spent the majority of my career working for myself. This is the perfect time to start a small business; in fact many big companies today had their beginnings during the Great Depression of the 1930's. Small business is what drives our country and you could be a part of that legacy to help the nation return to prosperity. I know that if these potential entrepreneurs give themselves a chance and use our services and resources to build something new, they will also experience the freedom of working for themselves and the financial success we are all looking for today."

If you are interested in learning more go to http://www.breakingfreeblog.com

CHAPTER 26

WHAT A DIFFERENCE A YEAR MAKES!

BY PAM MOORE

I always dreamed of being an entrepreneur. I dreamed of the lifestyle I knew would come with hard work and the right strategic moves. I imagined the freedom I would have to spend time with loved ones as I serve my community and my God.

I out-marketed my competition from the days of the lemonade, cookie and painted rock sales in the front yard that emptied my mom's cupboards. I remember a neighbor moving her painted rock sale to my yard as she was frustrated nobody was coming to her sale. What did I do different? I had music, a little sister that danced and I wasn't afraid to tell them why my goods were better.

Although I was being raised by a single mom, my cookies were generic and my lemonade was hotter than the pavement, I always sold out. They weren't buying the cookies. Instead, they invested in the experience and the way I made them feel when they came into my yard.

Why did I spend 15 years in corporate America? In the early years it kept me challenged with good food on the table. Eventually it kept me on an airplane, away from the ones I love. It kept me up late nights on projects I knew wouldn't bring a positive Return on Investment (ROI.) When you're in the rat race of life you have no choice but to zoom in 'turbo' regardless of your belief in the ride. I learned to do what I was told and didn't ask questions. After surviving 13 layoffs at one company, I became an expert at keeping a job in a bad economy. I avoided water cooler discussions with the motto, "to keep your job, just do your job".

My life in corporate felt "safe" but was it really safe? Or was it a fake safety net and in reality I was scared to death? If I wasn't scared why was I running like a hamster in a wheel? Why were my passions, dreams and life slipping away?

Did I feel appreciated or cared for? Nope, they definitely weren't words I used to describe the safety net I designed for myself. Time with family, time to live and pursue my dreams? Didn't happen. So why did I make myself believe I was safe?

YOU'RE FIRED!

On July 16, 2009 I was FIRED after I made recommendations and turned in a financial plan that took my life back. I share the full 'juicy' details in a book I co-authored with Mari Smith, Nick Nanton & 23 others titled "Social Media Relationship Age."

I started a business in a bad economy, savings depleted and husband out of a job. Many thought I was crazy for taking such risk. I knew being an entrepreneur was my '*zoom*' ticket to a better life!

TIME TO ZOOM!

On August 17, 2009, I officially incorporated my first business, FruitZoom, Inc., a social media marketing and branding agency.

Nobody pulled strings for me. There was no silver platter or rich uncle who gifted money to my bank account. My business was and is still being built on smart moves, sweat, tears and God's grace.

During September 2009, I met with my first client, Crossing Church in Tampa, Florida.

Within days of incorporation I leveraged social media to launch and *zoom* my business. I went from less than 500 to more than 30,000 followers on Twitter in six months. I do not count number of followers but instead focus on giving of myself to help other business leaders grow their business. I place priority on the value of authentic relationships and engaging with real people based upon content that inspires them to also build a better life.

People often ask me about my secrets to success and how I hit zoom speed in such a short time. I am going to share what worked for me including the activities that helped me get from idea to full execution in less than a year in a bad economy.

SAFETY IN CORPORATE?

We spend the early years dreaming about our life, educating ourselves, and planning for a great future. Yet, somewhere along the way as we take on big people responsibilities we become averse to risk. We work 24/7 to survive until the next paycheck, next layoff and the list goes on. Why is it we watch our life pass us by while we work to fill a bank account that's not our own? We watch our tank of passion, goals and dreams fall to empty.

We convince ourselves it's a safe place. Heck, at least we have a paycheck for the moment. We have a place to drive to every morning, even if we're miserable. We have so called friends and people we can relate to. We sit at happy hours, layoff parties and long lunches dreaming of what life could be like. We talk about our "big idea." Yet we lack the guts and time to execute because we're too busy running in the 'rat race'.

Why do so many entrepreneur "wanna be's" never make the move out of corporate? Is it a lack of motivation? The truth is, most lack confidence. We look at the statistics for how many small businesses fail and combine it with the last words heard from a mean boss before being fired or laid off. The two add up to self-pity and the belief it's safer to stay where you are, even if miserable.

We let the world and the corporate entity define who we are, what we are capable of and even what we're worth. We constantly seek acceptance. Confidence in self is 'flushing down' with the economy. Employees are drained emotionally, physically and mentally.

WHAT IS AN ENTREPRENEUR ANYWAY?

Entrepreneur, what does the word mean to you? Why do some succeed but most fail? Are the achievers smarter or prettier? Do you ever think, "why can't that be me?" The truth is that it can be you.

Entrepreneurs are simply the people who have the guts, the willpower and the faith in themselves to execute upon their dreams.

SOCIAL MEDIA: THE ENTREPRENEURS BEST FRIEND

Social media is a key component to the success I have achieved in launching and growing my business.

Generating buzz, awareness and brand equity are key requirements for a new business. Yet few entrepreneurs have the resources to do such when the business doors first open.

Social media can help you *ignite your business* into high gear. When efficiently executed as an integrated component of a broader marketing and business plan, social media will increase return on investment (ROI) exponentially.

Social media is about relationships and connecting one-on-one with real people. It provides you access to more people at a lower budget than you could achieve with any other traditional medium.

Despite what you may hear, social media is not free. Yes, access to Facebook, Twitter, LinkedIn and the millions of other tools are free. However, using them requires use of your greatest asset, your TIME!

I am going to share how I used, and am still using, social media as a competitive and strategic weapon to grow my business. The key to success with social media is to take the the time to learn the tips, tricks, best practices, lingo & strategies to maximize your investment. Social media is not one size fits all. Take the time to determine how you can best leverage social media to grow your business based upon your offerings, market and objectives.

KEY TRAITS OF A SUCCESSFUL SOCIAL ENTREPRENEUR:

1. Belief in Self
2. Forward Thinking
3. No Plan B
4. People, Passion, & Purpose!
5. Authentic
6. Share Best of Self
7. Work Outside of Comfort Box
8. Plan to Integrate
9. Balances Art and Science
10. Offer a "Safe Place"

SOCIAL MEDIA SUCCESS TIP #1: BELIEVE IN YOURSELF!

If you are considering entrepreneurship, what are you waiting for? A magic bus ticket to the land of the crystal ball telling you everything will be okay? It's never going to happen folks. Believe in yourself and make the move!

You CAN and WILL BE one of the POSITIVE STATISTICS if you make the right moves. The more you believe in yourself the more others will believe in you.

SOCIAL MEDIA SUCCESS TIP #2: LOOK FORWARD, NOT BACK!

Your passions, desires and dreams for a better life is what will provide you the endurance and agility to surpass your competition, weather a bad economic storm and achieve success.

Envision yourself and life as an entrepreneur. Regardless of your financial, personal or professional situation there is hope.

Had I believed everything the CEO of my last company told me I probably wouldn't be working anywhere. It is usually those who are most insecure that find joy in criticizing others. Do not let the words of someone who never knew the real you define what you are today. Your past is not your future!

Your only option is to look forward with your eye on the prize of a better life!

SOCIAL MEDIA SUCCESS TIP #3: NO PLAN B ALLOWED!

If your ultimate goal is to be a successful entrepreneur, then there is NO Plan B. I don't care how bad the economy is, how mean your last boss was. Your Plan A is you, your dreams, your business and your life. If you spend one ounce of energy on Plan B you set yourself up to fail.

Instead invest everything you have into your plan A! Believe and you will achieve. Don't look back. Look forward with confidence knowing you will achieve success.

Your commitment to Plan A will attract and inspire a loyal tribe of followers who will support you as you help them.

SOCIAL MEDIA SUCCESS TIP #4: PEOPLE, PASSION & PURPOSE!

If you are just leaving a bad situation personally or professionally, then take a mini-vacation. Get away if even for a weekend. Find yourself. Refocus and re-energize. Find that kid inside of you that dreams, plans and wants to live life! He/she is in there somewhere if you look hard enough!

Pick up the book *Crush It* by Gary Vaynerchuk. His story is amazing and is a testament to the power of passion.

By re-igniting your passion you will revive your mind, body and spirit. The passion will help you be yourself, create compelling content and connect with others of like interests.

You will know you are living your passions when you look forward to each day and it does not feel like work!

SOCIAL MEDIA SUCCESS TIP #5: AUTHENTICITY!

Authenticity is the turbo jet fuel of social media. There is only one you.

Do not hide behind an 'avatar' of your fancy logo. You must share a photo of yourself. Don't wait until you lose ten more pounds or until you get the perfect photo shoot. Instead, be proud of who you are!

You will be simply amazed at the reaction you will receive online when you share your true colors. If you are serious, don't fake you're crazy. If you're a nut, be a nut. Whatever you are, whoever you are, just BE YOU!

Make authenticity a priority and you will stand above the crowd.

SOCIAL MEDIA SUCCESS TIP #6: SHARE!

*Inspire – Connect – Achieve*I help customers build their business and life based on the belief that to *achieve* success we must first *inspire* with compelling content and relevancy. We then *connect* with a goal of building an authentic relationship. We last *achieve* success by leveraging the authentic relationships built on trust to grow and sustain our business long term.

To inspire we must share of ourselves. Don't be afraid to share your best goods. Share with the intent to inspire and you will keep people coming back for more. Share your passions, dreams, your ups and downs. Demonstrate daily that you are a real person with real content and that you want more from them than a credit card transaction.

We must give with no expectation to receive. Give with an objective to inspire and connect. Achievement of your objectives will follow if you focus on inspiring and connecting as a real person.

SOCIAL MEDIA SUCCESS TIP #7: WORK OUTSIDE OF YOUR COMFORT BOX!

Social media pushes us out of their comfort zone. I was terrified when I first got behind the video camera for my first video blog post. Yet I saw immediate results! Video is now one of the keys which helps me attract clients who bring me joy as well as shorten the sales cycle!

Spend time listening to and learning from leaders who inspire you. Enhance your skills with online webinars, local meetups and networking groups. Eventually you'll get a feel for how social media works and will develop your own personal style, format and platform.

Find colleagues who are at the same stage as you, and grow together. You can support one another to take risks and enable your business to *zoom* to new heights.

The same rules do not apply to small business and big corporations alike. Learning new skills will keep your business agile and ahead of competition!

REMEMBER: If you do what you have always done you'll get what you always got!

SOCIAL MEDIA SUCCESS TIP #8: PLAN TO INTEGRATE!

Social media does not replace traditional marketing 101. It does not stand alone and will not save your business by itself. However, it can be a powerful marketing weapon when used correctly.

Integrate social media into your existing marketing communications and activities. Add your social media profile links to business cards, email signatures, email newsletters, and event signage.

Establish an objective to build a community of loyal supporters with every marketing touch. It takes an average of 7-8 experiences with a brand before it is remembered. Make each touch count!

SOCIAL MEDIA SUCCESS TIP #9: BALANCE ART & SCIENCE

Social media is a balancing act of both art and science. The most important aspect of social media is the art of human connection via content and real conversation. Do not get hung up on the social media tools. They are needed only to execute social media and enable efficiencies. The tools are not the focus or where you spend the majority of your time. You can easily outsource the social media setup and execution so you can focus on the strategy, content and connecting with your core audiences.

SOCIAL MEDIA SUCCESS TIP #10: OFFER A SAFE PLACE!

Many people are looking for a safe place in life. They want friends they can trust, a home that is warm and inviting. They want to do business with people who make them feel good.

Be approachable, real and available. If you focus on what you can do for others as a top priority, you will find your ability to offer a "safe place" will be a key contributor to your success. It will help you connect in an authentic way to the people who want to learn from you.

I hope I have inspired you to consider taking that leap of faith you've been putting off. Please send me a tweet at @PamMktgNut when you leap and I'll be right there to cheer you on each step and tweet of the way!

ABOUT PAM

Pam Moore, CEO and founder of FruitZoom, Inc., an experiential social media, brand and digital marketing agency that helps business leaders leverage marketing that bears fruit. She teaches her clients to inspire and connect emotionally with target audiences by leveraging content, brand and integrated social media marketing strategies to nurture authentic relationships.

Pam spent 15+ years building brands in high tech marketing for Fortune 500 companies as well as smaller startups and business to consumer organizations. Her areas of expertise include engaging and developing communities in high technology, professional services, enterprise data storage and virtualization, natural lighting, database analytics, green/eco-friendly, online marketing, and web 2.0 ecommerce.

"At the heart of all business is relationships. Social media and that cute little blue Twitter bird simply make it easier to connect," said Pam. Pam's methodologies are based on the belief that we must first inspire our audiences with interesting content, we then connect and build authentic relationships, and last we help them achieve their objectives as well as ours. Inspire-Connect-Achieve is her tagline.

Pam left corporate America last fall and is seeing her business zoom in a short time frame thanks to a combination of social media, content and a focus on authentic relationships. She teaches social media seminars, is confirmed for several upcoming social media speaking engagements, is kicking off a "Women that Zoom" seminar series in addition to several joint ventures. She works with businesses small and large, local and national to help them zoom with integrated social media strategies and tactics.

In the book Pam will share her personal story and how social media and authentic relationships helped her succeed as a corporate business leader as well as ignite her business as an entrepreneur. Also included will be information regarding her proprietary methodologies for developing content and social media strategies that zoom with a positive ROI!

Pam goes by the code name of "PamMktgNut" and can easily be found with a Google search. "I am not afraid to show my nutty self. If I didn't I wouldn't be authentic, now would I?" said Pam.

Website: Http://fruitzoom.com
Facebook Fan Page (personal): http://www.pamsfanpage.com
Facebook Fan Page (Fruitzoom): http://www.facebook.com/fruitzoom
LinkedIn: http://www.pamslinkedin.com
Twitter: http://www.twitter.com/pammktgnut
Blog: http://www.pammarketingnut.com

CHAPTER 27

WAKE UP & GET PAID TO PLAY!

BY GARRETT J. WHITE - THE AUTHENTIC ENTREPRENEUR™

I lay there in bed staring at the ceiling as my wife cried herself to sleep - almost in a state of shock at where my life had ended up. Everything was gone, and the one thing I seemed to be succeeding at was hurting everyone around me.

"How the Hell did I end up here?" was the only thought crossing my mind.

Rewind seven months and I am speaking to over 2,000 of my peers at The Mortgage Planners Summit in Las Vegas. I was sharing the stage with Tony Robbins, who just happened to be one of my personal heroes in the world of speaking.

My presentation, The Mindset of an Investor, brought the house down with thunderous applause and cheers. As I worked my way off the back of the stage I can clearly remember thinking: "I have finally 'Arrived'."

My life experience at that moment felt like a drug. I was high 24/7 off of my own arrogant assumption that I was on my way to the "top", wherever that is. But like any artificial high, it was about to come crashing down.

The Banking/Credit Crisis was in full swing. We were some of the first hit by this massive tsunami that forever changed the face of banking and real estate in this country. Ultimately, my company proved unable to recover from the after-shock of these events.

By December 1st, 2007 my company was insolvent. By January 1st, 2008 I was personally insolvent and facing a possible personal bankruptcy.

I was angry. I was scared. I had no idea what to do.

Before my meteoric rise in the mortgage & real estate industry, I was a broke, divorced, cancer surviving PE teacher that had no clue what I wanted in life. And here I was back to square one!

But this time around there were 3 ***game-changing*** distinctions:

First: I already knew that it was possible to go from completely broke to insanely rich in a relatively short time period. This point of reference gave me the past evidence and future hope I needed to ultimately rebuild.

Second: Unlike my money driven, *"prostitute for profit"* 7-year run in banking, this time around I had a distinct feeling that all I was experiencing was somehow in alignment with a greater purpose for my life.

Third: There's nothing like a major crisis in one's life to get you to stop and re-evaluate everything. I started questioning my values, my priorities and my beliefs. I began to re-think my entire world view and the very meaning of my existence.

I was committed to create something significantly different than what I had built and lost. There were no "Sacred Cows" that would go unexamined.

Since that night I have built four profitable companies, co-authored two books with NY Times Best Selling Author Garrett B. Gunderson, hosted a weekly Radio & TV show on the new consciousness of Entrepreneurship, and I speak at workshops to thousands all over the country on the topic of *Getting Paid To Play.*

Even better, my marriage is on fire with a passion usually reserved for Hollywood movies.

I am driven from the inside out by a higher purpose that allows me to experience a HIGH that is like nothing I have ever experienced before.

I did it all in less than 18 months...

I *Get Paid to Play*, which is what I tell people I do these days. It is a world that is difficult for many to understand, similar to the recent attempt I made at explaining what a million dollars was to my 3 year old daughter, who just recently learned the concept of quarters and dollar bills.

My intention in this chapter is to give you a framework of how I rebuilt my world, and what I discovered about myself, my business and my life along the way. More importantly though, I will provide you with a MAP of how you can do the same. I will describe the four step process I went through, fully realizing that it is not a process that will resonate with everyone, but for those who are ready, hold on, your life is about to change for ever.

When the Student Is Ready The Teacher Will Appear
~ The Buddha

PHASE 1
ACCEPTING WHAT IS...

The first quarter of 2008 was a brutal fight. I was on an emotional roller coaster. It was a struggle to not retreat into self-defeating behaviors and addictions. I found most of my thoughts and conversation to be centered around why it wasn't fair that I had lost all of my money. It was exhausting to accept responsibility for the reality of my situation, so I argued with it.

During one of my many arguments with reality a mentor of mine, Byron Katie, introduced me to the idea that when I want reality to be different than it is, I might as well be wanting my cat to bark. I could try and try, but in the end my cat will look up at me and say, "Meow."

Wanting reality to be different is futile. I could have spent the rest of my life wanting my situation to be different than it was, but in the end the key to unlocking my power was to first surrender to 'what was'.

Ultimately, I came to understand and accept that I was a powerful creator of the results of my life and there was no one else to blame. Through this process I came to learn to love 'what is' - and own 100% of my perfect creation - regardless of what my *egotistical* mind thought it should be.

"The only time we suffer is when we believe a thought that argues with 'what is'.

When the mind is perfectly clear, 'what is' is what we want."
~ Byron Katie

Once I was able to acknowledge & accept the results of my financial life as perfect, I was positioned to take a hard look at who I was. What I saw was not what I expected. Once I was stripped of all my identity labels, my money, my "success", and my stuff, all I could see was nothing. I was speechless. I had no idea who I was, and for the first time in my life it caused me pain to not know the answer to "Who Am I?"

"It is only when we have the courage
to face things exactly as they are,
without any self-deception or illusion,
that a light will develop out of events,
by which the path to success
may be recognized."
I Ching,
Hexagram 5, Hsu,
Waiting (Nourishment)

PHASE 2
AWAKENING WHO I AM...

It seemed like a simple enough question. Little did I realize how simple and yet how complex this answer would be to uncover. Truth be told, a part of me feared that if I looked closely enough at what lay deep within me, I would find something horrible. I had resisted looking long and hard for fear of discovering someone I didn't like.

I was afraid of Myself. I felt Incomplete. I judged myself as not worthy or not "enough".

My self-judgment hit a climax in March 2008 in the parking lot of my friends business, as I read the words on the document in front of me, "Notice of Default". My home was going to be taken.

I sat in my SUV sobbing out of control. I have never cried so hard in my entire life. As tears poured down my cheeks, I looked up into my rear view mirror. Staring deep into my own eyes the word, "*Surrender*" rose from my heart up to my mind. I couldn't fight the illusion any more. It was time to hand my life over, it was time to surrender.

In words that could barely be understood I mumbled, " I surrender, I surrender, I surrender." An instant later I felt a warmth enter my body like nothing I had ever experienced before, a lightness, a peace and a certainty I could barely describe, but I could feel.

That afternoon sparked a 60-day journey that would ultimately unleash the truth of Who I AM.

So Who AM I?

I AM a powerful, passionate, spiritual man.

I AM a Spiritual Warrior.

These words defined Me. They had become my truth. I was ready to see my Purpose.

PHASE 3
ACTIVATING SOUL PURPOSE...

"Soul Purpose is your unique series of talents, strengths, passions, interests, hobbies, attitudes, and values that form the essence of the most magnificent version of you. When these qualities are intentionally acknowledged and cultivated, they coalesce into a specific mission in service to the world. These qualities already exist within you in a basic raw form. For most people they need to be clearly discovered, then nourished, studied and refined. Soul Purpose is like gold, hidden deep within."

~ Steve D'Annunzio

The sun was setting. My body felt strong. As nighttime descended on the Grand Tetons, I was 56 miles into my first 100 mile ultra-marathon in the summer of 2008. I found myself deep within the forest, alone with my breath, and my thoughts. That summer I had not only trained intensely on a physical level to be prepared for this race, but I had trained intensely with my Spiritual Mentor Steve D'Annunzio on the concepts of a higher purpose and spiritual enlightenment.

The words that he shared with me about Soul Purpose echoed through my mind, and I was left wondering...

What was My Soul Purpose?

As my mind searched for the answers, the forest grew very dark and still. I felt the stillness rest upon me as well. I paused to get a drink and turned my gaze to the heavens. Staring into the star-filled sky I vocally asked,

What is My Soul Purpose?

What is My Divine Contract?

At 31, I had lived a vast majority of my life oblivious to the true needs of others. But after the recent intense eight month Spiritual Awakening process I was experiencing, surrendering to my higher ***Soul Purpose*** seemed the natural next step.

"We cannot live only for ourselves, a thousand fibers connect us with our fellow-men; and along those fibers, as sympathetic threads, our actions run as causes, and they come back to us as effects."
~ Herman Melville

Was it possible that I was built and born for a very specific reason. Was I here on a mission?

From August of 2008 to December of 2008, I immersed myself in the pursuit of the answer to this question. What was my purpose?

When the dust settled, what was left was a Vision, a Stand that would radically alter my perception, not only of myself, but of my perception of business and making money.

Finally everything I had experienced in my life made sense, from my cancer, my divorce, my financial struggle and my rise and fall in business. It had all been necessary to create the favorable conditions to awaken me to my Soul Purpose Contract.

I had been sent here to serve a specific problem and a specific group of people.

We all have a Soul Purpose that gives us access to exactly what we need to serve our fellow man, to bring solutions, clarity and healing to their problems, uncertainty and disease. We're all here on a mission, even though many, like me, may have never bothered to uncover that Purpose.

Understanding this I spent weeks refining & clarifying what my *Soul Purpose Stand* in this life was.

It was absolutely inspiring to me to discover my Soul Purpose. So what is it?

1. To inspire, liberate and lead the Children of Light.
2. To unify the two conversations of Spiritual Transformation & Financial Production.
3. To redefine Spirituality and its application in business.

PHASE #4
ACCELERATING THE BUSINESS OF ME.

"I AM a Powerful, Passionate, Spiritual Man. I STAND to unify the world of Spiritual Transformation and Financial Production guiding humanity to Get Paid To Play".
~ Garrett J. White

By December 2008, almost one year after that dark night when I lay awake wondering 'what the hell had happened to my life', I found myself in a place of peace and power I had never known before. I knew who I was, and I knew what I was called to do.

Next?

How to put that purpose into action?

The model was simple.

Step #1: What Soul Purpose Plane did I feel most passionately called to?

(Physical Body, Mental/ Emotional, Social/ Relational, Financial/ Resource, Spiritual/ Mystical)

The Plane: Financial & Spiritual

I felt passionate about two dimensions, Financial & Spiritual dimensions. Great! Now I had the playing field I would create my business on. The next step was to identify the problem.

Step #2: What is the problem, challenge or obstacle others are facing in these dimensions that I am fired up about solving and serving?

The Problem: Financial: Unconsciousness in Financial Production. Producers working hard to make money with no clue why they are making it. No sense or undertone of power or purpose. Ultimately "prostitutes for profit", who feel dissatisfied with life.

Once I was able to identify the problem/pain, the next step was to identify the people.

Who was my target market?

Who was suffering from this problem and did I feel drawn to work with them?

Step #3: Who are the people I feel passionately drawn to serve, based on the plane and problem?

The People: Primary: Warrior Men & Women between the ages of 25 and 45 who have had some financial success in business but are struggling to recover from losses financially in the past three years or are still in the beginning stages of getting a purpose driven business off the ground.

The next step was to identify the Product, the Platform, the Plan and finally the Production strategy that I was going to create to solve the problem. Because of the length of this chapter I will be unable to go fully into detail. To access the full content go to http://PaidToPlaySecret.com

The Product: What is the tool I am going to create as the solution?

The Platform: What form of business and Team will I use to provide the solution?

The Plan: What are my Marketing, Sales, Fulfillment and Systems?

The Production: What are my first 30, 60, 90 day targets and measurements?

I repeated this cycle with 4 different businesses serving the same Plane, the same Problem, and the same People. I simply adjusted the Product, the Platform, the Plan and the Production to meet different needs within the same Plane. Soul Purpose in action is the greatest thing I have ever experienced.

GETTING PAID TO PLAY – A CONCLUSION.

"How could I serve more people?" I asked a friend of mine as we sat out on the patio of a local hot spot in SLC, UT in November 2009 during a late lunch appointment. The sun was shining and like most years in Utah, summer was still in full effect heading into fall. I was at peace.

As I sat there my mind reflected over what I had created in the previous twelve months. I had four successful companies, financial liberation, and an offline Intensive Workshop process entitled "Awaken Soul Purpose" that was radically altering Entrepreneur's lives.

Truth be told my greatest passion at the time was the Intensive. Through the four day Intensive, I was able to assist over 1,000 students across the USA & Canada to:- Accept, Awaken, Activate & Accelerate the "Business of Them". Although it had cut literally 10 years off of the process for my students vs. other methods, it was still too slow compared to what I sensed was possible. Also the price point made it out of reach for many ($2,000 per ticket).

As I pondered this, I gazed across the parking-lot to the main road just a short distance from where we were sitting and watched as hundreds of cars passed by - traveling home from work.

I wondered how many people inside those vehicles were living lives of quite desperation, like most of my students prior to attending the Awaken Soul Purpose Intensive.

I wondered how many were getting Paid To Play every day vs. getting Paid To Work?

I wondered how many were stuck just like I once was.

I had to do more. Now that I had the resources, the networks, the knowledge and the experience it was time to launch something huge. Something that would allow me to touch not just 1,000 people a year but over 10,000 lives a month.

Awakening Soul Purpose and Getting Paid To Play had to reach the masses.

With this vision, I launched an online version of my offline Intensive experience. I call it My Paid To Play.

Between November 2009 and March 2010 we experienced our first round of beta tests. I was convinced that we could create a transformational on-line experience that was affordable, and yet at the same time could guarantee the results, using high-end technology.

Our results were off the charts.

In May we launched and enrolled 400+ students in three weeks - and are projected to hit 10,000 students in 2010.

When I die, whenever that is, I want to be known as one of the preeminent Leaders on the planet that forever transformed the conversation of Spirituality and Business.

My Legacy will be a tsunami of “Purpose Driven Producers” getting Paid To Play.

Will you be next?

As a gift for reading this chapter - I would love to serve you with a 30 day FREE trial membership to the On-Demand Paid To Play Today program to see for yourself why the program is to transformational.

Go to http://PaidToPlaySecret.com right away.

With Love, Your Brother In Light,

Garrett J. White | The Authentic Entrepreneur

ABOUT GARRETT

Garrett J. White ~ The Authentic Entrepreneur ™ is a passionate, powerful, spiritual Man who's transformative 10 year journey from broke P.E. teacher to powerful Entrepreneur and thought leader in the world of Spiritual Transformation and Financial Production is nothing short of Inspirational. He has become known as the 'Guru of Getting Paid To Play'.

At the young age of 22, Garrett began his transformational journey from the pit of despair to the peak of possibility. He was divorced, bankrupt and physically recovering from a 2 year battle with cancer and felt completely alone. Later he would say that he had arrived at the primary crossroads of his life. At this crossroad he could see two choices. The choice to live a life of darkness, poverty and mediocrity or the choice to live a life of light, prosperity and greatness. He choose the light.

At the age of 24, Garrett unleashed on the world of Investment Banking and Real Estate Investing. Over the next 6 years Garrett exploded on the world of business becoming a multi-millionaire while building 3 national mortgage companies, an empire in Real Estate, and a professional speaking career traveling, training and connecting with thousands of people around the United States. In his arrogance, he felt he had arrived, how wrong he was.

At the Age of 30, Garrett lost everything. His empire in Mortgages & Real Estate was unable to recover from the impact of the credit crunch and mortgage banking crisis. He was broke, in debt beyond belief, and felt yet again completely alone. The pressure of providing for a family and the financial explosion in his personal life, created a dynamic tension that drove him to ask questions of himself he had never asked before. Who Am I? What is my purpose? What do I really want? These questions led him on a journey of self-discovery that would ultimately liberate and awaken him to a place of wholeness he had never know before... Prosperity Economics!

At the Age of 32, Garrett uncovered the formula of Peace, Power & Productivity in life - Stop doing what you hate and Start doing what you love! This discovery lead to the co-creation of the Freedom Fast Track & Paid To Play training processes. Paid To Play focuses on 'Awakening, Activating & Accelerating the Business of YOU', while Freedom Fast Track focuses on transforming your potential Into profit.

At the Age of 34, Garrett has co-authored two highly acclaimed books, The Money Tree™ & The Economics of Soul Purpose™ and is currently co-writing his third book, Game Changers, The new rules of Enlightened Entrepreneurship, due out in late fall of 2010. He hosts a weekly TV & Radio Show entitled "Stop Doing What You Hate & Get Paid To Play". Both shows are committed to Inspire, liberate and empower the 'Modern Male and Female Entrepreneur' on the new consciousness of spirituality & business.

Garrett and his Goddess of Light Danielle have two brilliant, powerful children of light, Parker & Bailee, who bring constant contrast and expansion to his life. He attributes his success in business & life to a passionate purpose-driven perspective that he feels is divinely inspired. His ultimate desire? To leave this life being known as the Man who bridged the GAP between the contrasting worlds of Spiritual Transformation and Financial Production.

CHAPTER 28

BUILD YOUR DREAM BUSINESS

BY DR. ARIF BALAGAM

Imagine transforming an ordinary, every-day, often dreaded event, like going to the dentist, into an extraordinary, positive experience for the patient, the team and the dental practice owner. This statement describes not only the vision that I had for a bold, new type of dental practice but the reality that it has become in the form of Lumina Dental Spa.

Over the past 18 years, I have had a successful career setting up and managing dental practices. Although they were successful from a financial standpoint and the care they provided, the setting, the business practices, the team and even the apparel were very traditional in nature. The mundane, mechanical aspect of the routine that these businesses had become lacked excitement and led me to believe that there was no alternative. Quite frankly, I was bored, to the point where, in 2008, when I began asking myself, *"How can I create a breakthrough type of practice that overcomes all of the negative connotations typically associated with going to the dentist?"*, the seed of an idea started to germinate.

As we all know, an idea or opportunity is a form of potential energy. Action is the catalyst which converts it into kinetic energy. I was now faced with having to take the right series of actions, supported by my values and principles, to create Lumina Dental Spa. My inspiration was Michael Gerber's "Dreaming Room", which challenges you to use your "right brain" to visualize your dream business in a whole new way by letting go of all of your old preconceptions about the kind of business you run. Rather than focusing on how to fix a business, Gerber advises you to reinvent it from the bottom up, in an organic way that frees your imagination to discover exciting, innovative new business models and systems. The pivotal question is: *"If you had a choice to start your business all over, and if you knew it would never fail, how would you create your business?"*

Embracing Gerber's approach, my first step went well beyond the typical visualization. Yes, I had to visualize the waiting room, the furniture, the artwork and the attire, but more importantly, I had to *feel* what it would be like to be a guest, not merely a patient, at Lumina Dental Spa, what it should *feel* like to work at Lumina Dental Spa, and what it would be like to own Lumina Dental Spa. Through this uninhibited thought process, I realized that by melding excellent dental care with an inviting, soothing environment and a caring team, I could redefine the dental experience as the patient experience, and have fun doing it.

The more I focused on the new reality, the more clearly the total picture emerged and the more excited I became. I could actually see a new guest coming into the office, being warmly greeted by name while being offered a fruit drink, coffee in a mug or protein shake. A calming effect overtakes the guest as the artwork, décor and soothing sounds envelop the pleasantly surprised person. Customized choices of movies viewed through eye-goggles, pillows, blankets, hot scented towels and other forms of relaxation set the stage for a stress-free and pampered experience. Our Guest Concierge attends to the appointment details with the optimal balance of professionalism combined with the personal touch. Every concern is pre-empted or explained to the satisfaction of the guest and no guest ever leaves the office in pain, unhappy, or with an unanswered question.

To augment the "feeling good" atmosphere, Lumina Dental Spa has consciously elected to focus primarily on cosmetic dentistry. Using state of the art technology, we show the guest comparative 'before' and 'after' images to visually present the outcome beforehand, not merely from a technical standpoint, but to demonstrate the renewed confidence and poise that a winning smile can command. We offer many solutions such as whitening, Invisalign , Veneers and Lumineers so that each guest has options and can make an informed decision. Behind the scenes, our team is a cohesive unit that collaborates to achieve common performance and qualitative goals, based on the underlying supposition that when we take care of our guests in an extraordinary way, the business will be taken care of above and beyond our expectations.

Now that I had the fully developed image of Lumina Dental Spa firmly in place, I implemented the concept by applying these principles:

CLARIFY YOUR VISION

Clarity and focus are key elements to honing your vision, which must have a fair degree of specificity for it to be achievable. In my case, I narrowed my vision by choosing the aspect of dentistry which I found the most exciting and that I felt has the most significant impact on the whole person, not just from a medical perspective. There are limitless possibilities of what you could do. However, the goal is to decide what you will do and what you won't do in the scope of your business. This is your chance to ignite your passion and infuse it into your business.

REBRAND YOUR IMAGE

Your brand is the complete visual representation of your business, from the name that you choose to the colors on your website. As we all know, a brand is a powerful image, in that it evokes ideas and emotions in the people who see it and make a lasting impression. In defining your company's values and culture, a word portrait will begin to develop. Branding then immerses those concepts into everything relating to your business, to reflect at all levels who you are and what you do.

When it comes to rebranding, be brutally honest and relentless in examining every aspect of your business. Then break the mold by creating something totally fresh. My traditional dental practices felt very clinical. They were making money, but they lacked vitality. Once I had clarity of vision, I knew exactly what I wanted to do. Instead of casting a wide net, I carved out a very specific target market: people who wanted or needed cosmetic dentistry. I became totally jazzed about branding my practice as a dental spa. The name itself sparks curiosity, which initiates a conversation, which leads to a new guest, which evolves into repeat business and referrals. Then I had fun choosing the name, designing the space, selecting the colors, creating the marketing materials and inventing the details to present a cohesive and compelling message, every step of the way. So, what jazzes you, and to what extent does your brand tell the story of your business?

INFLUENCE THOSE AROUND YOU

There are many definitions and characteristics of a great leader, but what leadership really 'boils down to' is wielding influence, which can be in a positive or negative way. Taking a negative stance will instill fear and resentment in those around you, whereas a positive attitude will nurture trust and commitment. It's your decision. Since leadership emanates from the inside out, you have to change yourself before anything else in your business will change. Your thoughts, language and actions have to align to embody the change that you want to precipitate. Adopt the philosophy of doing whatever it takes, rather than merely doing your best. Create a positive environment and relationships that remove drama from the equation. Ignite the fire within people, instead of lighting a fire under them. Emphasize and reward the positive, and when times are tough, keep the message upbeat while being realistic about what has to improve. Wow your team by doing unexpected things! Leadership starts from the top. What kind of leader do you want to be?

PAMPER YOUR TEAM

As the heartbeat of your business, your team can make or break your success. The single most critical attribute that your team members should possess is a positive attitude, since skills and procedures can be taught easily enough, while attitude is ingrained. Just as I have passion for my business, I expect my team to have a passion for coming to work where the environment is conducive to creating something exciting, contributing and making a difference. Once the goals and guidelines, which the team helps to establish, are in place, they individually and collectively assume ownership, responsibility and accountability for delivering the results.

My role is to provide the leadership and the tools and to eliminate roadblocks for them to get the job done without compromising our principles and values. It all starts with hiring people who are fun and interesting, want to connect on a personal level with our guests, have some business experience and share the ethic of a positive attitude and commitment. Once the staff is 'on board', it is your duty to pamper them and to appreciate and reward them commensurately with the value they bring to the company. Morning group huddles are a sure-fire way to keep the energy level high and set the priorities for the day! Have you huddled with your team lately?

NEVER STOP LEARNING

Many business people read books and attend seminars for self-improvement. Doing these things is an admirable first step, but only provides a fraction of their potential value. More than a task or an event, personal growth is a lifestyle that doesn't begin and end with the classroom or the front and back covers of a book. Self-awareness is not an end in itself; the magic lies in what you do with it. By reading a book or attending a seminar, you become the conduit of that information, which only gains meaning and power by how it is applied for your direct benefit, and by how it is shared for the benefit of others around us. I personally surround myself with coaches, experts, workshops, conferences and any tool that can be considered a knowledge resource. I then find ways in which to implement the ideas and I observe the impact. Then, from my direct experience, I make decisions about incorporating these techniques into my way of doing business. The message that I want to share is that by improving yourself, you improve others, your business and the world around you.

FOCUS ON CUSTOMER SERVICE

At Lumina Dental Spa, we actually believe that we work for our customers, who indirectly sign our paychecks. While it is true that exemplary customer service takes many forms, it starts with a strong customer-service-oriented attitude as its foundation. Customer service can be an elusive concept because of its qualitative nature and often means different things to different people. In reality, customer service consists of the planning, design and execution of many small things that show consideration, respect and surprise for the guest. Our philosophy is to educate and to explain, not to oversell. In this way, our conversations are elevated. In addition to the thoughtfulness and attention that we lavish upon each guest, Lumina Dental Spa has a breadth of customer appreciation programs for being a loyal patron, for referring new guests and for providing their feedback. To assess your own level of customer service, ask yourself if you would like to be a customer of your own business. Think 'out of the box' to make minor or radical changes and plan to enjoy dramatic results.

BE CREATIVE

This is the time to tap into the powers of your "right brain" by dispensing with logic and relying on feeling instead. This shift may be challenging for many people, but it can be cultivated through practice. Force yourself to use your intuition instead of analysis. Conjure up your imagination, by asking, *"What if...? "* , and then brainstorm a multitude of ideas without critiquing them. Creativity can manifest itself in simple or big ways. For example, instead of being situated in a strip mall or a professional building, Lumina Dental Spa is located in an upscale setting, a radical departure from the typical dental office. We replaced common place medical scrubs with professional suits and colorful shirts. We serve water in a glass instead of in a plastic bottle. Our team now includes a full-time aesthetician who offers chemical peels, Botox, facials and micro-dermabrasion treatments. These services contribute to the overall feel-good outcome and complete the total look, but we are not stopping there. We continually look for ways to creatively solve problems and keep things interesting and dynamic.

GIVE BACK

For me personally, giving back is one of the key drivers for me to be in business in the first place. This gesture can take many forms, such as time, money or knowledge, and it can be big or small, depending on the situation and your own comfort level. For example, all of our staff receives complimentary dental work from our office. Another example comes from the situation of one of our guests who was enjoying the dramatic results of her veneers. She was 20 years old and her mother had paid for the treatment at our office about 6 months earlier. The veneers got knocked out when the woman got into a fight. Distraught, she came into our office. After hearing her story and not wanting to add to her trauma, we replaced them, foregoing the $8,000 fee. We now have a fan for life and felt good about doing it.

So, what has been the result of Lumina Dental Spa? I'm thrilled to say that after being in business for just over a year, we exceeded our aggressive targets despite a distressed economy. Thanks to our innovative concept and exemplary service to our guests, we see 60 new patients a month, half of whom are from referrals. For the record, our success extends well beyond the financial aspect. Our business processes are fine tuned and our staff is happy. Patient response has been tremendous, as evidenced through expressions of how wonderfully they are treated and the amount of referrals we have. We did lose some patients who did not embrace the changes, but that is to be expected. The most rewarding outcome is, by far, that my dream has finally become a reality, and I can honestly say that I am now happier and more energized than I have ever been in my entire business career.

In closing, I challenge you to ask yourself:

"What will it take for me to be deliriously happy with my business?", "How will I do it?", **and** ***"When will I do it?"***

ABOUT ARIF

A 25-year veteran of dental practice management, Dr.Arif Balagam moved to the United States from his native Pakistan in 1980 after graduating from dental school. Motivated by a drive to master the business aspect of the dental profession, Dr.Balagam initiated his career with a Houston firm where he learned dental practice management from the ground up. His savvy business sense and his keen instincts quickly made Dr.Balagam an invaluable asset to the leadership team. Over the 15 years that he remained with this practice, Dr.Balagam was instrumental in driving the company's annual revenue from $1.5 million to a $7 million.

In 1992, Dr.Balagam purchased Smile Dental Group which consisted of three practices. Out on his own for the first time, he faced the challenges and reaped the rewards of managing his own practices while continuing to hone his vision and his skills.

Dr. Balagam's evolution achieved a breakthrough in 2009 when he launched his dream practice, Lumina Dental Spa, a revolutionary model that embodies his complete value system and makes dentistry appealing to people who are afraid to go to the dentist. His approach of nurturing the emotional while treating the physical needs of patients has proven to be a winning formula – for the patient and for the practice.

Dr. Balagam, a firm believer in personal development, attributes much of his success to mentors such as Werner Erhard (EST),Tony Robbins, Bob Proctor, Brian Tracy, and Michael Gerber. Dr.Balagam stays on the cutting edge of personal and professional growth by regularly attending conferences and listening to audio books. Through continuous learning, introspection and overcoming obstacles, he was able to not only define his vision with clarity, but also to create something that he is passionate about and benefits others.

On the horizon for Dr.Balagam is the opportunity to impact practices in other cities, states and countries through his consulting practice using the Lumina Dental Spa model.

Arif Balagam lives in Houston, Texas with his wife of 15 years and their three daughters.

CHAPTER 29

THE DELEGATION BREAKTHROUGH

BY DANIEL R. MCCABE

At heart, I am an entrepreneur. For whatever reason, the idea of working for anybody else just never sat well with me. I couldn't even stomach paying rent in college. I talked my parents into co-signing on a loan for me so that I could buy a house, rent out rooms to my friends, and thus live for next to nothing. Of course, I gave myself the master bedroom and the single stall in the garage. But that seemed fair to me, because it was all my idea, and more importantly I was the one who had the courage and drive to make it happen. Many of my friends thought I was crazy to buy a house at such a young age, but what I later learned is that they were only *saying* that I was crazy, the truth was they just couldn't grasp the concept of stepping 'outside the box' and doing something similar themselves.

The same is true in business today. I talk to people all the time about starting their own business. These are good, smart, hard working people who would do very well if they ever decided to go out on their own. But grasping that concept of "Business owners are people just like us, they just decided to start a business" is difficult for them. They almost always feel that they are not worthy of being top boss at their own company, and regress into the comfort of working for someone else.

Since I bought that first house at age 19, I have bounced all over the entrepreneurial map. Fortunately, I am pretty sure that when you start your own business there is no perfect straight-line route to get to your destination. You will face twists and turns, challenges and opportunities on your path to success, but if you keep fighting and stay focused on your end goal, you will always get there.

I started right out of college, real estate degree in-hand and energized to start my first business. I became a real estate agent. I wanted to be an investor, but it was the early 2000s and houses in our area were appreciating in double digits every year and it seemed like a scary proposition. Regardless, it was a great time to sell houses! As a real estate agent you are the epitome of a small business. You are responsible for everything in your business and you only make money when you work. I was my own sales rep, chief marketing officer, receptionist, courier, janitor, you-name-it-I-did-it business owner. I had to work at a feverish pace just to keep up with everything, but I did, because nobody could ever possibly do it as well as I could. Why would I pay an assistant $12/hour to do something I could do myself and do it better? (Please note the sarcasm in the last sentence.)

As an entrepreneur I believe we are all built with a do-it-myself attitude. That is what makes us entrepreneurs. I had a successful real estate business, which lead me into owning my own brokerage, and eventually, a successful real estate investment firm as well.

I maintained the do-it-myself attitude right up through the real estate brokerage by working long hours, making sure everything was done properly and up to my expectations. Finally in late 2008, the real estate market was in the tank and I was spending long hours managing and training agents who simply weren't producing at a level I needed for the brokerage to be worth my while anymore. Not to mention there was a golden opportunity to invest in real estate, which was what I always wanted to do in the first place. The nice thing about real estate is that there is always an opportunity. In a booming market: Sell real estate, there is a ton of money to be made there. In a down market: BUY! BUY! BUY! So I started my investment company.

With a small group of investors we started buying distressed homes. I ran every aspect of every transaction, rehab, rental, maintenance problem, everything. About 6 months into this new company I had what I like to call "My Delegation Breakthrough." Or, you could call it a breakdown, as I was working way too many hours on things that I finally realized someone else could do for a very minimal amount of money. My breakthrough came as I realized what it was costing me NOT to delegate. It was costing me, not only in the form of money, but also in the form of time. I had never put a value on my time before, and when I made this mental shift and realized that my time is worth a lot more than the $12/hour it would cost me to hire an assistant, my world changed and I haven't looked back.

I started with the obvious choice and brought in a property manager. Soon after, I made a deal with my contractor that put some of the maintenance in his lap. At this point we had created a rehab template, which saved me from having to visit each house continuously through the rehab. With the standard template the contractor always knew what colors to use, which cabinets to use, where to order windows, etc. I later hired a real estate agent to help with the buying and selling of the properties to free up more of my time. This is when I realized that even though I was an integral part of the business, pulling the strings from behind the scenes, that I was really only putting about 5 hours a week into the business. The truth is, I could have probably even pared that down, but I was bored and liked being around. I had effectively delegated myself out of a job! The positive side is that now things ran so much more efficiently that we are actually making more money.

I still have that investment company today. It has been just over two years now and that company has afforded me the opportunity that I have now to work with, and train, real estate agents and other small business owners. I still spend a couple of hours a week on the investment company, but that time is really spent meeting with my employees while they tell me what is going on, and me nodding with approval. They are doing an excellent job. As an entrepreneur I like to think that I could do it better, but in this case I know I couldn't.

With my new-found time I was able to get to work on an idea I had for years and Fuzed Marketing was born. Fuzed Marketing is dedicated to creating efficiency solutions for real estate agents and small businesses across the country. We do this by helping them focus on where their time is best spent so they can add the maximum to their bottom line. We also teach them how to create 'killer' marketing campaigns that produce results and are fully automated. The best part is that I have been using my Delegation Breakthrough to the Nth degree on this new company. I went out and found the absolute best team I could to carry out this vision, and I could not be happier with all of them today. Before we even began development on our initial core products, I hired a top-notch national sales rep, then a Chief Operating Officer, a head trainer, a designer, a web team, copywriter, and 5 more regional sales reps! With all these great people in place, this brand new company that I was so excited to get going barely needs me! I get to spend my time working on customizing plans with our clients, which is what I love to do. I am home every day at a reasonable time, I haven't worked a weekend in who knows how long, and my future looks brighter than ever. Maybe I should start another company just to fill the day?

Hopefully you were able to catch some of the sarcasm above as I laid it on pretty thick at times. I actually thoroughly enjoy the fact that my life has made the turn to working less hours and making more money. My companies are growing without me setting foot in the building some days, which is the true definition of how a BUSINESS should operate, and what the business owner should expect once they have built it. Anyone can start a business, be their own boss and go to work every day fulfilling their customers' needs. But if that is the case they don't have a business, they have a job. They just happen to work for themselves. There is nothing wrong with doing it that way if that is what you want, but I have found that is not exactly what most entrepreneurs had in mind when they opened the doors. That is why they come to us.

The people I work with now want to own businesses. Whether they are real estate agents or not, people want to make more money working less hours... which makes sense, I would question anyone who says they want to work more hours for less money.

Aside from great marketing and sales (which are both grossly overlooked by most new businesses), a key element to taking your business to this next level is to delegate responsibilities to others. Telling you to do this is easy, and executing actually isn't that hard. You just need to make sure you follow a few crucial steps when you are considering this bold step and while you are hiring your new employees, contractors, or companies to fulfill your businesses needs.

Below are 7 considerations to take into account when you are having your Delegation Breakthrough.

1. How are you spending your time?
2. What is your time worth?
3. What are the roles that your company needs to be filled?
4. Are you really the only one who can do what you do?
5. What will adding a person do to your bottom line?
6. Do you hire an employee, an independent contractor or a company?
7. What will you do with your 'new-found' time!?!

Your time should be spent doing what you are good at. Do what makes you unique and the expert at what your business does. If you find yourself cleaning the bathroom at the office to save paying someone a minimal amount of money, this is a great place to start outsourcing.

Only you can answer the question, "What is my time worth?" I encourage you to put a fairly high number on it, though. For argument's sake, let's say your time is worth $100/hour and you are cleaning the bathroom, which would cost $15/hour. You are losing $85/hour by not doing what you do best in your business!

One thing that helped me a lot was creating a flow chart of the positions and responsibilities that I knew would ultimately need to be filled to make my company become what I envisioned. In the beginning I needed to fill many of those positions myself, but slowly, I was able to fill them with other qualified individuals. This gave me a plan. I knew what I needed, was able to prioritize what I needed most, and bring people in when it made sense. In this way, I could start removing myself from the day-to-day operations.

It is important to realize that there are a lot of smart people out there; some are even smarter than you. One of my favorite lines is, "Hire people smarter than you to do the things you can't do." Often times when these people take one aspect of your very broad business and focus on it full time, you'll find they can do it much better than you. Bringing in enough of these people will ultimately help your bottom line explode. A good employee should bring in three times what you are paying them.

Just to be clear when you begin your delegation, it is important to realize these don't necessarily need to be employees. It might not always make sense to have them full time. You wouldn't need a full time person who only cleans the bathroom. In these cases you might hire an independent contractor, or even a cleaning company to handle these services for you. You can do the same with your marketing, design, copywriting, etc… Hiring independent contractors or companies is a little more expensive on a per-hour basis, but definitely makes sense until you grow big enough to bring someone in full-time.

Hopefully you are now ready to make your mental shift to freeing up time and getting your business to make you money even when you are not there.

My goals include coaching my son's baseball team and making sure that I am always there for him during these formative years. I also plan on enjoying time with my wife and time at the lake, while knowing that my businesses are doing their jobs by keeping my bank account healthy.

What would you do with extra time? More money?

I wish you much success in your endeavors, and am confident you will succeed as soon as you make that choice for yourself.

ABOUT DAN

Daniel R. McCabe – **The Big Picture Entrepreneur** – is the entrepreneur's entrepreneur. He's always innovating. Looking at things broadly. He has an eye toward not only generating the big ideas, but also executing on the concept to actually deliver something meaningful to his customers.

Dan started out early by buying his first investment property at age 19. He hasn't looked back since. Little did anyone else know that this was just the beginning. After receiving his degree in finance and real estate from the University of St. Thomas, Dan began a successful career as a Realtor. This quickly led him to opening and running his own real estate brokerage. Anyone who knows Dan understands that this was not enough. So, during this time he also opened his own real estate investment company, which he describes as a very successful and fulfilling venture.

Dan, being a true entrepreneur, couldn't stop there. Around every corner he saw an opportunity to help others run their businesses more efficiently, thus reducing his cost. It's this kind of "big picture" thinking that has constantly led him to new success. He understands the environment around him and capitalizes on the fact that we can all benefit from one another in some way. He believes there is nothing 'sweeter' than making more money by helping you make more money.

A perfect example of this is the construction company that he formed with his lead contractor. The business plan was to combine the contractor's expertise in construction, and Dan's expertise in business. Since starting out, they have grown from just an idea, into a company with a full time office staff and multiple crews out in the field. And, he did it in just over a year. A major component of this growth was the addition of a complete marketing strategy and a full time sales rep.

Dan's focus has always centered on real estate. Real estate has been his passion for many years and continues to be a driving force for him today. He has learned though, that his winning strategies are universal. They can be applied to any number of businesses to help them grow and reach a higher level.

The culmination? Fuzed Marketing is offering a unique tool, specifically designed for real estate professionals – Fuzed Agent (www.fuzedagent.com). Since every Real Estate agent has to run his/her own unique business, Fuzed Agent is designed to help them create effective, business-changing marketing campaigns, as well as automate their communication tools. Why? So Real Estate Agents can spend time actually SELLING real estate.

The one thing Dan wants everyone to understand is that your business is only as good as your marketing. You are encouraged to talk to someone at Fuzed Marketing/Fuzed

Agent for a free business assessment. We'll help identify areas of your business that need improvement, or even a complete overhaul.

Fuzed Marketing has sales and marketing experts around the country who are looking forward to helping you and your business reach the next level.

Dan can be reached at 612-208-1071, info@danmccabe.com, or by visiting www.fuzedmarketing.com

CHAPTER 30

THE 4 ESSENTIALS FOR BUILDING BRAND VALUE

BY JOHN BEJARANO

IF YOUR BRAND SUDDENLY DIDN'T EXIST, WOULD PEOPLE MISS IT?

Enduring brands leave long-lasting impressions and cultivate relationships with their customers by becoming part of their culture. The brands that understand and use branding effectively in order to build brand value are usually the most impactful and earn a loyal following. Question: What are you doing to build value in your brand?

In this chapter you will learn 4 essential elements of branding and how to use them to build brand value. Whether you have no branding experience or are a seasoned strategist, my goal is that you find this information insightful and thought-provoking to help you build a stronger brand.

Keep in mind that branding is not exclusive to corporations, and that these principles can also be used to build your personal brand and shape your career. You are also a brand, and I'll explain this further later in this chapter.

Let's begin by asking a fundamental question, **"What is a brand?"**

When I get asked this question I like to start by saying what a brand is not, because some people think it's just a logo, trademark, product, or service. A brand is more than that. The logo and product names are just symbols or elements representing the brand. A brand is a set of expectations, memories, stories, and emotions that collectively create a meaningful experience for an individual and allows them to distinguish, associate a value, and chose one brand over another.

Simply put, a brand is a collection of meanings defined by an individual.

If a person cannot distinguish a brand over another or associate a value with it, then that brand does not exist, at least to that individual. In a way, a brand is elusive and only exists in the minds and hearts of the people who experience it. A brand is also not what a company says it is either, but rather what the person experiencing the brand thinks and feels it is. Companies can influence our perception of the brand, but ultimately it's up to the individual to make up his or her own mind on what a brand means to them. Eventually, the brand will make or break the business or organization.

Branding is nothing new either, although we didn't always call it that. Cowboys helped make the word popular when they needed a way to distinguish their cattle from others. They took a hot uniquely shaped piece of metal and pressed it against the hide of the cow until it left an imprint, and the cow was then "branded". But the history of branding takes us even further back before pre-industrial times, thousands of years ago. Some of the first forms of branding began as storytelling, which at its core is what branding still is today. We used storytelling then for "personal branding", which is the process by which individuals express their unique values and differentiate themselves from others. The legendary people that were talked about around a campfire in a tribe or the people who created the cave paintings of their hunt in Lascaux, France some 17,000 years ago, branded themselves with stories of their efforts that stood long after they were gone. The great Pyramids of Egypt also served as branding tools for the Pharaohs that once ruled the land. Personal branding was mainly used to gain power and respect from others, leave a stamp in history and, well…to make babies. What others think of us, our reputation, our accomplishments, our perceived value, is all part of our personal brand and it's just as important today as it was then.

Today we live in a fast-paced technological world, a digital revolution where new media channels are consistently emerging and forever changing the way in which we communicate. Our advances in technology and daily overexposure to brands are forcing marketers to come up with new and innovative ways to compete for our attention and influence our actions. Though the tools of communication are changing, the core essence of branding is still the same and we can use that to our advantage.

Throughout my marketing career I have had the privilege of working with numerous brands across a wide range of media. This has allowed me to gain an accurate sense of a truly integrated marketing approach using a set of proven principles. Looking at what made my best performing campaigns very successful led me to develop a set of branding and marketing principles around which I base all my work. In this chapter I will focus on four of these essentials, which I feel are the most basic and important elements of branding - to build a strong foundation for a brand to expand and last.

The 4 Essentials for Building Brand Value are:

1. Differentiate Your Brand
2. Be Authentic
3. Engage Emotionally Using All 5 Senses
4. Be Excellent at Every Touch Point

People love to buy, but they don't want to be sold. It's our job as marketers to create the perfect environment for our audience to take the desired action.

Here is what I mean by each point:

1. Differentiate Your Brand:

Your audience needs to be able to remember your brand, connect with it, and be able to chose it over others. Your brand identity, all the way from the name and logo design, needs to be different from others and expressed through a unique promise of value. This will determine how you will be seen by others and help you stand out. Pricing is another way to differentiate yourself from others; whether you are more expensive or lower in cost, this can say a lot about your brand.

Here are some basic questions to help you define how your brand is different and develop your brand strategy. Write out the answers and discuss them with your team.

- What makes your products or services special, better, different and stand out?
- Who needs to know? (your target audience)
- Who does not need to know?
- What is your promise to your target audience?
- What does your brand stand for?
- What are your strengths?
- What does your target audience expect to gain from your products or services?
- What do you want others to think about your brand?
- Why should they care?

These fundamental questions can help you get a better sense of what your brand is and what you brand is not, and how to best differentiate from others. If you have a competitor that has a gain in your market or has been established before your brand, you don't want to be just like them. You need to be unique and find ways to be different that are true. Wal-Mart is known for low prices. So Target positions itself as low prices but chic, and made a strong # 2 brand. Kmart got caught in the middle where it didn't differentiate itself enough, and eventually filed for chapter 11 bankruptcy.

Keeping the concept of a brand as a set of meanings, write down what your brand means to you. Write down five to ten different meanings about your brand and save them along with all of these other exercises. They are all essential brand research and it will help you track your progress and further develop your brand.

"In order to be irreplaceable one must always be different"
~ *Coco Chanel - House of Chanel*

The origin of the company, product or service can help you stand out and create a story to differentiate your brand. Try out this brand building exercise by writing out the answers to these questions to create your brand story:

- What accomplishments and credibility do you have in the

market place?

- What is the origin or history of the brand?
- How was the company or brand founded?
- How many years have you been established?
- Are your products made differently?
- Do you have a specialty or niche?
- What are your strengths and business values?

Combining what you wrote down from the first exercise, create a story around your brand. This story can help you communicate valid points of why your brand is special and worth paying a premium for, or choosing over others. At its essence, branding is about the art of storytelling and the story about your brand can be a powerful way to stand out from your competitors and create a special place in the hearts and minds of your target audience.

Here is an example. Let's say I handed you an ordinary looking rock and I didn't tell you anything about it and then asked you how much would you pay me for it. You would look at the rock and probably not think much of it. After all, it's just an ordinary looking rock. There is no perceived value, so how much is it worth to you and why would you pay me anything for it at all?

Now let's say I revealed to you that the truth about the rock you are holding is that it's the first rock sample taken by Neil Armstrong during the first landing on the moon. This rock is extremely rare and has a lot of symbolic meaning to mankind with only a few other moon rock samples in existence. What would you say is the value of that same rock now, after I told you the history behind it?

Once I told you the story about the rock, it's perceived value instantly changed because this rock was no longer ordinary, it is now different and special. Using the history behind the brand can help you increase the perceived value and if it's good enough, it can command a premium.

Using your story and brand attributes, create a shorter company profile about a paragraph long that can be used for PR purposes, hiring, media kits, investor, stocks, and so on. You can adjust your messaging to your audience, but it's generally left very similar.

What do you want people to think about your brand? Use the same questions in the previous exercises but this time make your message more concise, and highlight what's most important to your target audience.

The information should include:

1. Your brand name and marketplace credibility
2. The major benefits your product or service provides to your target audience
3. An easy-to-understand description of your products, sub-brands, or services.
4. What makes your brand unique and stand out in your marketplace
5. History and elements of your brand story that are most important to mention
6. If used for PR, a reference to where they can learn more about your brand

Here is an example of what I used for PR purposes from one of the brands I've worked with in the spirits category:

> ***BOMBAY SAPPHIRE*** *is the best selling super premium gin in the United States. The combination of its ten unique botanicals, vapor infusion process and authentic British heritage secure* ***BOMBAY SAPPHIRE*** *as a leader among gins, as well as a symbol of style and sophistication.* ***BOMBAY SAPPHIRE*** *strongly supports inspired adult individuals who create passionate work in design, film and other artistic arenas. For more information, please visit www.BombaySapphire.com*

From this you can create a Unique Value Proposition (UVP) which is about a 'sentence long' and summarizes what your brand stands for. Your UVP should be an easy to understand, simple and quick statement, communicating the unique value your company, product and services provide, that is different from your competitors. The UVP can also be utilized to inspire a brand slogan or marketing taglines.

> Example: *Amazon: Low price, wide selection with added convenience anytime, anywhere.*

With what you developed so far, you can create a wide range of additional messages that are important to differentiate and build a strong foundation. This includes your mission statement, positioning statement, your brand values, unique sales proposition, and your "elevator pitch" to name a few. These messages, stories and brand elements should all work together to create an impactful experience for your target audience and help develop a positive meaning for your brand that they can relate to.

2. **Be Authentic:**

   Effective branding starts with authenticity, also known as "Keeping it Real!". You need to be true to what your brand stands for and what the brand is really about. Brands can only go on so long until people figure them out and validate if they are authentic or not.

   Great brands are authentic to themselves, and realize that you can't please everybody and that's ok. Your brand must take a stand for what it believes in and expect some people to disagree. It is important that people choose your brand and not the other way around. Now this does not mean that you don't listen to your customers, but it means that the brand remains true to itself and does not pretend to be something it's not.

   The authenticity of a brand begins with the people in the organization or the person. The culture of the organization must be true to what the brand claims to be. There must be consistency within the organization, among the people who live the brand, and that culture must be visible to others.

3. **Engage Emotionally using all 5 Senses:**

   Most of the time we make decisions based on how we feel, and then we justify our decisions with the facts. If someone is emotionally engaged, they are more likely to pay attention to the reasons why they should buy. Therefore, capture your audience's interest with a powerful emotional appeal and engage their feelings first, before you engage them intellectually.

   When most people are shopping for a new car they first fall in love with the car design, the smell of the new leather, that shiny fresh coat of paint and how it feels when you turn on that engine. But afterwards, when it comes down to making a rational buying decision, they'll talk about gas mileage, safety and maintenance. If our hearts are in it first, we are more likely to find a way to rationally justify the buying decision. 'If we can reach the heart first, the wallet will follow.'

Stories are a great way to engage emotionally, but you will need to do more than just documenting it to truly stand out. You can bring your story to life by appealing to all human senses and looking at every 'touch point' as an opportunity to create a lasting experience. Taste, touch, sight, smell, and hearing all contribute towards the experience of the brand and you should use them when appropriate. By the way, that new car leather smell that you love, well it comes in a can and it's called something more like RDX9500.

Engaging your audience using all five senses will help your brand create a deeper bond and produce a meaningful and hard-to-forget experience. If you've ever been to an Abercrombie and Fitch store, you may have noticed a signature fragrance that lured you in to the store, which happens to get pumped into the air ducts; or the model standing at the door and the models in the signage inside, which all just make you want to try on one of those new pairs of jeans and purchase them - to take home a bit of that sex appeal.

Let's outline some of the major deep motives why people do anything in life. Though there are more, these are the 10 basic motives that move us to action. I listed them here so you are aware of them, because they are a part of us all. The more motives you can provoke, the more likely they will be willing to take action.

The 10 Basic Motives that motivate our actions are:

1. The Emotion of Love
2. The Emotion of Sex
3. The Desire for Material and Financial Gain
4. The Desire for Health and Longevity
5. The Desire for Freedom of Body and Mind
6. The Desire for Self-Expression and Recognition
7. The Desire to Be Liked and Accepted By Others

8. The Desire for Revenge
9. The Emotion of Hate or Dislike
10. The Emotion of Fear

Most of these emotions are positive but some are negative and can be very powerful in motivating us to take action. Fear is used commonly in advertising and you can find it not only in slogans but in the actual brand names as well. Take Johnson and Johnson's classic baby shampoo: No More Tears®. If you have ever gotten shampoo in your eyes you can remember that it stings 'pretty bad'. By bringing the focus to "No More Tears" it plays with our emotion of fear because you don't want your baby to feel that awful burning sensation. So you say "yes, no more tears".

Think about what your product or service helps people with, and mix in some strong emotions when appropriate, in order to connect with people on a deeper level. Brands are created only by humans, and therefore by nature, people can relate with them because of their human origin.

4. **Be Excellent at Every Touch Point**

Great brands are good at what they do and are consistent at it. You don't need to have the best product or service in the world, but you need to deliver what you promise, your brand promise. Every 'touch point' matters, including your products, services, customer service, and so on. Even after you've made the sale, your return policy and customer satisfaction follow-up all play a role in the brand experience. Your standards must be consistent throughout the entire customer experience - before, during and after interactions.

For instance, there is a Pizza restaurant that I go to because they have some of best tasting pizza in town. The staff is friendly and the pizza is second to none, but there is just one big problem. Their bathrooms are filthy, things are broken, and I noticed that they ran out of soap. This changed the way I felt about the restaurant and the brand, because it made me wonder what their kitchen was like and the cleanliness of the staff's hands. Is it really that difficult to keep a toilet clean? Though the owner has taken great pride in delivering a great tasting pizza and friendly service, he left out a very important piece. The bathrooms alone have tarnished my experience and even though I still order carry out, it bothers me and eventually there may be a point where I may chose to take my business elsewhere.

The design of a store, knowledge of the staff, the checkout process, the packaging of the products it comes in… it's all part of the brand experience. In this next exercise, write how each 'touch point' makes you feel about a brand you like, one you dislike, and your own. I included several 'touch points' which might not all be relevant to you, but feel free to customize this list to your brand. Write down how you feel next to each point. This will help you 'hone in' on any 'leaky buckets' that are affecting your brand experience and learn from the others as well.

Corporate Communications:

- Advertising
- Public Relations
- Direct Marketing
- Sponsorships
- Events
- Customer Service Experience

Online Experience

- Visually appealing website
- Usability
- The information is accurate and relevant
- Check out process
- Online return policy
- Online support
- Packaging

Retail Store or Branch Experience

- Design of the location
- Cleanliness of the place
- Friendly and knowledgeable staff
- How products are organized
- Product selection
- Follow up experience

- Return policy
- Openness to complaints

So there you have them, the 4 essential principles of branding and how they can help build value in your brand.

As far as next steps, this is what I recommend; reinforce with creativity. Once you've created a great brand story and identity, you want to look for creative ways to reinforce your positioning. If you are getting started, you don't need to spend all of your budget on advertising, but rather start with a narrow focus. Deliver your message to the people that matter most, your target audience. A strong brand identity and a carefully designed marketing strategy will advance your brand. Listen to your imagination for new ideas to help build your brand and treat each idea with civility. An idea that may seem crazy at first can sometimes be the answer to what you are looking for, and in this competitive world a single idea can make all the difference.

True brand loyalty is not about teaching people how to be loyal, like you would with a puppy, but about getting people to love your brand, and that is what keeps them coming back. Building a brand is a never-ending process because it exists in the minds and hearts of the people to whom you gave it meaning. Get excited, you are on a wonderful journey of storytelling and as you continue to build your brand, the story will continue to unfold.

ABOUT JOHN

John Bejarano - Brand Strategist | Interactive Marketing Consultant | Event Producer

At the eager age of 6, John Bejarano's entrepreneurial spirit began to take shape when he founded his first business of selling cakes and coffee to his local community. Fast forward twenty plus years, and John has built a solid reputation as a hands-on, strategic thinker known for delivering dynamic and impactful results in interactive marketing, sales and event management.

As the Chief Strategist for First Class Alliance (FCA), an ROI-centric marketing consultancy that develops brand strategy, John is responsible for leading the firm's creative vision and partnerships, as well as overseeing the development of its innovative marketing programs. Key campaigns have included Office Depot, where John developed the Business Solutions Division (BSD) Email Marketing program for North America.

Prior to FCA, John was the Senior Account Executive covering Florida and Latin America for ValueClick Media—a leading digital advertising network. At ValueClick, he oversaw successful, multi-million dollar marketing programs for well-established brands across multiple online marketing platforms, including Westgate Resorts, QuickBooks, Sol Melia, Orkin, Kaplan, AOL Latino, and CitiFinancial. Other previous key positions included Senior Account Director for SendTec/RelationServe—a multi-channel direct marketing agency and Strategic Alliance Director at Slip-N-Slide Records—a leading independent record label, where John was responsible for all brand partnerships between the label's artists.

John has also served as a Strategic Advisor for numerous Fortune 500 companies, including GE Money, Bombay Sapphire and Coca-Cola. In his campaigns, he has also had the privilege of working with leading ad agencies such as Crispin Porter & Bogusky, World Media and Sapient.

John currently sits on the Board of Directors for the South Florida Interactive Marketing Association where he frequently produces marketing workshops and educational events. In John's spare time, he enjoys traveling, learning photography, writing music and helping others in their quests for greater professional success.

CHAPTER 31

EXPERIENCE TRANSPARENCY TRUST

THE KEYS TO YOUR BIGGER FUTURE

BY PHILIP BENNETT

An early morning awakening on a cement floor in Mexico left me searching for truth for my life. In the early dawn hours, I discovered that I had been emotionally bankrupt, spiritually dead, and void of relationship. My poor choices were physically killing me. I had found my life story, and I realized that I wanted to rewrite the main character.

Four months after fulfilling my life dream of being an independent business owner, my then wife walked out the door, leaving me with no income, all of the household expenses, and my three children to support. Eleven months after leaving my very lucrative and self-defining career, I found myself growing a business in a very unconventional way—divorced, emotionally unavailable to my children, and battling 'stage four' melanoma. I had no training to prepare me for what was to come, and I was 'too damn proud' to admit it. I adopted an "I can still make this happen" attitude which ultimately lead me on a journey that has changed my life. After waking up on the cold floor of a Church in Ensenada, where my kids and I had gone to serve, I felt for the first time in months that I was quiet enough to hear that faint voice whispering, telling me I was dying and that I needed to fix things soon.

I had to reconnect with who I was and who I wanted to be. Money and business success were no longer going to define me. I would make choices to become who I was created to be: secure, humble, and FREE. On this journey, God sent me a life boat to get off of the island I had created for myself. I immediately went home and 'rolled up' the best contracts, sold off assets, rewrote my business plan, and dove head first into getting the tools I needed. I went to seminars, read books, listened to recordings, attended webinars / teleseminars, created a network of geniuses, took lots of vacations, and ultimately reconnected with my loved ones.

Now, this is a very short version of a very real story. I wanted to give you some context as to why I can say the title of this chapter is true. My search for doing it better, easier, more fun, and more lucrative has landed me where I am today, and that includes my privilege to be sharing my story with you.

What can we glean from my story? Well, just as my relationship with my family suffered from my lack of availability, so will your relationships with your clients. Get more of what you want by giving more of your client wants seems easy enough, yet the noise of life and running a business often keeps us stuck. I have heard it said that an hour of focused thinking is worth more than a week of unfocused work. It is time to put the pieces together before you end up on the cold hard floor one morning, alone.

Experience is defined as:

1. The apprehension of an object, thought, or emotion through the sense or mind (e.g., a child's first experience of snow).
2. Active participation in events or activities leading to the accumulation of knowledge or skill, and the knowledge or skill so derived (lesson taught by experience).

You are the only one with your experience. Period. No on else has your perspective. The idea of being an expert in most people's minds just does not come naturally or even easily. Yet, I would argue that we are all experts just by being human. Just enter a conversation with someone and they will argue their point of view until the end of time, if you let them. The way our minds sift and sort data and file it in the appropriate file for us to draw upon at any time enhances our life, shortens the learning curve, and even protects us from negative events and threats.

Is your company's unique selling proposition connected to your experience and who you are? More than likely. What is a unique selling proposition? It is a marketing concept that was first proposed as a theory to explain a pattern among successful advertising campaigns of the early 1940s.

It states that such campaigns made unique propositions to the customer and that this convinced them to switch brands. The term was invented by Rosser Reeves of Ted Bates & Company. It is defined in three parts:

1. Each advertisement must make a proposition to the consumer. Not just words, not just product 'puffery', not just show-window advertising. Each advertisement must say to each reader: "Buy this product, and you will get *this specific benefit*."
2. The proposition must be one that the competition either cannot, or does not, offer. It must be unique—either a uniqueness of the brand or a claim not otherwise made in that particular field of advertising.
3. The proposition must be so strong that it can 'move the mass millions', i.e., pull over new customers to your product.

If you're not leveraging a USP, how are you standing out from your competitors? It's imperative that you set yourself apart from your competitors or your clients, or worse, your unrealized potential clients, who may not know why you are unique and why they should choose you over everyone else.

In addition, it is essential to educate your customers and prospects on the value you create and the solutions you deliver. There are many ways to look at how to deliver that message. One very powerful way is to let your best clients tell them by promoting a referral program that creates, trains, and rewards a behavior you want.

The other key element is your experience. You are an expert if you follow the thinking you are the only 'you' there can be, and there is no better expert on the subject of your qualification. Don't be shy. Your freedom in business and the way you experience life may depend upon it. Once you have identified this experience leverage, use it to gain recognition as the expert that you are. Find a way to gain credibility, for instance write for a trade publication, create consumer awareness pieces to help give your clients more information (such as: questions one should ask before hiring within your industry), teach a class, speak at an event, share tips and "how to's", and the list goes on and on. Find what fits, then do it.

EXPERIENCE

Direct personal participation or observation; actual knowledge or contact.

This is the heart of the matter. In the ever-increasing speed at which business happens and information is compiled and delivered, businesses come into success and soon are copied. This sameness is boring and uneventful, and soon becomes commoditized with everything else and devolves into being about nothing but price. We can use the fast food industry as a model.

I can say that the one dollar value menu will never go away, and if it does it will take a long time for it to disappear. McDonalds thought they could win at this game, and guess what? Now everyone has a dollar menu. Flame broiled, best fries, hand-scooped ice cream shakes—none of this is important! Look at the ads in the window. The original ideal of fast food has been completely 'murdered', and eating fast food has been repackaged to the point of identity crisis and who can produce the cheapest hamburgers.

Folks, it has to be about experience, and true, authentic, emotional, deliverable experience at that! When you allow your dream to over-deliver on your promise, to exceed the expectation and reward it, your company will deliver experiences that consumers dream of, and they will skip the cheap hamburger meal to pay for the experience you deliver every time. Find out what those areas are that you excel in. Ask your best clients what they like best about you and your company, and give that to everyone—even if it is several different qualities.

If you are not giving the best experience ever, then I hope I am competing with you. "I promise to over-deliver on my commitment to give you the best experience ever. That is just what we do." …is a tagline I have been living by for years. I started making more money as soon as I started using it. Overnight I became a welcomed guest because of my experience, and the experience I promise.

Transparent

1. Having the property of transmitting rays of light through its substance so that bodies situated beyond or behind can be distinctly seen.
2. open; frank; candid.

If we use the idea of being transparent in our business, it will help us to remain focused on what is important to us as entrepreneurs, and people in general. It speaks to our beliefs and values in such a way that authenticity and trust worthiness are the natural byproducts. When people know, like, and trust you and you are giving them the experiences they desire, you lose sight of what may now be the competition, and you create a whole new level of doing things. Let's face it, when you have educated your clients, delivered an experience beyond that which is expected, nurture the relationship, and get referrals, you will get what you want—more business, more freedom, and the money to be able to put the FUN back in your business.

It is much easier to live in a state of transparency than in the darkness on the island. When we adjust the lens and put some light behind our authentic selves, it will project a much bigger and brighter future. If we want something different, we have to do something different. Albert Einstein once said, "Problems cannot be solved by the same level of thinking that created them."

If you can imagine a small slide behind the projector, and with the use of focus we can magnify, enlarge, and bring to clarity whatever we are projecting, the image should be your authentic self. Eventually this image will become how the world around you experiences you and your business. Businesses are nothing more than an expression or extension of who we are.

TRUST

A firm reliance on the integrity, ability, or character of a person or thing.

When you are known as the expert in your respective field and community, you deliver experiences far beyond what is expected, you are transparent with who and what you are …and you are posed for explosive growth in every area. The more you focus on experience, transparency, and trust, the greater the multiplier will be for your business. The benefit is that you can now have more of what you want. *It's your story, you get to write the script.*

Because I paused that day and realized that the freedom I was seeking was nowhere to be found, my joy had been robbed and I was alone. I decided to be real and authentic with myself and others, and it has enriched my life fully and completely. My clients see that within me, and they respond to it.

I asked my clients why they did business with me, why they referred me, and why they kept coming back. The answer was always that they trusted me. I took the time to share with them about the process that we would be going through together, I expressed to them what they could expect from their experience, and I had taken the time to share with them what others had experienced when dealing with the same issues, and what we did together to solve it.

I reached out and created a community around me with like-minded entrepreneurs, friends, and family. I asked for feedback on my ideas and I asked for accountability in what I knew was my purpose. I now make more money doing the work with much less effort, and spend most of my time doing what I want. As a part of the re-writing process, I discovered a new way of getting what I sought after and fulfilling my desire for helping others. Out of this desire I discovered a way to help the consumer get what they want —"Value you can trust, and solutions you desire"— a way to help entrepreneurs get what they want, and a way to get what I want.

ABOUT PHILIP

For over 25 years, Philip Bennett has been contributing to a better way of doing it. As a father of three amazing children; a recognized leader in retail management, sales, and marketing; an entrepreneur; developer; writer; speaker; missionary; and volunteer, Phil has been able to use his diverse journey both professionally and personally to achieve expert status in life and people. This has ultimately landed him with a passion for business, personal growth, and success as an entrepreneur. For the last six years he has run as many as 6 service companies at one time and helped many others with market positioning, branding, and gaining the freedom to live a joy-filled, abundant life outside of the office. Phil is passionate about life and sharing his experience in human performance, human behavior, and how each applies to your business - and more importantly, to your life and relationships. His situational awareness, creative mind, and energy have helped him accomplish much.

On May 1, 2010, Phil launched ethicalpro.com—the best place to find a professional business. This site was created to take the fear out of the consumer's mind and to help answer the question, "Who can I trust?". Ethical Pro does this by providing a directory of reviewed and rated companies that have signed a code of ethics. Coinciding this launch, Phil is also working on the launch of Prodromos Central—an online community for businesses in the directory. Prodromos provides information on tools and strategies to run a very lucrative company—"get them off the island and into the community". Phil has also recently agreed to collaborate on the new book, "Game Changers", with other recognized experts. "Game Changers" will be available in November.

"When we understand that all of our activities connect one to another we can leverage each individual activity to the greater whole" ~Philip Bennett

CHAPTER 32

BUILDING BLOCKS – DIRECT MAIL & REAL ESTATE

BY JUSTIN C. CARTER

Remember as a child playing building blocks with our parents? I do, except my building blocks were real buildings and my parent was my dad, Jeff Carter.

My dad, a lifelong union worker who woke up early, got home late, working 60 hours a week for as far back as I can remember, had an epiphany about the time I entered high school. He had read a little book by Robert Kiyosaki, *Rich Dad Poor Dad*. That book was the defining "ah ha" moment for my father and the springboard that would challenge and motivate him to leave his conventional life behind and build the next life chapter - where there was more fun, more meaning and more life in living - a life rich in personal development and financial success.

That one little building block, a book, stacked many more blocks. Dad read more books, attended real estate seminars, and networked with others who shared the same passion. Within seven years of reading that first book, Dad's life and mine changed in many ways. A 25 year veteran in the sheet metal union, he retired and became a real estate investor. He created his own company amassing a portfolio of real estate worth several million dollars in just a few short years. I watched, took notes, and decided that real estate investing was much more exciting than the union world. Dad left behind the standard two weeks of vacation per year to enjoy months or more vacation even during the busy times. How did he do this? It was all in the MARKETING!

My father marketed himself and his business very purposefully. He talked to everyone, creating relationships. He wrote numerous offers and letters of intent on properties and he organized direct mail campaigns. Those direct mail campaigns attracted the right people, the right deals, and the results that rebuilt our lives, taking my family and myself to the next level.

Dad learned early on how valuable direct mail and building a consistent, targeted campaign is to generating the leads you need to succeed in real estate investing. It doesn't matter how many seminars you go to, how many books you read, or how many real estate experts you network with, they all agree that direct mail marketing is the building block to your success.

How do you build your own direct mail marketing campaigns? My dad's attended dozens of expensive seminars and all the experts tell you to mail but what they don't tell you is how to mail. If you don't know the details and subtle nuances of direct mail marketing and don't have a strong marketing strategy to make the phone ring, nothing else matters. You can be the best at the rest of your business but if you don't understand how to market what you're good at, then success is harder to come by. My father quickly learned this lesson, and was able to create a successful real estate business using direct mail marketing that he tested and honed over time.

Our marketing success started with the foundational building block - defining your market. Dad started his real estate portfolio by acquiring single family homes, because these properties were relatively inexpensive and easier to obtain. We decided to send letters to owners of foreclosure properties or expired listings. The letters generated a strong response rate, which was a vital first step to growing his business. This strategy entailed sending multiple letters to several different mailing lists. You can imagine the difficulties we incurred keeping all the letters organized. There were multiple lists, multiple letters, with different mail dates. My dad developed a colored envelope system to help keep it all straight. He had red envelopes for the first letter, blue for the second, green for the third, and so on. Although time consuming and took up a lot of space storing the letters and envelopes in the house, this marketing strategy was very successful. Dad continued this way for several years.

At one point, I asked him why he didn't just let one of those big bulk mail houses I had heard about send his mail for him? He said that because he was mailing small quantities, the big mail houses didn't want his business or were too expensive. He also believed it was better to control the process himself and provide a level of personal touch mail processors couldn't easily provide. This is why he continued to do his direct mail for years on the kitchen table in the evenings. Although he has bought dozens and dozens of properties through different lead sources, direct mail always gave him the best return on his investment in time and dollars. Even today while investing in multi-unit properties, land entitlement projects, and commercial developments, he will tell you that direct mail should be the backbone of any marketing plan for generating leads for properties, buyers, sellers, and investors.

Over the last few years, with the coaching of my dad, I have taken each building block and lesson learned to build my own real estate portfolio of single family homes. I've attended seminars, read the books, and networked with the best of the best, just like Dad. Best of all I market using direct mail. I have experienced and feel the pain my dad has gone through for years. The least fun part being a real estate investor is developing and executing the direct mail campaigns. I would much rather meet with homeowners, contact lenders, or rehab an old dusty house than do my direct mail marketing. I know how important it is, but sitting around the dinner table addressing labels, stuffing letters, licking stamps all night wasn't the family bonding I was wanting. I decided there had to be a better way. I've grown up with the world wide web, technology, cell phones, internet, email, and all the other cool things that come with it. How could we integrate technology and direct mail marketing to make the process easier, faster, more targeted, and ultimately less expensive?

THE NEXT BUILDING BLOCK

In 2008, I approached my dad with the idea of a website that could manage, process, and fulfill direct mail for real estate professionals - even small campaigns at a reasonable and affordable cost. No more dinner table envelope stuffing. Neither one of us knew anything about building a website, let alone launching a sophisticated web application. Over the course of 2 years and many building blocks that toppled down, we've designed that website that can manage our direct mail - from finding and selecting that qualified list, mailing to them, and getting the phone to ring. Our businesses are growing. Regardless of how you process your direct mail, here are a few proven tips that Dad and I know can help you see results to grow your business too.

Here are 5 Direct Mail Tips that can build your business and elevate the success of your direct mail campaigns forever. (And you probably wont find these in your college marketing books.)

1. **Qualified Mailing Lists:** You must have a qualified list! This is a list that is targeted to just the people you want to mail too. The list is the foundation of any direct mail campaign, especially in real estate. Without a qualified list, you stand little chance of success. In most cases, your total campaign cost is determined by the size of your list so don't make it any bigger than you have to. Depending on who you're marketing to it's also important to have a list that excludes non-desirables and eliminate names that won't produce results. There are plenty of ways you can narrow down your list and save yourself some money. Some lists like pre-foreclosure, foreclosure, and probate are published in newspapers or on websites and are very easy to obtain. Make sure you research the source of the list, understand where the data comes from, and how current it is before you purchase and acquire your list. Remember to update the list often as it becomes stale and won't produce the same results or generate as many leads unless it is 'scrubbed' between mailings. After all, people move, properties exchange hands, and circumstances arise that make an old list fatigued.
2. **Targeted Messages:** You must have a clear and compelling

message or offer that is targeted toward your audience. If you're trying to tell your whole life story or explain why your business deserves a call, you're probably not going to get one. The message needs to be short, concise, and direct, informing the people on your list exactly what they need to hear so they understand your business proposition and are comfortable enough to call you. If your targeted message appeals to an affluent, wealthy client, but you are mailing to a 'blue collar' list, the recipients will miss your intentions altogether. You want to look professional but also appeal to your audience. If your list contains different socioeconomic classes, then divide the list into those classes, creating a different message for each one. The recipient who receives your mail piece should be able to fully understand your product or service without feeling intimidated or unsure whether your prospects should know exactly who you are, what you are offering and what is in it for them. Depending on who you are marketing too, you may find that letters work better than postcards and *vice versa*. If you're sending multiple letters, then make sure the first letter leads into the second, and the second into the third, and so on. If someone throws away your first letter but sees your second letter and it references the first letter, you have a better chance of getting a response. Sending multiple letters allows for you to test and use different verbiage and marketing techniques. Overall, testing should always be an element of developing highly responsive direct mail strategies.

3. **Repetition & Timing:** The timing of your mail piece can make the difference between getting your message read, passed over, or thrown in the trash. It has been proven time and time again that your response rate will increase when you send your message multiple times to the same prospects. Your ratio of number of contacts to close will greatly improve with qualified lists and targeted messages like I mentioned before. If your list is time sensitive, i.e. a foreclosure list, consider mailing it at least three times. This may mean once a week or once every two weeks, depending on your budget, your time, and your desired response rate.

4. **Quality not Quantity:** If it looks like Junk Mail then it will be perceived that way. Don't underestimate the importance of good design. This doesn't mean the most expensive design, the most colorful, or the most graphic. All of the elements of the card or letter must work together cohesively to present you, your business, and your message clearly and professionally. The message should "pop" and have no chance of being missed. Choose a good design artist who understands direct mail. Send out a mail piece that you would save and put on your fridge, and you will see an increase in your response rate. Don't send out something that you are embarrassed by.

5. **Mail Smart!:** Standard Mail is just as good as First Class! In the past standard mail was reserved for "Junk Mail" but not any more. Even though the USPS says "allow 2 weeks for delivery", I have done multiple tests and standard mail arrives within 1-2 days of the first class mail 98% of the time. The only time you really need first class mail is if you would like it returned. Depending on the size of your list, paying for return mail may not be worth it. If it fits with your campaign timing or isn't time sensitive, trying sending standard mail. And remember you can always add a pre-canceled stamp to your mailer for a little extra cost and you get the first class look.

In the past, direct mail has been time consuming, very expensive and hard to mange especially for the small business owner. Technology is changing the way people do business in many ways and direct mail is no different. The internet makes acquiring targeted lists easier than ever. Professional mail pieces can be created quickly and easily, and the management and execution of your direct mail campaigns can now be done with the click of a mouse. Right now is the best time to be sending direct mail. Today there is less and less direct mail showing up in mail boxes… and more and more email. Don't be fooled into thinking email is the only way to go. Direct Mail Matters. Integrate 'snail mail' with technology. Build your direct mail marketing blocks and build your business. It will be an important strategy for any successful real estate professional for years to come.

ABOUT JUSTIN

Justin C. Carter is an active real estate investor, consultant, and life long entrepreneur, having initiated and managed a variety of small businesses from a young age. As a freshman in high school Justin purchased a lawnmower, edge cutter, and leaf blower and built a neighborhood landscaping business to 20 weekly accounts. While attending college he established a very successful DJ & Entertainment business that serviced dozens of weddings and hundreds of gigs per year. Having a real passion for real estate, Justin applied profits from those businesses and private investor funding to acquire his first foreclosure investment property at age 19. In the next six years Justin would be directly involved in the acquisition and sale of over 100 properties, concentrating on residential and multi-unit rental properties. He credits a lot of his knowledge and experience to the "Mom & Pop" real estate companies he worked with, including his association with a national real estate investment company that specialized in creative real estate acquisitions and sale. Consequently, Justin has extensive experience in acquiring properties through short sales, subject to existing financing, and lease option agreements. He's quite handy at rehabbing properties and is a skilled property manager. Still an emerging entrepreneur at age 25, Justin owns a small portfolio of properties and continues to search for the next great deal!

Having his father, Jeff Carter, as mentor, Justin paid attention to how his dad grew his business, taking copious mental and physical notes on the numerous steps and activities it took to operate a successful real estate business. He learned that for many small business owners direct mail was an important lead generator. He also learned that as a small business owner, direct mail isn't easy to manage. It takes a lot of time, organization and financial resources to effectively manage a campaign that returns a constant supply of leads and prospects to build the business.

Knowing that there must be an easier way, Justin combined his passion for real estate investing and his technology expertise into a dynamic internet business, designing and developing a disruptive web-based application that specifically assists Real Estate Professionals build their business through direct mail campaigns. Technology has now made it possible to turn a once painful but necessary task into something virtually effortless. With less effort needed logistically, more emphasis can be placed on the effectiveness of the mailings, creating less waste and a higher return on investment. Direct mail marketing has combined with all the right technology resulting in more targeted and focused campaigns, conveniently and more cost effectively than ever before.

Justin is Chief Technology Officer as well as Co-Founder of BuildFive.com BuildFive.com is pioneering the innovative way small businesses view and use direct mail. www.buildfive.com launches Summer 2010. Check it out: www.buildfive.com

When it's time to shift gears, Justin loves to rock climb and ski in beautiful Colorado where he currently lives.

Justin C. Carter

twitter: Justin_C_Carter